Public Controls
for
Nonpublic Schools

Public Controls
for
Nonpublic Schools

Edited by
Donald A. Erickson

The University of Chicago Press
Chicago and London

Library of Congress Catalog Card Number: 68–55149

The University of Chicago Press, Chicago 60637
The University of Chicago Press, Ltd., London W.C.1

Acknowledgments

The materials for this book grew out of a national invitational conference on "State Regulation of Nonpublic Schools," sponsored by the Midwest Administration Center, University of Chicago, and held at the University's Center for Continuing Education on March 28 and 29, 1967.

Funds for the conference were provided by the Danforth Foundation. Created in 1927 by the late Mr. and Mrs. William H. Danforth of St. Louis, the foundation exists to strengthen education, through its own programs and through grants to schools, colleges, universities, and other educational agencies.

The conference was organized and directed by the editor of this volume, with the counsel and assistance of many people: Julia Ashenhurst of the Center for Continuing Education; John deJ. Pemberton, Jr., of the American Civil Liberties Union; Brevard Critchfield of the Council of State Governments; Dean M. Kelley of the National Council of the Churches of Christ; and scholars such as C. Arnold Anderson, Roald F. Campbell, Francis S. Chase, Luvern L. Cunningham, Jacob W. Getzels, Philip B. Kurland, George R. LaNoue, Frederick F. Lighthall, Dan C. Lortie, Margaret Mead, George D. Spindler, and J. Alan Thomas.

Contents

Donald A. Erickson

Introduction:
Beech Grove Isn't Far from Andover

While the March wind howled in Kansas in 1967, LeRoy Garber's attorney mounted an appeal to the Supreme Court. Garber's daughter seemed well educated, yet he was fined for failing to send her to a conventional classroom.[1] At the same time, in Iowa, the legislature struggled to end a destructive confrontation. Frightened Amish children fled through the cornfields, and their parents' possessions were seized and sold.[2] Similar troubles were brewing in Kentucky. Men of varying commitments wondered whether issues of state control and educational dissent had been properly assessed, with respect both to the Amish and nonpublic schools generally.

In the shadow of this concern, a diverse centumvirate gathered at the University of Chicago. Bearded Amishmen journeyed from Ontario, Iowa, and Ohio, breaking precedent to appear in a public forum. State administrative officers, legislators, a governor, constitutional lawyers, professors, social scientists, school administrators, and men of the cloth came to talk and listen and think. Their ideas appear in the following ten chapters.

The author is associate professor of education at the University of Chicago.
1 Very shortly I will publish an analysis of this episode under the title "LeRoy Garber's Ordeal: What It Costs To Be an Amishman."
2 See "Showdown at an Amish Schoolhouse," chapter 2.

Both the conference and this volume could have been arranged in other ways. Presentations could have been apportioned among the generic problems of policing nonpublic schools. The terrain could have been surveyed sequentially through the lenses of several disciplines, such as law, history, social psychology, anthropology, and political science. Our plan was more radical. We began, as the first four chapters indicate, by analyzing the Amish school controversy in some detail, delaying scrutiny of the larger picture. This approach was calculated to bring dialogue firmly to earth, inducing contemplation of the feelings and beliefs of living men. But would the Amish situation prove atypical, only elusively illustrative of the broader context?

Either our stars were well aligned or the conference participants were unusually perceptive. I think the tactic worked. What was lost in comprehensiveness was apparently more than gained in focus and immediacy. The basic enigmas seemed remarkably similar in Beech Grove Amish School, St. Anne's in the middle of Detroit, and Philips Academy at Andover. It may eventually be acknowledged that the Amish made a weighty contribution to education, giving distant early warning of dangers affecting all nonpublic schools.

A single leitmotif is sounded throughout the following pages: How can nonpublic education be both responsible and free? Responsible to serve the public interest; free to experiment and disagree. *Without* regulation, some schools may victimize patrons and endanger the general welfare. *With* regulation, dissent is jeopardized. Where should the balance be struck?

In chapter 1, Governor Hughes reflects on the paradox that plagues public leaders when the laws they must uphold violate sincere religious convictions, when the might of the state is marshalled against the meekest of men — devout pacifists who pose no threat to the common weal. The conflict the governor deescalated is described and analyzed in chapter 2. There is disconcerting evidence that local officials did not act through solicitude for Amish children.

In chapter 3, Franklin H. Littell provides the most luminous explanation I have seen of the Amish educational posture. The Plain People are not simply "backward." They fear, not learning itself, but the cunning artificer — the technocrat, his incompassionate world, and his version of education. Theirs is the pursuit of wisdom, the quest of the harmonious and humane. They are haunted by their history. Their landmarks are martyrs, victims of "technically competent barbarians." "But who is so bold as to say that the depreciation of the technological is more dangerous to the future of the human race than the neglect of wisdom? Who will deny that for the present, at least, the twin policies of learning are best secured by avoiding an educational monolith, by providing for effective dissent from a single set of scientific goals?" More recently, other commentators warn that lionized technology ("the American theology") may now be subtracting from human welfare as much as it is adding, if not more.[3] We may need in the future, much more than we foresee, the cultural options our minorities keep viable.

In chapter 4, Jules Henry suggests a seldom-discussed motive for some statutory decrees: We must destroy anything that menaces our political economy, as if the national well-being were wedded to the status quo. "Materials suggesting the possibility of an austere life [such as the Amish lead] threaten the gross national product. . . . People must be portrayed as spenders." Our educational system is no cafeteria where children choose freely among alternatives. It "tirelessly corrects deviations from the culture."

With chapter 5, consideration broadens to nonpublic education as a whole. John Elson discusses the general legal basis of governmental intervention. Rather incidentally, he begins to explain the lack of uniformity among states: The legislatures, far from functioning as long-range planners, mostly react to problems. Where nonpublic schools occasion no alarm, there is little state surveillance. They arouse anxiety, one would predict, mostly through nonconformity. And powerful groups of schools, not markedly

3 Wilbur H. Ferry, "Must We Rewrite the Constitution to Control Technology?" *Saturday Review*, March 2, 1968, pp. 50–54.

unorthodox to begin with, probably extract more genteel treatment than is experienced by impotent subcultures. Where tolerance is plentiful, it is not needed.

A critical component of the constitutional structure is then perused by Norman Dorsen in chapter 6 — the condition of the struggle for racial equality in nonpublic schools. There are complex implications in his statement, "I believe that the 'law' is there and waiting under which an enterprising court could rule that nonpublic schools are subject to the constitutional demand to desegregate."

I attempt, in chapter 7, to propose a framework of public accountability for nonpublic schools that is grounded in a consistent philosophy. At the conference, several students of the law and politics thought the approach was workable. It requires further criticism.

In chapter 8, William J. Sanders reveals the perceptions of a state commissioner. Citizens deserve protection, he observes, from unscrupulous schools that have sprung up in several areas. We could profitably have probed this exigency at greater length. If we err in terms of balance, we slight the reasons for regulation of nonpublic schools, rather than the peril it involves. Perhaps state departments of education themselves should now organize an exchange of information and viewpoint in this regard.

Sanders contends, further, that nonpublic schoolmen are unusually accepting of edicts that come wrapped in dollars. In chapter 9, William B. Ball tweaks some of his brethren for this tendency. If they overemphasize their commonalities with public education in an effort to obtain financial relief, they may sacrifice important liberties. Ball sees public funds and public stipulations as closely linked but feels that " '*any* aid justifies all control' is a slogan as dangerous as it is absurd." Government should be permitted to legislate only for the parts of the program it supports. This conception contradicts the broad court doctrine of "state action," discussed earlier by Dorsen, a doctrine which would vent the full thrust of the Fourteenth Amendment on nonpublic schools that receive any shred of public assistance.

Chapter 10 preserves a sampling, virtually verbatim, of the lively swordplay that occurred at the conference. Here is Leo Pfeffer's impassioned protest against the role some nonpublic schools play in impeding social justice, along with the sharp retorts his thrust elicited. Here, too, are suggestions time did not permit us to unravel. To mention just a few: Littell urges a special position for groups like the Amish that do not aspire to full political participation — "strangers in the land." Anne H. Strickland requests more systematic differentiation between schools that are merely permitted to operate and those that are accorded public approval. T. Raber Taylor asks for legal acknowledgement that in some settings high school instruction is less necessary than elementary schooling to good citizenship. In other notable paragraphs, John A. Hostetler makes moving observations on the Amish culture (he himself was reared in an Old Order Amish home), and Miss Strickland comments incisively on the First Amendment.

Finally, I must attempt to muffle the thunder that may be anticipated from perceptive critics. As I mentioned earlier, this book represents an initial reconnaisance of a complex topic. It is neither exhaustive nor comprehensive. It was not intended to be. Not all kinds of nonpublic schools are given the notice they warrant. Our stethoscope leaves untouched the nonpublic academies in Maine that have long functioned in a quasi-public capacity. They are now being forced out of existence — sometimes, their headmasters claim, through stipulations designed to harass them. We provide but limited diagnosis of the precepts high-prestige college-preparatory schools find bothersome. We neglect comparisons that should be made among nations with varying modes of support and control for nonpublic schools. We fail to trace the development of competing philosophies on unity and cultural pluralism. It would have been illuminating to detail the total system of regulation in a particular state — in Iowa, for instance, where the Department of Public Instruction was at loggerheads until recently with a variety of nonpublic schools.

The preannounced intent of the conference was to bring a

broad range of scholarly and practical viewpoints to bear on matters of freedom and control in education that had been widely overlooked. I believe that purpose was achieved to a decent if modest extent. The issues will no longer easily be ignored. Perhaps our chief accomplishment was to demonstrate that current state enactments for nonpublic schools, and perhaps for public schools as well, lack a defensible, well-integrated rationale. They may threaten individual liberty, cultural diversity, and badly needed instructional experimentation. These are sobering possibilities. We hope that our discussions have just begun.

1 Harold E. Hughes

The Amish School Controversy in Iowa: The View from the Governor's Office

In the hills along the Mississippi River in northeast Iowa is the village of New Vienna, population under 300. This is in a Catholic area of predominantly Protestant Iowa. The most prominent landmark of the town is a large church. For years, almost ever since anyone could remember, the bells of the church had sounded the arrival of the noon hour for the town and surrounding countryside.

The priest in charge of the church was a monsignor of strong convictions, devoted to tradition. He had an obsession against daylight saving time. Nonetheless, one day the town council had the temerity to adopt daylight saving time. The priest refused to recognize the change. And the church bells were not available for sounding the hour-early noontide.

Some devout citizens thought the world might come to an end as a result of this unfortunate misunderstanding. But it didn't. From that point on the town officials used the whistle of the volunteer fire department to sound the noon hour, daylight saving time. And one hour later, the church bells, mellow and clear, sounded the second noon hour, God's time. In no time at all, the people got used to this double standard, and life in the New Vienna area went on with its customary peace and tranquillity.

The author was governor of the state of Iowa when this chapter was written.

I think perhaps this true story summarizes how I feel about such matters as state regulation of nonpublic schools, particularly nonpublic schools maintained by ethnic minorities.

So far as I know, there is no neat solution to minority problems in our society — no "pat hand" answer that will meet minority needs and still preserve the letter of the law and the rigid uniformity of the regulation. If anyone is of the impression that I have found such a solution in Iowa, I must quickly confess that this is not the case. There is often no solution — only accommodation. And the accommodation must be sought patiently, imaginatively, and devoutly. Basically, what is required is the willingness to make the exception — to refrain from closing the door, whatever the provocation may be, on human needs and the dictates of someone else's conscience.

How does the state deal with minority groups in the controversial area of education? It seems to me that this issue is symbolic of what must be faced in our present-day society if we are to consolidate the social gains we have made through the years and move ahead. We must yield some ground where we have traditionally been unyielding if we are to have the cooperative strength we need in order to move on to the next plateau. The nonpublic school issue could well be the proving ground of our ability and willingness to face a whole bevy of subtle interpersonal problems that must be faced if our society is to continue to advance.

In January of 1963, I delivered my inaugural address for my first term as Governor of Iowa. In this address, along with the recommendations that were expected, I released a bombshell that was not expected. I recommended that private school children be allowed to ride on public school buses.

"Why did you do this?" my political associates asked me. "The issue wasn't up — you didn't need to bring it up." I recall that two of the leading political commentators of the state were reported to say: "That's the end of Hughes, politically. Why did he do such an asinine thing?"

I recommended this measure in Protestant, Masonic Iowa because I believed in it and I felt that the state needed it. People in our state had gone along convinced for too long that the world would come to a flaming end if some private school children were permitted to ride on a school bus. And yet, public school costs were going up by leaps and bounds and we were expecting citizens who sent their kids to private schools to support the public bond issues.

I felt that this issue was the key to many other issues in our state. If Iowa was to move ahead, we needed to relax our prejudices, to give a little ground in this and other areas where we had been adamant before, in order to create the spiritual unity in our society that was needed to meet the complex problems ahead. As a Methodist and Mason myself, I felt that I could make the recommendation with maximum effect. Judging from the irate letters I received from Methodists and Masons, it had that effect, all right.

Today, four years later, we still do not have public bus transportation for private school pupils, but we are gradually and inevitably getting to it. In the current session of our state legislature, for example, a school bus bill has been passed by one house, and although it may be killed in the second house, it has come closer to enactment by a country mile than at any time in the past. I don't want to overstate such change as I think there has been. The school bus issue is still bitterly controversial and divisive in our state. But I sincerely believe there has been a substantial relaxation of prejudice on this matter and that this relaxation of prejudice has spilled over to other areas, resulting in a degree of spiritual liberation for the state.

We all know the arguments relating to the separation of church and state and the uniform application of the laws. We know these arguments well because most of us wholeheartedly believe in the principles involved. But in dealing with the subtleties of minority problems, I believe that sometimes we must depart from logic and consistency, must sail by instinct instead of mathematically precise navigation. Those whose political views are shaped more than a little by religious prejudice are not the only "purists" when it comes to nonpublic schools. Some of my friends who are both political and religious liberals can exceed all others in intolerance as they fiercely proclaim their tolerance. They get themselves painted into a corner, as I see it, not realizing that their hard-line liberalism becomes bigotry for all practical purposes when carried to the extreme. Personally, I am more willing to bend laws and logic than human beings.

It was in 1965 that a school controversy involving a small religious sect in northern Iowa known as the Old Order Amish flashed into the national news in a big way. Through national press and television sources, it became known almost overnight that school authorities in the Oelwein area in northern Iowa were trying to make this quaint religious sect obey the school laws, relating particularly to the use of certified teachers in the private schools. The issue of religious persecution was raised, although denied by the school authorities. In the course of the efforts of school and civil officials to make the Amish conform, some of the parents were jailed; property was confiscated for nonpayment of fines; and an unsuccessful effort was made to physically round up the Amish children and transport them by bus to public school.

Although the matter hit the big-time news at this time, it had been brewing for a number of years. Events got started on their present course in 1947 with a school consolidation in the area where the Old Order Amish lived and farmed. At that time, most of the rural schools were closed in the district, and rural pupils began attending school in town. The Amish community purchased the one-room former public schools and set them up as private schools. The two Amish private schools were operated from 1947 until 1961 with certified teachers paid by contributions from individual Amish families. Then the Amish elders began to be dissatisfied with the certified teachers and the burden of supporting them, and from that point on to the present day, there has been continuous trouble and disagreement between the Amish and the public authorities.

The Old Order Amish, admitted by all to be good and law-abiding citizens, simply wanted to live their own lives in accordance with their religion and their old-fashioned customs, and they wanted to have their children taught only what they felt they should be taught. Specifically, they wanted their children in rural schools and believed that Amish teachers with eighth-grade educations were best for their children. The school and civil authorities, on the other hand, were charged with the enforcement of the law. Under the law, the Amish children were entitled to the same quality of education as all other children of Iowa — and it was the job of the officials to see that this was carried out.

It would take a long time for me to relate to you the chronology of events that took place during this period involving the school board, the sheriff, the courts, and, finally, the attorney general of the state. By late 1965, all efforts to come to any satisfactory understanding between the Amish fathers and the school officials had failed, and the prospect of getting out of the impasse seemed to worsen, rather than to improve. This is where I became involved in the Amish problem — for better or worse, only time will tell.

I will not burden you with a detailed recitation of all of my negotiations with the Amish fathers and the Oelwein school board, some when they came to my offices in the Statehouse and some when I went to the city of Oelwein and to the farmsteads of the Amish elders. I have participated in a number of negotiations in my time, but these were the most sensitive of all. At times we seemed near agreement, only to have it crumble when all seemed assured. Communication with the Amish elders was perhaps the most difficult of any I have undertaken. Yet I felt a sense of brotherhood toward these people that was perhaps greater than I had felt toward any fellow human beings before. There may have been times when I felt utterly discouraged with their other-worldly stubbornness, but I never stopped liking them and believing in them.

The belief in the Amish fathers and in the school board as well paid off ultimately when an agreement was reached for a temporary solution to the Amish school problem. The agreement between the Old Order Amish fathers of the Hazelton area and the Oelwein school board, which I announced at a press conference on February 22, 1966, has made it possible for the Amish children of that area to be taught by certified teachers paid for by nontax funds furnished by private sources. A "statement of understanding" was agreed to and was signed by representatives of the Amish and of the school board a week earlier when I flew to Oelwein and met with the Amish fathers and members of the school board. This arrangement was designed to hold until this year when the 1967 Legislature would be asked to enact a permanent solution. Funds to pay the certified teachers have been provided by the Danforth Foundation of St. Louis, a private foundation devoted to educational causes. The school board, at my request, agreed to act as the recipient and disbursing agent of the private funds to be expended in the operation of the two rural schools involved.

The problem of arranging for the instruction of the children of the Old Order Amish community with certified teachers in conformance with the law and without violating the religious convictions of the Amish posed one of the most sensitive problems in human relations that we have ever encountered in our state. Only those who know these good people personally and who have the patience to understand their utterly sincere devotion to a way of life prescribed by their religious convictions can appreciate the delicate communication problems involved. That a temporary solution was reached attests to the good will and good faith of the Amish, the members of the Oelwein school board, the civil authorities, and the people of Iowa who had hoped and prayed that this dispute might be solved in a just and peaceful manner.

Under the terms of the "statement of understanding" agreed to, at my request, by the Amish and the Oelwein school board, the two Amish schools are rented to the Oelwein Community School District and thus have become a part of the public school system. The two schools are staffed by two certified teachers assigned by the Oelwein school board. Standard public school requirements relating to attendance and curriculum are being met except that certain adjustments have been made to avoid conflict with Amish religious beliefs. These adjustments include the right of the Amish to provide for instruction in the German language in the schools for at least two hours a week. There can be no religious instruction in the schools.

Basically, this has been a delicate problem of communication between devout people whose religion requires them to live in accordance with old ways and customs and a modern society whose educational system is based on the proposition that all children have an equal right to be taught by properly qualified teachers. The Amish live their religion. Their clothing, their beards, their shunning of modern conveniences, and their resistance to certain phases of our modern educational programs are all part of their religious beliefs. The public officials involved — both the school officials and the civil authorities — are persons of good will simply trying to carry out in a conscientious manner the public responsibilities they have sworn to uphold. There was never any intention on their part to deny the Amish their religious freedom or their right to observe their cherished customs. However, it was understandably difficult for the Amish to understand this. They are a people who live devoutly by God's law as they interpret it, and it is their strict conviction that divine law transcends any law made by man.

I felt it was the responsibility of those of us outside the Amish community to exercise the utmost patience and good faith in communicating to the good people of this minority group that we prize and cherish their religious freedom and their right to live in their own way, and that these rights need not be violated by conformance with man-made laws which we must observe if we are to have an orderly society. The arrangement arrived at permits the Amish children to be taught by certified teachers without violating the religious principles of the Old Order Amish, on the one hand, or the state school laws, on the other. The temporary agreement between the school board and the Amish has worked out beautifully.

Now the matter of a permanent solution of the Amish school problem is before the Iowa Legislature. I have proposed that the state provide special school funds to carry on an arrangement similar to the temporary plan that has worked out so well. Legislation to implement this has been introduced. According to the news surveys, the prognosis for passage of this legislation is not good. In the event that the legislation is not enacted, where do we go from here?

I am not precisely sure where we will go from this point, if our legislature does not provide a solution.[1] I can only tell you this — that as long as I am Governor, I will never stop seeking a solution. I acknowledge the logic and consistency of those who disagree. I simply believe that the human values are more important than all of these. And I believe that the strength of America in the complex, dangerous days ahead will be determined, to a large degree, by our ability to reach a peaceful settlement of such touch-and-go, interpersonal problems as the Iowa school controversy with the Old Order Amish.

By way of conclusion, let me repeat what I said thirteen months ago when I announced the temporary agreement in the Amish school problem:

I will always believe that Iowa and America are big enough in space and spirit to provide a kindly place for all good people, regardless of race, creed, or custom. One of the most precious parts of the American heritage has been our willingness as a people to lean over backwards to assure minority groups freedom of conscience. It is a tradition infinitely worth preserving.

1 Editor's note: Subsequently the Iowa legislature did provide a solution, though not of the type Governor Hughes originally advocated. See chapter 2, pp. 47–48.

2 Donald A. Erickson

Showdown at an Amish Schoolhouse: A Description and Analysis of the Iowa Controversy

The Showdown

Its engine sputtering against the cold, the school bus left Oelwein, Iowa, for the Old Order Amish settlement a few miles southwest. Aboard were a superintendent of schools, a school nurse, and a driver, all intent on bringing some forty children to a public school, against the wishes of the Amish leaders. The Plain People had been violating the law, staffing their private schools with uncertified teachers. It was 7:45 a.m. on Friday, November 19, 1965.

On the way to the Amish settlement, the bus stopped momentarily in the tiny hamlet of Hazleton, and Owen Snively, principal of the Hazleton Elementary School, climbed aboard. He had been appointed temporary truant officer for the task at hand, for the Amish had long regarded him as a friend, and it was to his school that the youngsters were to be brought. A homespun

In lieu of detailed documentation, an appendix on methodology is provided at the end of this chapter. Much of the material discussed here has appeared in "The Plain People vs. the Common Schools," *Saturday Review*, November 19, 1966, pp. 85–87, 102–3; and "The 'Plain People' and American Democracy," *Commentary*, 45 (January, 1968): 36–44.

warmth and candor about him reflected boyhood years on an Iowa farm. In his love of the land and the outdoors, he had much in common with the Plain People. But he was apprehensive concerning the events that lay ahead.

The superintendent, Arthur Sensor, counted seventeen carloads of newsmen and sightseers, waiting outside the school for the drama to begin. "If I'd had any sense," he says, "I'd have gone back home the moment I saw those cars." Sensor had avoided action against the Amish for most of his thirty-eight months in office, for he was fond of many of the Plain People, and he knew where national sentiments lay in this regard.

With one exception (Abe Yoder had his driveway blocked so the bus could not enter), the delegation called at the homes of all the Amish who had been breaking the school code, occasionally stepping inside to talk. At each stop, Truant Officer Snively declared that he had come to take the children to the Hazleton school, under the authority of Iowa's truancy statute. Many of the parents, knowing what was planned, had hid their young in the fields ahead of time. Though Christ Raber reported his offspring were "not here," the driver claimed to see them peeking through a doorway. William Schmucker's children were present when the bus arrived, but he would not willingly let them leave the premises. Still hoping to avoid trouble, the group moved on from farm to farm, emptyhanded. After the last home had been visited, the bus turned back down the gravel road to Amish School No. 1 (also known as the "South School"), where many of the pupils had already arrived for their studies. By the time instruction was scheduled to begin, the sheriff, deputy sheriff, and county attorney appeared on the scene, along with numerous fathers and mothers.

Entering the building, Snively explained that it was legally necessary to transport the pupils to the school in town. He said he was their friend, wanting only to help them, and promised a warm welcome in Hazleton. Now, he asked, would they be good children and quietly file into the bus behind Sheriff Fred Beier. The sheriff started slowly toward the bus, the boys and girls following in an orderly single file. Suddenly, when most of the youngsters were outside, either the teacher or one of the mothers shouted in German, "Run!" The pupils bolted for the field at the rear of the schoolyard, scrambled through the barbed-wire fence, and ran through the adjoining cornfield into the woods beyond. Some never stopped running until they reached their homes. Wisely, the officials declined to give chase. Emanuel Borntreger, a portly boy of thirteen, could not keep up with his peers, waddled confusedly into the deputy sheriff's arms, and was led weeping to the bus. Sara Schmucker, a tiny six-year-old, was left behind in the cornfield, shivering and screaming distractedly. Tears coursing down his own face, Superintendent Sensor took her to the sheriff's heated automobile and tried to calm her.

On the lookout for interesting pictures, a newsman told Truant Officer Snively, "Some kids are hiding in the classroom. You can see them through the window." Peering through the pane on tiptoe, Snively provided a scene that appeared in papers across the nation the next day, along with photographs of children hightailing for the corn; a doe-like girl with stricken eyes, fleeing in blind panic while looking over her shoulder; Teacher Katie Miller, wiping her cheeks while her charges disappeared; Emanuel Borntreger, whimpering in the grasp of two husky officers; and the county attorney, stalking along the fence as if in search of some vanished quarry.

When no other pupils could be found, the men left Sara and Emanuel in the schoolhouse, urged the Amish to return the children to their studies at once (it was bitter cold), and announced that no further interruptions would occur that day. On the way back to Hazleton, however, Snively suggested that "since the Hookies pulled a fast one on us, we should pull a fast one on them." (The Amish, who fasten their clothing with hooks and eyes because of a taboo on ornaments, are often called "Hooks" or "Hookies." The non-Amish nearby are frequently referred to as "Buttons" or "English.") During the noon hour, Sensor and the sheriff suddenly appeared at Amish School No. 1 ("South School"), and Snively and the deputy sheriff at Amish School

No. 2 (also known as "North School" or "Charity Flats School").
Soon the bus followed, first to one school and then to the other,
and the pupils were carefully loaded aboard, one at a time, and
whisked to Hazleton. No parents or newsmen were present, and
the youngsters offered no resistance.

At Hazleton, preappointed pupil hosts met the bus, welcomed
the Old Order children, and escorted them to classrooms, helping to settle them and provide them with books. During the
afternoon, the newcomers took part in studies, played games with
their classmates, and were treated to cookies and milk. Many of
the Amish youngsters viewed the whole affair as high adventure
and sang and joked all the way home. But some were emotion-
ally shaken as a result of being forced to disobey their parents.
According to reports, a few were punished for going too enthu-
siastically to Hazleton.

The Plain People assumed that on Monday the authorities
would arrive via the same route as on Friday, calling first at
South School; so the most important Amish leaders and their
attorney, William Sindlinger, were posted there. Instead, the en-
tourage entered the community from the north. As before, the
officials went first to several homes along the way, and most of
the youngsters had fled. Abner Schwartz's children darted for the
cornfield just as the bus turned in at the gate, but Truant Officer
Snively was agile enough to retrieve them. Mrs. Schwartz dropped
to her knees in tears, pleading with the men to leave her little
ones alone. Her husband angrily kicked a milk pail all over the
barnyard. Superintendent Sensor refused to let the children leave
the bus, but assured Mrs. Schwartz they would come to no harm.
She then asked to be allowed to come with them to the school,
and when Sensor assented, climbed inside.

At the North School, a large horse-drawn wagon sat astride
the driveway, blocking passage, and the Amish attorney's colleague, Wallace Read, stood nearby, reading aloud from a document. Anyone but Truant Officer Snively would be liable for
trespass, Read intoned, upon entering these private grounds.
Snively huffed that he was entitled to bring assistants. Sheriff

Beier said he had responsibility to take action wherever the laws were broken in rural Buchanan County, and he proceeded to move the team and wagon, permitting the bus to enter.

Mrs. Schwartz and her frightened brood scurried into the schoolhouse. The entry-room was full of weeping women. A group of stern-faced fathers stood outside, guarding the door. Truant Officer Snively pushed his way through the men (the Plain People are pacifists), and brushed off the mothers who pulled at his clothing and begged him not to proceed. Sheriff Beier followed soon after. As Snively stepped inside, the pupils began singing, half-hysterically, chorus after chorus of "Jesus Loves Me," led by a teacher who circled the room in agitation. Soon mothers entered to embrace their children protectively. Snively attempted to pry a screaming schoolboy loose from a desk. A group of girls ran into a corner to huddle and sob as Snively approached them. Fathers burst in to protest. County Attorney Lemon shouted his disgust at the way the Amish were behaving. Newsmen came in, scribbling madly. Children wailed, women whimpered, flashbulbs popped, and tides of emotion swept the room. More than sixteen months later, the officials still show their embarrassment when asked about this event.

Retreating outdoors, Superintendent Sensor, Sheriff Beier, and County Attorney Lemon decided to fly to Des Moines for assistance. By 11 a.m. that same morning, the three men were airborne for the capital. Themselves upset, they left behind them an Old Order community in a state of shock. Some children could not be composed for the rest of the day.

As news of the showdown spread, citizens in the area sprang to the defense of their representatives. Strong support was soon expressed by the Oelwein *Daily Register*, the Rotary Club, and the Chamber of Commerce. Two statewide organizations, the Iowa State Education Association and the Iowa Association of School Administrators, applauded the "firm position" that had been taken. But in general, an opposite trend appeared outside the immediate vicinity. Hostile phone calls, telegrams, and mail poured in from all parts of the continent. Many commentators blistered Sensor, Snively, and their colleagues in the nation's news media. In Cedar Rapids, some eighty miles away, WMT-TV had supported Oelwein's leaders up to this point. Now it condemned what it called "legalized kidnapping":

> Force had been used on the Amish before, but always on the Amish parents who were guilty of violating the law. Now, force has been used against the Amish children, who are guilty of nothing. They have done their parents' bidding as good children do; and as a reward, they have been frightened, man-handled, and forced to violate their religious convictions. . . . Mr. Lemon [the county attorney] and school officials have acted most unwisely. Their ultimate weapon has turned public opinion sharply against them, as ultimate weapons always do. . . . Whatever the final outcome of this distasteful controversy, we urgently suggest that any future prosecution of the Amish be directed only against the guilty. Leave the innocent children alone.

The confrontation was obviously harmful to the Amish youngsters, damaging to Iowa's public image, and destructive of trust between the Plain People and local authorities. What circumstances can explain such hostilities between a gentle farming folk and apparently well-intentioned public officials?

The Cause Célèbre

There is an obvious linkage between the showdown with the Amish and an informal agreement in the fall of 1961. Until that time, the Hazleton and Oelwein public schools were located in separate districts. It had been suggested for years that the two districts merge and all high school students be educated in Oelwein, for Hazleton High was too small to offer adequate programs. The proposal was supported by numerous Hazletonians, especially those who wanted to give their young a strong preparation for college. A few families were paying tuition and providing their own transportation to send their offspring to high school in Oelwein.

But many Hazletonians opposed reorganization, remembering years of rivalry between the two towns and thinking that the loss of high school and school board headquarters would seriously weaken their community. Many felt the proposed merger was tantamount to a take-over by the city of Oelwein, which had threatened for years to eclipse its tiny neighbor five miles south. Some Hazleton people still complain that the Oelwein *Daily Register* trumpets the escapades of Hazleton teen-agers and ignores similar high jinks at home. In Oelwein, where nothing was to be lost through reorganization, sentiments were strong for approval. There, the school district would be enlarged, the high school program broadened, the tax base improved.

The Hazleton school board unanimously fought the projected merger and refused to put the matter before the voters. Residents who desired the alliance with Oelwein then formed a committee and, abetted by Oelwein school officials, filed enough petitions to require a referendum, scheduled for November 8, 1961. Issues of school district reorganization are often severely contested in rural America, but the Hazleton-Oelwein fracas grew unusually bitter. Those who supported the proposal were described as "for Oelwein"; those who damned it, "for Hazleton." Old friends stopped talking. Secret meetings were held. Vicious rumors spread. Each faction accused the other of lies and distortions. On both sides a few hotheads who normally lacked an audience found attentive ears.

As for the Plain People, they petitioned a joint meeting of the Buchanan, Fayette, and Bremer County school boards, which was to draw the boundaries of the new district, asking to be excluded from the jurisdiction of Oelwein officials. (In Iowa and several other states outside the South, the county level of school government is intermediate between the state and the operating districts. Generally overlying several local school districts, the county unit provides services that small districts would have difficulty maintaining by themselves.) The Amish wanted to be attached to the adjoining Fairbank Township area, where one-room public schools were still maintained for Old Order pupils. Hazleton's two Amish schools were themselves once public. But when the Hazleton Consolidated School District was formed, back in 1947, farm boys and girls were transferred to the consolidated school in town, and the Plain People, unwilling to have their young educated in environs they saw as hostile, bought the abandoned one-room schoolhouses and "went private." Where farm children attend nonpublic schools, income from school taxes on their parents' land is $99\frac{44}{100}$ per cent gravy for the public school districts. Even when rural pupils attend simple one-room public schools, the potential tax income from the area often exceeds the school expenditures. Coveting these resources, Oelwein officials helped arrange the rejection of the Plain People's request to be "set out."

At the time in question, Sensor's predecessor, A. A. Kaskadden, was still superintendent of the Oelwein public schools. "Kas" is described by those who knew him as brilliant, expert in virtually every aspect of school affairs. But he was nervous, anxious, and full of self-doubt. He drove himself mercilessly and worried about everything. Kaskadden was distraught about prospects for the reorganization referendum. He knew Oelwein citizens would support the merger overwhelmingly, but the approval of the voters in both districts was required. Hazletonians, he thought, would split fifty-fifty on the issue, and the Amish, perturbed because they were not permitted to stay out of the proposed new district, might sabotage his efforts by casting their ballots negatively.

In September, 1961, Kas wrote Paul Johnston, State Superintendent of Public Instruction, asking for help in putting the referendum across. A little later the two men conferred at a meeting of professional educators. Johnston was known in Iowa as "an apostle of school district reorganization." He had already attempted to influence Hazleton voters by announcing that state approval of their high school would be withdrawn after July 1, 1962, the date on which the projected reorganization was to take effect. Johnston suggested that Kaskadden win the Amish vote by promising to revert to a practice still followed in nearby school districts, maintaining simple one-room public schools in Amish communities. The new board, Johnston suggested, could reincorporate Hazleton's two Old Order schools into the public school system by leasing the buildings for a nominal fee, could provide two certified teachers at public expense, and could adapt the programs to the convictions of the Amish leaders. The fiscal advantages for the Plain People would be considerable, and they would lose practically nothing in the process.

But Johnston had fought for the elimination of one-room schools in Iowa! "If we are caught maintaining one-room schools for the Amish," Kaskadden demanded, "what will happen to our state approval?" Johnston replied that the State Department of Education, knowing the particulars of the situation, would raise no embarrassing questions. Kaskadden predicted that the Amish would vote for reorganization if such a compact were arranged, but he insisted he would take no steps in that direction unless Johnston sanctioned the strategy in writing, promising in a letter that the status of the Oelwein schools would not be jeopardized. Back in Oelwein, Kaskadden confided to his board members, "Johnston will never write that letter!" A few days later, the following communication arrived:

October 12, 1961

Mr. A. A. Kaskadden
Oelwein Public School
Oelwein, Iowa
Dear Mr. Kaskadden:

I am in receipt of your letter concerning your reorganization and I am sorry that you have not been able to get in touch with me before this.

I recall our conversation concerning the Amish settlement located in the Hazleton Consolidated School District. I am glad to set forth in this letter my views concerning the situation as it exists.

I think that because of the situation as it exists and the feelings of the Amish people that the Board would, and should, recognize that they have to give consideration to the people making up the new district. As I suggested when we were visiting, I would recommend that if the reorganization took place that the Board hire teachers and provide supervision for the two schools which the Amish people are now operating. I think the new Board should provide good facilities and equipment, and good teachers for these schools but in so doing recognize these people's feeling concerning education.

I think this would be a good solution for these people and also I think your board and the future Board should undertake to understand their beliefs and work with them in giving their children the basic education that they firmly believe in. We would, I am sure, raise no questions concerning this arrangement so long as the facilities were adequate and well qualified teachers furnished to teach these children along with the type of instruction materials that I am sure your Board would insist upon providing. We would not adversely judge your school because of this as we do have an understanding of the situation.

Trusting this gives you the information you requested, I remain

Sincerely yours,

(signed)

Paul F. Johnston
State Superintendent of
Public Instruction

Kaskadden wasted no time at this point. He held several discussions with Dan Borntreger, venerable chairman of the Amish School Committee, bringing copies of Paul Johnston's statement. Gentle in mein but renowned for his shrewdness, with aquiline profile, white beard, and silken hair around a bald pate, Borntreger is well cast as biblical patriarch. He was not easily persuaded that Kas and the board could make a lasting covenant, for he knew that they had no legal authority to bind the board that would be elected after reorganization. "I expect to be superintendent for many years to come," Kaskadden said, "and I will always recommend that the board honor our arrangement." At least one board member talked with Borntreger; the member said he had every anticipation of being reelected, and he, too, would keep faith. Buck Kjar, chairman of the Hazleton reorganization committee, urged the Amish to place confidence in the promises of Kas and his colleagues. Finally convinced, Borntreger set about to persuade his confreres to vote for reorganization. C. J. Arthaud, then president of the Hazleton school board, tells of spending several hours with Kaskadden at this juncture, trying unsuccessfully to persuade him not to bargain for the Plain People's ballots.

Just four days before the referendum, Johnston's letter was published in full in the Oelwein *Daily Register*, which thirty-two Amishmen were receiving at the time. In the same issue, a letter to the editor complained that "the Oelwein Community School District has promised the Amish people tax paid schools for their children. . . . It looks to these writers that someone is buying votes." In addition, the Oelwein board inserted a statement of its own:

> Should this reorganization proposal pass on November 8th and the newly elected board of education see fit to concur in Mr. Johnston's recommendation and again take over the operation of the rural schools in the Amish area, the same curriculum, the same standards, and the same quality of teachers would be used as in all other schools of the district.
> . . . To transport these children to Hazleton at taxpayers [sic] expense would probably cost as much as to educate them in the rural schools as the Amish desire.
> The present Oelwein Board of Education feels that the desires of all minority groups should be given full consideration whenever possible providing these desires are legal and lead to better education. . . .
> The Oelwein Board of Education could not legally and did not make a definite commitment to the Amish people. We simply passed on the recommendations given us by the State Department of Public Instruction that legally the newly elected board of education for the new district if reorganization passed, could and should give consideration to the Amish peoples' request that their schools be operated under the full jurisdiction of the duly elected board of education.

On November 8, 1961, citizens in the Oelwein school district approved reorganization overwhelmingly (993 to 231), while in Hazleton, with 44 Amishmen voting, the measure passed by a margin of only 49 (264 to 215). Assuming that the Plain People supported reorganization, in accordance with the agreement, it is obvious that they could have defeated the measure by voting negatively. But Dan Borntreger and the Oelwein school officials had underestimated the reaction that would follow. Hazletonians who had opposed reorganization were furious concerning the behind-the-scenes compact and the Amish role in the election. Key Hazletonians to this day insist that the followers of the Old Order "swung the election and forced us to come under the Oelwein board." Residents who wanted the referendum to pass had brought several carloads of Amishmen to town to cast ballots. Seeing the Amish at the polls, numerous local people were so incensed they left without voting, and others angrily stayed home as the news spread. The resentment was exacerbated when, in March, 1962, not one member of the Hazleton board was elected to represent the new district, while Buck Kjar, who headed the despised Hazleton reorganization committee, was placed in office with all five members of the old Oelwein board. Ancient grievances against the Plain People were revived. Hazleton citizens vowed to take stern steps against any Hook caught breaking the law. Intense pressures were exerted to prevent the new school board from taking over the two Old Order schools in accordance with the agreement, and a close watch was kept to determine "whether Oelwein will make the Amish obey the school code the way Hazleton always did."

By this time, it appears, many Hazletonians had developed what a former Oelwein school board member describes as "very deep, bitter prejudice" against the Amish, comparable, he avers, to attitudes toward Negroes in Selma, Alabama. Local leaders confess they cannot quite understand how these antagonisms arose, except that the circumstances of the referendum played an important part.

The Plain People are the object of some criticism wherever they are found. Their nonconformity is itself a mild insult to the larger society. Generally preferring to limit contacts with Buttons, the denizens of the Old Order sometimes seem cliquish and unfriendly. On occasion their refusal to retaliate when attacked is viewed as cowardice. In a number of areas, the existence of many Amish conscientious objectors meant that a disproportionate number of "English" were sent to battle during World War II, for a county-by-county quota system was in force. Forbidden to possess radios, television sets, automobiles, plumbing, washing machines, refrigerators, sofas, sports equipment, and "fancy" clothing, they put little money into local purchases and much into land and ironware crocks. Yet they frequently ride in their neighbors' cars and ask to use their neighbors' telephones. Since each church district is autonomous, some bishops permit what others prohibit. Even within a single community, what is allowed at one time may be forbidden at another. Now and then the Amish are exempted from legislation concerning schools and social security, and a few Buttons object to this "unfairness." But in most areas, the Amish are admired, in spite of these foibles and inconsistencies, for they are usually skillful farmers, industrious, self-reliant, and honest. They never leave a brother in need.

Around Hazleton, however, they are subject to a dismal list of charges, often exaggerated, unsupported, or inconsistent. Two or three Legionnaires were fiercely offended by a juvenile prank in Amish School No. 1 that left the American flag on the floor, and by doodlings, interpreted as disrespectful, found in some civics workbooks. A few residents who lost sons in the war still act as if the Plain People were entirely to blame. When a member of the Old Order recently bought up a deceased friend's mortgage, apparently to protect the widow from an "English" creditor, this was evidence to local people, strangely, that "the Hooks want to be in a position to coerce each other financially." As sociologists and anthropologists recognize, many issues that are secular in the urbanized world are sacred in folk societies. But when Amishmen cite religious principle as the basis for most decisions, Hazleton people accuse them of "using religion as an excuse for anything they want to do." The Plain People say their community needs isolation to survive; consequently their young must be limited to a simple elementary education in rural schools. Scholars who have studied the culture agree. But locally the Amish are branded as hypocrites, motivated by economic greed, wanting only to keep their schooling costs down, and hoping to exploit child labor in the fields. Not all Amish are honest, of course, but as a people they are acknowledged by social scientists and most businessmen who serve them to exhibit unusual integrity. But because a few young blades hide transistor radios under broad-brimmed hats and buggy seats, citizens nearby declare the Old Order "makes people deceitful." Neighbors almost universally aver that the Plain People are happy and carefree — "perhaps happier than we are." Yet some of the same individuals describe the Amish community as if it were a concentration camp — where children are chained to beds, where barefoot women run farms while their husbands loaf and travel, where the young are "worked to death," and where aging wives are allowed to die in childbirth as a substitute for divorce. The Amish are depicted at some times as so wealthy they should be ashamed to let sympathizers pay their fines, but at other times as unsuccessful and poverty stricken ("they don't use enough fertilizer"), living in dilapidated lean-tos. Out of a community of at least five hundred, local leaders identify about fourteen Amishmen who have left the fold in recent decades, yet argue that the young are deserting in such alarming numbers the community will soon disintegrate. Defectors from the subculture are depicted as "getting along beautifully" in their new surroundings, but their education is condemned as cutting off all chances of survival in the outside world. Old Order adolescents are pitied for their drab, iron-clad lives, yet their purported barnyard orgies are discussed with evangelical indignation ("They aren't as righteous as they claim to be!"). One board member recently emphasized that modern agriculture demands a far better schooling than the Plain People receive. Almost in the next breath, in response to a question, he described some of the Amish as unsurpassed as farmers.

The post-referendum animosity in Hazleton could hardly be ignored in Oelwein. School leaders were particularly sensitive to voter opinion at the time, for a bond issue referendum to finance an urgently needed high school addition had recently been defeated. Now that Hazleton youths would be bussed to Oelwein, the space shortage was especially critical. Hazletonians had been alienated badly enough through the reorganization itself. It seemed that the second bond election, soon to come, would fail if the school board further angered local people by complying with the compact with the Amish. What could Superintendent Kaskadden do?

The Double Standard

In a communication dated May 7, 1962, the Oelwein school board announced two conditions which, according to the Amish and several board members themselves, had never been mentioned to the Plain People before the reorganization referendum of November, 1961. First, if the board took over the two Amish schools, there could be little or no tailoring of the academic program to suit the religious convictions of the parents, even though State Superintendent Johnston's now-famous letter had urged the board to "recognize these people's feeling concerning education" and "undertake to understand their beliefs and work with them in giving their children the basic education that they firmly believe in," and in spite of Kaskadden's repeated assurances to Dan Borntreger. Second, the arrangement must be *temporary*. "It would appear obvious," the board declared, "that Mr. Johnston's letter advising us to work with the Amish people in these schools . . . [was intended] to make the transition of these [Amish] pupils to a public school setup easier. Realistically and in all honesty and fairness, it should be pointed out that the ultimate state requirement will demand that these pupils will be incorporated into the school at Hazleton where we have a reasonable chance to have at least one teacher for each elementary grade."

In the Oelwein *Daily Register* for November 4, 1961, four days before the referendum, the board had said: "Should . . . the newly elected board . . . again take over the operation of the rural schools in the Amish area, the same curriculum, the same standards, and the same quality of teachers would be used as in all other schools of the district." The Amish paid no attention to this one statement, however, for no such idea had been brought up in their several conversations with Kaskadden and his colleagues. It was easy to assume that this isolated utterance, appearing in the newspaper virtually on the eve of the referendum, was public relations copy and nothing more, intended to pacify a few citizens who were complaining about the understanding with the Plain People. If Kaskadden and the board had wanted to apprise the Amish of a new condition, stating it in a single sentence in a small item in the *Register* was the wrong method, and four days before an election that had involved months of haggling and planning was the wrong time.

As the Amish see it, the sudden introduction of two far-reaching provisions represented a deliberate attempt to back out of the compact, for Kaskadden and the school board knew the Plain People would never accept such demands. "They wanted to be able to say that they offered to run our schools but we wouldn't cooperate," one Amishman declares.

The second blow fell on May 14, just one week later. In response to inquiries from Kaskadden, State Superintendent Johnston sent two of his regional consultants to Oelwein, ostensibly to advise the school board and the Amish concerning the specific improvements that would have to be made in Hazleton's Old Order schools before they could be taken over as public schools. The consultants, Melvin Anderson and Thomas Green, inspected the two buildings, along with Kaskadden and several members of his board.

The delegation found the schools primitive, as indeed they still are. The Amish are committed to the simple life, shorn of many conveniences the outside world regards as necessities. In the manner of a bygone era, they know how to maintain healthful conditions without benefit of plumbing and electricity. They scorn many modern educational materials and devices, for they want merely to rear their young to manage farms and kitchens. But people who have seen only tiled bathrooms are certain to be shocked by a privy. In contrast to a chrome-plated faucet, a simple well and pump may seem unsanitary. It is easy to forget that generations of Americans learned to read without light bulbs.

In keeping with the Plain People's philosophy, their schools are rustic, reflecting little attention to esthetics. The two buildings near Hazleton are reasonably clean and cheerful, though finished rather roughly inside and out and marred in spots by flaking paint. Each is furnished with two outdoor privies, a coal shed, and a well with a manual pump. The North School boasts two see-saws, two swings, and some old tires as playground equipment; the South School has none at all.

In each case the only entrance is through a small vestibule, with shelves and nails for lunch buckets and coats. Each classroom has rough board floors, generations-worn; extra-tall windows on two sides for ventilation and light (no electricity); short shelves holding a potpourri of dog-eared books; home-made cupboards for construction paper; a kitchen sink with water crock and paper towel dispenser; a large Regulator clock clucking high on the wall; bits of blackboard; five rows of ancient desks; a teacher's desk and chair; a hard bench or two for recitations; two or three sturdy work tables; cardboard boxes full of discarded textbooks; and some roll-up maps that should be priceless as antiques. Heat radiates from a massive stove at the rear, stoked by boys assigned to the task. Pupils' drawings (virtually all brightly colored rural scenes) are tacked here and there.

The South School had been closed for the summer (in violation of the statutes) when the inspection team arrived, but Amishman Andy Kaufman provided a key. The officials professed profound shock at what they saw. They had never imagined, they said, that conditions were so bad, so utterly degrading. One man stuck his head into a privy, emerged with a grimace, and commented, "Ugh!" Another protested the presence of a bird's nest on an exterior window sill. Still others worried about mud puddles near the well. Virtually no supplementary reading materials were available. Several texts and workbooks were badly outdated. In a meeting that very night with the Oelwein board and two representatives of the Amish community, without contacting Des Moines for Paul Johnston's approval, the state department officers suddenly reversed the recommendation contained in his widely publicized letter of October 12, 1961. The Amish schools were impossible, Anderson and Green announced, and could never be brought up to an acceptable standard. The State Department of Education would permit the Oelwein Board to operate these schools *for the first six grades only and for two years at the very most.* Before this could be done, furthermore, the Amish must agree to send all seventh- and eighth-grade pupils to Hazleton at once, with the other children to follow within two years. From that point on, the Oelwein board could say it was powerless to help the Amish unless they agreed to the state department's conditions, which of course the Plain People were unlikely to do.

This dramatic reversal of state department policy is the most puzzling event in the entire controversy over Hazleton's Old Order schools, not only because two men in the field purportedly took it upon themselves to countermand their superior's recommendation without even checking with him, but also because of its blatant incompatibility with state department policy less than twenty miles away. At the time of Anderson and Green's ruling, public school districts just west of the Hazleton district were operating seven one-room schools and one two-room school in the countryside for Amish pupils. State department consultants made regular visits to these districts, but the schools were never condemned, although, as late as March, 1967, all eight lacked plumbing, all were served by wells similar to those at Hazleton's Amish schools, two had no electricity, and at least one looked considerably more neglected than the schools pronounced impossible by Anderson and Green. In March, 1967, a regional consultant for the state department visited five of these schools (including the two without electricity), now maintained by the Wapsie Valley Community School district, and expressed his delight at the way the district was providing for the education of the Amish.

Until recently, these primitive public schools for Old Order pupils were maintained by small rural districts whose boards were composed mostly or entirely of Amishmen. By July, 1966, under a new Iowa law, all public elementary schools were required to belong to districts providing instruction at the secondary level. Many observers predicted that the remaining one- and two-room public schools in Amish settlements would be closed as a result, and that Oelwein's debacle would be duplicated elsewhere as the Plain People established more schools of their own, staffed with uncertified teachers.

Three of the schools in question became part of the Jesup Community School District, southwest of Hazleton, and five joined the Wapsie Valley Community School District to the northwest. But leaders in Jesup and Wapsie Valley cleverly avoided Oelwein's dilemma. The town schools, they argued, would be overcrowded if the Older Order pupils were assigned to them, and to make space for the Amish would entail serious expense. It would be financially necessary, then, to continue operating the primitive schools in Amish neighborhoods, at least for the present. The Jesup district has candidly left the schools for the Plain People much as they were, doing little to alter either physical facilities or academic programs. The teachers, though provisionally certified, have but meager formal qualifications, are paid at a rate considerably below Jesup's salary schedule, and would never be tolerated by the state department, Jesup officials declare, if used in other public schools. Science instruction is omitted in compliance with the wishes of the Amish leaders. In Wapsie Valley, similarly, teachers in the one-room schools for the Amish are remunerated at levels considerably below the regular salary schedule, and the buildings are similar to those maintained by Dan Borntreger's committee. The superintendent has made a special effort to gain the confidence of the Plain People, however, and they have agreed to the addition of courses in science.

Clearly, a double standard has been in force in northeastern

Iowa for the past five years. The Oelwein, Jesup, and Wapsie Valley school districts all have benefited fiscally through the annexation of Old Order communities. Oelwein alone argues that it cannot justify the costs of maintaining rural schools for the Amish. By state department edict, furthermore, Hazleton's Amish have been forbidden the very accommodations the department has lauded elsewhere.

In terms of local attitudes, however, the difference in policy between Oelwein and the other two districts is not difficult to explain. Only around Hazleton is hostility toward the Plain People so intense that officials have dared not give the Amish access to simple one-room public schools. But why the conflicting actions of the state department? Perhaps the department innocently blundered into inconsistency, as every large bureaucracy occasionally does. The inconsistency came, however, at the very time when Superintendent Kaskadden needed an excuse to abandon his covenant with the Amish. As a long-standing friend of Kas, State Superintendent Johnston had previously invented a maneuver that helped guarantee passage of the reorganization referendum. Was he now taking Kaskadden off another hook? Could Anderson and Green have come to Oelwein with orders to be surprised and shocked and to reverse Johnston's recommendation accordingly? The theory cannot be proved, but it fits the circumstances well.

But Kaskadden is gone, and leaders in Hazleton and Oelwein seem genuinely unaware of the double standard. The most common explanation for the controversy over Old Order education is that Dan Borntreger and some sixteen families in his group are being unusually stubborn. "All the other Amish in the area are attending public schools, but these Hookies refuse to send their children to Hazleton." However, the Hazleton school is radically different from the schools the other Amish attend — in its physical make-up, in the nature of its surroundings, in its programs and activities, and in the composition of its pupil population. And Borntreger once covenanted with Oelwein officials to obtain schools precisely like those his confreres nearby have patronized.

A few months later, in September, 1962, for the first time in history both of Hazleton's Amish schools reopened with Old Order teachers who were equipped with only an eighth-grade education (the Amish generally do not believe in instruction beyond that level). The Plain People have steadfastly refused ever since to employ certified instructors. This comparatively new stance is defended as a matter of religious principle. But do the Amish commandments change, local citizens ask, permitting state-approved tutors for fifteen years and then forbidding them? It is difficult to determine exactly why the Amish suddenly refused to comply with the Iowa law they had obeyed for so long a time. Their leaders were never happy, it appears, with the certified teachers they imported from outside. It is widely conceded that Dan Borntreger's group had to pay a premium to obtain legally recognized instructors and generally obtained poorly qualified individuals even then, for those who could obtain positions elsewhere were usually unwilling to work in such primitive schools. Apparently several of these schoolmarms lacked initiative, communicated poorly with the pupils, failed to maintain proper discipline, and reacted defensively to suggestions from parents and community leaders. It is probably true, as the Plain People argue, that many bright Amish girls, available at far less cost, could have functioned at a higher level. Financial considerations may have played some part in the decision to hire no more state-approved teachers, for the school committee was having to pay considerably higher salaries as time went on. Disillusionment was almost certainly involved. Apparently the Amish were complying with a law that did not make sense to them partly in deference to public officials they trusted and admired. They had particular respect for Kaskadden. But now they felt they had been betrayed. Perhaps the convictions of the Amish School Committee members concerning the religious defensibility of certified teachers did genuinely change when a traumatic series of events forced a reexamination of relationships between God and Caesar. Some local citizens insist that Dan Borntreger lost face in his community when his compact with public officers turned out to be worthless, and he had to take some kind of dramatic counteraction to reestablish his influence. Or a complex combination of factors may have been involved.

Whatever their logic, the Amish played into the hands of their antagonists by suddenly refusing to comply with the law requiring certified instructors. Previously, hostile Hazletonians lacked a legal reason for demanding action against the Plain People. The Amish had bypassed several requirements of the school code, but common citizens had no right to inspect private schools; so most shortcomings were largely unnoticed. Whenever violations were visible, as when buildings went unpainted or vacations began too early, neighbors would complain, public educators would issue a few threats, and the faults would be rectified. For a brief period during September, 1961, one school was staffed by an uncertified teacher, but the Buttons noticed right away (a buggy rather than an automobile was parked outside), the county superintendent uttered thunder, and the situation was soon corrected. But in permanently renouncing state-approved instructors in the fall of 1962, the Amish gave their angry neighbors the clear-cut instance of law-breaking they had sought. There was an immediate, vehement demand that the Amish be prosecuted.

From Bad to Worse

As pressure mounted for action against the Amish, local leaders at first avoided involvement by raising jurisdictional questions. In time, the officials were forced into several futile legal proceedings, interspersed with scapegoating and efforts to achieve a compromise. But the problem only worsened.

The reorganized Oelwein Community School District, which has responsibility for enforcing the compulsory attendance law, includes parts of Fayette and Buchanan counties. Since the district headquarters are in Fayette County, the attorney for that county acts for the school board on most litigative issues. But Hazleton's two Amish schools are in Buchanan County. Each county attorney argued, then, that the other was responsible to move against the defiant parents. Finally, someone thought of requesting a ruling from Des Moines, whereupon the Buchanan County Attorney, then William O'Connell, was identified as the proper person to act as prosecutor. O'Connell insisted, however, that he could do nothing until some school officer filed informations against the Plain People. Under fire from citizens who wanted immediate action, he protested that Oelwein school board members, who didn't "have guts enough" to do their duty, were to blame for the delay. Oelwein officials announced that the county school superintendent should be the one to institute proceedings. While the law merely *permitted* local school boards to prosecute in such cases, they argued speciously, it *required* the county superintendent to do so. Oelwein leaders also insisted that they could do nothing until state agencies took the first step. The attorney general and state superintendent of schools, in turn, declared that the controversy was purely local in character and as such was a matter for local people to handle.

On the morning of September 25, 1962, Kaskadden complained to Bruce Girton, then school board president, of exhaustion and dizziness. Reorganization had burdened Kas heavily, along with lengthy and frequent board meetings to deal with the Amish problem. On the evening of that day, he puttered a little in his basement, came upstairs, and slumped dead into a chair. At an emergency board meeting the next morning, Arthur Sensor was appointed acting superintendent.

After Kaskadden's death, the Amish were less hopeful of reaching an equitable settlement with the authorities, for Kas was one of the few school officers they trusted. Even today, they attempt to rationalize the broken agreement in terms of Kaskadden's passing, preferring to ignore the fact that the board had changed its tune when Kas was at the helm. Intransigence set in on both sides. The Oelwein board began to deny there ever was a behind-the-scenes arrangement with the Plain People. On November 29, 1962, the *Daily Register* reported, "At least one news agency stated to Sensor that they had conclusive evidence that the Oelwein Community School District had promised the Amish two schools in the Amish settlement. The school board felt that this and other similar statements were untrue." In the next issue of the same newspaper, Board President Bruce Girton "emphatically denied that any deal had been made with the Amish and said there had absolutely been no doublecross in the situation." Several local people think it conclusive to point out that no one had authority, before the reorganized Oelwein district was formed, to make a legally binding covenant in behalf of the district. Neither Kaskadden, his board members, nor the Amish ever pretended the compact was legally binding. It was an informal understanding that public officials as individuals promised to honor. The Plain People, accustomed to loaning money to each other over a handclasp, simply relied on the personal integrity of these officials. According to some observers, the Oelwein board's reluctance to prosecute the Amish was partly attributable to embarrassment, for the Amish kept mentioning the shattered covenant.

J. J. Jorgensen, then Buchanan County Superintendent of Schools, was the first educator to yield to demands for punitive action, possibly because his board, unlike Arthur Sensor's, was drawn entirely from the county where the hostility was centered. Jorgensen did not proceed on his own volition. According to several observers, he was a tired, noncommittal office holder who hoped nothing controversial would arise to disturb his plans for retirement. On November 24, 1962, acting on information filed by Jorgensen, Buchanan County Attorney William O'Connell prosecuted ten Amishmen before a justice of the peace for failing to send their children to schools with certified teachers. All ten were fined. Eight refused to pay on religious grounds and served three days behind bars. Newspapers across the continent published pictures of black-bonnetted Amish mothers on the way to visit their husbands in jail. Local officials were deluged with insulting letters. Soon there was talk of how O'Connell was "bungling the Amish affair." Next, O'Connell sought an injunction to close the Old Order schools, but the district court pointed out, somewhat tartly, that there was no statutory basis for such action. In the next Republican primary, O'Connell's handling of the case was widely debated, and he was trounced. Other men, sobered by these events, sought the more to avoid involvement. To act against the Plain People was "quicksand," "political suicide," "taking a bear by the tail." The controversy was "one of those affairs that tar everyone with the same brush."

In January, 1963, at the urging of the beleaguered county superintendent, the Oelwein board offered once more to run the two Amish schools temporarily if Dan Borntreger's group would agree to send all seventh- and eighth-grade students to Hazleton at once and all other pupils within two years. The proposal, no different from previous ones, was rejected. In October, 1963, the attorney for the Amish, William Sindlinger, sought unsuccessfully in district court to have his clients exempted from the law demanding certified teachers. Arguing that "this may be a way out of the impasse for us all," he tried to persuade the Oelwein board not to oppose the petition. The board refused. Its position was becoming more rigid.

In September, 1964, another compromise was attempted. At the suggestion of State Superintendent Paul Johnston, the Oelwein board offered to provide special ungraded classrooms for Amish children in the Hazleton school on a one-year trial basis. The Amish would not concur. Later, officials proposed that Borntreger's people hire a certified Amish teacher (a virtually unheard-of species) from Kalona, Iowa. The Amish School Committee interviewed the teacher and announced that he was "not our kind of Amishman." If forced to accept a certified instructor, Borntreger said, his group would prefer a total outsider.

The turning point in the long series of delaying actions came in September, 1965. An Oelwein school board member whose term was not expiring resigned, and several others decided not to seek reelection; so four new members were placed on the seven-man body. The Amish affair had been an important behind-the-scenes issue in the election. In response to adverse national publicity, sentiments in Oelwein had become less sympathetic toward the Amish. The new members of the board had implied they would deal more firmly than their predecessors with the Plain People. At the first meeting of the reconstituted board, the new Buchanan County attorney, Harlan Lemon, was present. Repeatedly during his campaign he had promised "to enforce all laws," and he urged the Oelwein board to file informations against the Amish immediately. Almost simultaneously, a leader of the anti-reorganization faction in Hazleton announced that he would ask a court to remove Sensor from office for failing to make the Amish obey the school code. In the words of Sensor, "We didn't give him a chance to act. We acted first." Oelwein officials filed informations against the offending Old Order parents in the court of Justice of the Peace Minnie Wengert.

For a number of weeks, local leaders had known they were in for trouble. In response to their call for aid, Iowa's attorney general, then Lawrence Scalise, had summoned County Attorney Harlan Lemon and two Amish representatives to Des Moines "to work something out." Scalise first persuaded the Amish to accept certified teachers once more — so long as the Amish School Committee did not have to pay the salaries. (The Amish often make a distinction between what they may do for themselves and what it is permissible, under duress, to let Caesar do.) Then Superintendent Sensor of Oelwein was convinced, according to Scalise, that the only way out of the impasse was for the Oelwein board to take over the Amish schools quietly and run them for two years, during which time a more permanent solution could be found. For example, two Amish teachers might take some courses by correspondence, qualifying for special certificates that would be valid only in Old Order schools. Scalise emphasized, however, that hotheads in Hazleton and Oelwein would quickly sabotage the arrangement if it were publicized before the board had acted conclusively. Scalise insists that Sensor agreed to bring the matter before his board with as little fanfare as possible.

As it turned out, the board meeting at which Scalise's proposal was considered was a virtual press conference. While the board was still in session, Scalise phoned County Attorney Lemon to see what progress was being made. Lemon observed that reporters had been invited to the discussion and that the board was about to reject the proposal. Scalise relayed a plea to the board that they defer action until he had a chance to discuss the matter with them personally. Then he talked to the members of the press by telephone, begging them not to publicize the mater until it had been resolved. When he watched the news on television that night, the issue was exposed in great detail.

Still not willing to concede defeat, Scalise pressed for a closed consultation with the Oelwein board. The meeting was scheduled for September 28. In the meantime, the Oelwein board decided the meeting should be held in public "so everything will be in the open." Plans for the discussion with Scalise were revealed in a major story in the Oelwein *Daily Register*. But Scalise was not informed of the change. A Democrat, he was widely disliked in Oelwein, a Republican stronghold, not only because of his political affiliation but also because he had publicly castigated Oelwein officials for their "inflexible approach" to the Amish problem. On September 28, Scalise flew to Oelwein, hurried to Sensor's long office, where the board usually met, and chatted with Sensor while munching a sandwich (he had missed dinner). When time for the meeting approached, Sensor announced that it was open to the public and ushered Scalise onto the platform of the junior high school auditorium nearby. A belligerent crowd of three hundred had gathered. What happened next has been generally described as a "three-ring circus." Board members and people in the audience fired a barrage of loaded questions at Scalise, and each time he winced or faltered, the crowd clapped and cheered. Scalise said later he had "lost fifteen pints of blood" at the meeting, and felt Sensor was responsible. Sensor insists, however, that he tried to persuade the board to hold a closed meeting. A "side show" of this kind is always a mistake, he says. He would never deliberately subject anyone to the embarrassment Scalise suffered that evening.

After an hour or so of high humor at Scalise's expense, the

board summarily rejected his proposal. Board members claim that he was simply trying to trick them into taking over the two Amish schools, establishing a practice that would be difficult to abandon. Near the end of the meeting, Scalise said he had been asked for advice in a strictly local affair, had offered assistance in good faith, and had received only insults as a result. From now on, he declared, Oelwein could worry about its own problem. He would have nothing more to do with it. "But don't come running to me for help the next time you get yourselves in a jam!"

Shortly thereafter, Justice of the Peace Minnie Wengert began to process charges against the Amish in her renovated porch in Hazleton. For more than three weeks, fourteen bearded Amishmen showed up each night, Monday through Friday, beaming good will and bearing gifts of garden produce for Mrs. Wengert, the sheriff, and other officials. As if to provide a little variety, Adin Yutzey stayed home from time to time and had to be fetched by the sheriff. It soon became the custom to arrive early and stay late, for Mrs. Wengert would pour coffee and the antagonists would munch and visit. But occasionally a certain bitterness was detectable beneath the outward amity, and a few of the smiles came out a bit grotesque. At 7:30 each evening, officials testified that the Amish had once more refused to obey the law, the Amish acknowledged that the charge was true, each defendent was fined $20 plus $4 costs, and each refused to pay on religious grounds. Occasionally Dan Borntreger showed up (he was not a defendant) to administer a lecture from Scripture, and Mrs. Wengert retorted with some well-chosen Bible quotations of her own. It was announced that the fines and costs would be exacted at the end of each school day, indefinitely, until the Plain People complied with the Iowa code. Furthermore, Amish properties would soon be seized and sold to pay the levies.

A clever young man with a lean and hungry look, County Attorney Harlan Lemon was in no mood to be accused, like his predecessor, of botching the Amish issue. He sought, not punishment, but compliance. As the weeks wore on, he worried. The nightly sessions were robbing important leaders of an unconscionable amount of energy and time, and the Amish showed no sign of relenting. It would not take long at this rate to ruin the Amish community financially, and the political consequences of that eventuality were unthinkable. Lemon began to explore ways of ending the impasse in off-the-record discussions with Superintendent Sensor and two or three Amishmen who secretly disagreed with the Amish School Committee and Dan Borntreger. Toward the end of October, the Oelwein board renewed its offer of an ungraded classroom for the Amish in the Hazleton school on a one-year trial basis. The Plain People again rejected the compromise, even when it was suggested that their fines could be waived as a part of the package. Finally, the behind-the-scenes negotiators agreed, according to Lemon and Sensor, that everyone would save face if the Old Order pupils were escorted to Hazleton in accordance with Iowa's truancy statute. Since the Amish will not resort to violent resistance, Borntreger would be powerless to prevent officials from transporting the children to the public school and thus could claim that he was overcome by force rather than modifying his convictions. Those who disagreed with Borntreger would have their way without causing a serious schism in their community. Public officials would succeed in enforcing the law without jailing or bankrupting the Plain People.

A plan was mapped out. Working sub rosa, the two or three Plain People would prepare their brethren for the coming events. Early one morning, public school busses would quietly arrive at the Old Order schools. Amish leaders would remonstrate appropriately, for the record. The children would be loaded onto buses in spite of the protests and taken to the public school. After a few days of ritual, a pattern of compliance would be set, and the trouble would all be over.

In the meantime, County Attorney Lemon phoned Attorney General Scalise about another matter, and in the process casually mentioned the strategy for dealing with the Amish. "What you do is strictly your own business," Scalise responded. "Count me out. Enforce the truancy statute if that's what you want to do.

But if you manhandle those little kids, you will be in trouble with the state!"

On Thursday evening, November 18, 1965, Lemon announced in Minnie Wengert's court that a school bus would call at the Amish homes and schools the next morning and take all the pupils to Hazleton, in keeping with the law. He requested that the Amishmen explain the situation to the children to avoid undue excitement. The fathers who were present neither assented nor protested. The Amish often refuse to respond to a new proposal until they have a chance to confer with their leaders. But as the explosive showdown of the next two schooldays demonstrated, the two or three Plain People who previously agreed to this approach had certainly not spoken for their community!

The Truce and Settlement

When County Attorney Lemon, Superintendent Sensor, and Sheriff Beier arrived in Des Moines a few hours after the showdown at the Amish schoolhouse, Governor Hughes was out of town, not expected to return until late afternoon. Attorney General Scalise was still very angry with Sensor at the time, believing Sensor had doublecrossed him on at least two occasions. Scalise invited Lemon, a fellow Democrat, into his office, leaving Sensor and Beier to stew in the waiting room for nearly two hours. According to Scalise, Lemon said the group had come to ask that Scalise deputize one officer for each Amish child involved in the controversy or that the governor call out an equal number of national guardsmen. With one official to escort each Old Order pupil to the Hazleton public school, the trouble could quickly be ended. Scalise responded that the idea was unspeakably stupid and threatened again to take strong action if any Amish youngsters were handled roughly. William Sindlinger, the attorney for the Plain People, reports that the three officials were overheard discussing this plan before they left the North School to journey to the capital. Sensor and Beier deny that such a proposal was ever considered, and Lemon has recently been unavailable for comment.

At any rate, Scalise made sure that Sensor and Beier were kept waiting long enough to feel insulted. When he had nothing more to discuss with Lemon, Scalise busied himself with other matters. Finally, his secretary reported that Sensor was threatening to leave for Oelwein. Scalise summoned all the newsmen he could find, ushered them into his office along with Sensor and Beier, and proceeded to discuss emphatically and at great length the unreasonable approach he thought Sensor and other local officials had been adopting.

Around 4:00 p.m., Governor Hughes returned to his office. He closeted himself with Lemon and Scalise, leaving Sensor and Beier waiting once more. A little later, he proposed to Sensor and Beier, first privately and then at a press conference, that a moratorium of at least three weeks be called to permit him to explore alternatives. Sensor and Beier had little choice but to agree, and the Oelwein board later ratified the arrangement reluctantly. During the moratorium there were to be no further attempts to take the Amish children to Hazleton, and the prosecution of their parents was to cease.

Shortly thereafter, Buchanan County officials announced that grain and livestock belonging to nine Amish farmers would be auctioned to pay the fines and court costs that were levied before the moratorium began. Amid an outcry that the Amish had again been betrayed, the governor observed that, though the action of the county leaders was unfortunate and would "not create any good will," technically the truce had not been violated. At the last moment, an anonymous donor in Des Moines came forward with $1,511 so the sale could be cancelled (some people believe the governor raised this money). In January, 1966, two businessmen from Independence, Iowa, eleven miles south of Hazleton, donated $282 to prevent another auction. A few days later, 980 bushels of Amish corn were sold to pay fines and court costs, and further auctions were threatened. But before long the governor remitted more than $8,000 that the Amish still owed the state.

Some local leaders are unhappy about this. "The governor made asses of us. We went to court every night for all those weeks, and nothing ever came of it."

On January 10, 1966, Governor Hughes conferred separately with Amish leaders and the Oelwein school board. Three state patrol cars and two dozen newsmen were at the Oelwein airport when his Piper Aztec touched down, and a long procession trailed behind as he sped down the dusty roads to Dan Borntreger's house. Several Amishmen drove up in buggies to attend the meeting, some came on foot, and a few were dropped off from automobiles driven by their neighbors. The conference lasted for nearly two hours, while the blankets on the horses flapped in the breeze, the windmill creaked, and sheep and pigs meandered in the fields. Finally the governor emerged and drove to Amish School No. 1, half a mile west. There he was photographed talking to Andy Kaufman while the American flag flew upside down nearby. No insult or distress signal was intended. The Amish are not too attentive to such details.

In the afternoon, Governor Hughes spoke briefly to students in Oelwein's junior high school auditorium, remarking that "we must respect the right of others to live differently, . . . if it is an honest and decent way of life." Then he met for two hours with the Oelwein board around the long table in Arthur Sensor's office. Simultaneously, Adin Yutzy, whom the sheriff had fetched to court on several occasions, was auctioning his last pieces of farm equipment before moving to Wisconsin. He wanted to get away from all the trouble.

As it turned out later, the Amish agreed that day to lease their schools to the public school district for a nominal sum; the public school board promised to supply certified teachers to the two schools for the rest of 1965–66 and during 1966–67; and since the board refused to pay the salaries of the two teachers, the governor promised to find funds for this purpose elsewhere. In a signed statement, the school board went on record that "adjustments will be made in the curriculum offered and in the teaching aids and methods used in these two schools, consistent with Iowa law, to avoid conflict with Amish religious beliefs." The Amish promised that, since the schools would be publicly maintained during this period, no religion would be taught.

In search of the needed money, Governor Hughes asked Francis Keppel, then U.S. Commissioner of Education, if federal funds could be made available. Keppel pointed out that the church-state overtones of the Amish problem made it too sensitive for Washington to handle and suggested that the Danforth Foundation of St. Louis might help. By February 22, 1966, Danforth consented to provide the needed $15,000, and the agreement was publicized. The governor said he would ask the 1967 session of the Iowa Legislature to create a fund for school boards that wished to make special schools available to minorities like the Amish.

During the rest of the 1965–66 school year, certified teachers were in charge of instruction in the two schools, with the former Amish teachers as assistants. The arrangement led to difficulty, for the Old Order assistants sometimes contradicted statements by the teachers in charge. During 1966–67, the Amish permitted the certified teachers to proceed alone, and few problems arose. The Plain People objected to some extent when they saw that a course in social studies was to be offered, emphasizing that they would prefer history and geography to be taught separately. The *Fayette County Union* commented: "Most of us had the impression old Dan [Borntreger] came away from the bargaining table with everything but Governor Hughes' suspenders. Now it would appear he wanted them too." To avoid trouble, the public school authorities refrained from introducing science into the curriculum of the two schools.

In its 1967 session, the Iowa legislature refused to establish the special fund requested by Governor Hughes, apparently in response to the wishes of the state superintendent, associations of educators, and other conservative elements. For a time, in fact, the lawmakers were unwilling to make any concessions to the Amish. The governor was forced to circumvent these tendencies. He established a special advisory committee of influential citizens who, armed with new arguments and evidence from interested scholars, worked through key senators and representatives to arrange an amendment to the state's minimum educational standards law. It was provided that religious groups could apply for exemption from the provisions of this law. Exemption would be granted for two-year periods only, and only at the discretion of the state superintendent, who had shown little aversion to the treatment the Amish had been accorded thus far. But so long as national outrage seems certain to be aroused by further heavy-handedness with the Plain People, peace may be maintained. At this writing, Hazleton's two Amish schools have been granted the necessary exemption and have reopened under the tutelage of uncertified instructors from the Amish community.

An Analysis

The action against the Amish in Hazleton was prompted, it seems clear, not by concern for the well-being of Amish children, but by antagonism. The Iowa school code, however it was intended, provided a convenient instrument for the persecution of an unpopular minority, harnessing public power to the wagon of local prejudice. But could public officials have condemned the Amish schools on more rational grounds? How should educators view the way the Plain People prepare their young for adulthood?

On the surface, the issue seems clear-cut. Demanding that all children be given a "decent education," numerous state legislatures have established minimum standards for all schools. Repeatedly the Old Order Amish violate these standards. A small but growing proportion of Amish children are in public schools; however, the private elementary schools most Amish youngsters attend are of the primitive one-room variety described earlier. To stay out of the forbidden secondary grades, many Amish boys and girls begin school a year later than usual, repeat the eighth grade, attend part-time Amish "vocational high schools" — which some states refuse to recognize — or simply drop out, compulsory attendance laws notwithstanding.

With their education thus limited, the Amish cannot produce their own certified teachers; so when they refuse to hire personnel from the outside there is trouble, at least in states like Iowa that require certified instructors for all schools. But often many other state standards are violated. During 1959–60, after visiting twenty-two Amish elementary schools, representatives of Ohio's Department of Education judged all to be in violation of eighteen of the state's thirty-nine minimum standards for nonpublic schools, while only one standard (relating to length of school day) was met by all twenty-two. All of the schools were reported as failing, for example, to comply with state demands for a term of specified length; teacher personnel records; graded courses of study in language arts, geography, history, mathematics, natural science, health and physical education, fine arts, first aid, safety, and fire prevention; provisions for staff growth; teaching aids, adequate instructional materials; supplementary textbooks and references; and satisfactory heat, light, ventilation, water, and sanitary facilities. When nine Amish "vocational high schools" were visited, all nine were judged to violate seventy-nine secondary school standards. According to Ohio authorities, the Amish schools have not improved significantly since then.

But contrary to a common view, this noncompliance represents more than stubbornness or stupidity. It is calculated to preserve the highest Amish values. At the heart of the Amish culture, reinforced by religious tenets and a long history of persecution, is the view that the larger society is evil. The Amish are taught to keep themselves peculiar — a separated people. They are knit together by kinship, common unquestioned values, and customs that mark them off visibly from everyone else. By emphasizing mixed farming as a way of life, they limit the need for outside contacts. Reliance on horse-and-buggy transportation keeps the basic social unit small, facilitating surveillance of behavior. Community norms prescribe ways of acting in such detail that most early symptoms of rebellion are detected. The *streng meidung* —

the strict shunning of those who violate Amish rules, even by spouses and other members of the immediate family — is a powerful enforcer of obedience.

Like other social systems, Amish society is organismic, composed of mutually dependent parts. Alter one component and the rest will change in response, often in irreversible, self-reinforcing fashion. Allow automobiles, radios, telephones, and modernized clothing, and the individual feels less distinct from the dominant social order and starts to assimilate its values. Take away farming as the predominant occupation, and exposure to alien folkways is vastly increased, for more complex callings demand more formal education and bring interdependence in their wake. Inure the child to the consolidated public school, replete with such luxuries as bus rides, plumbing, and electrical devices, and he is less likely to tolerate the taboos of his culture as an adult; furthermore, his peers and teachers will often influence him to defect. Give him a modern secondary education, or even too elaborate an elementary education, and he will frequently gain aspirations for, and access to, pursuits that are outlawed for an Amishman. Expose him too long to the lure of learning and he will hunger for the higher education that will alienate him still further from his origins.

On the other hand, rapid assimilation is not the only danger confronting the Old Order. If the Amish permit no adaptation to their changing environment, their culture will soon prove unworkable and the community will disintegrate. This eventuality may be most imminent when the Amish are threatened, for then, rather typically, they seem to emphasize norms that otherwise would have been abandoned; as a result, disruptive pressures are created, particularly for the young. When overt attacks cease, the settlements appear to strike a more realistic balance between rigidity and capitulation. It is in these relatively peaceful situations, one suspects, that the Amish are most likely to perpetuate important cultural distinctions while avoiding alienation, marginality, and anomie.

One fact is often ignored by public officers: In terms of the Amish culture, the Plain Peoples' approach to education may be one of the most effective yet devised. Their success in training the young to be farmers has impressed many agricultural experts. Unemployment, indigence, juvenile delinquency, and crime are surprisingly infrequent. Amish prosperity and self-sufficiency are legendary. These are not the characteristics of a preparation for adulthood that has failed.

Like Iowa, nevertheless, most states with Old Order Amish populations have attempted, at one time or another, to compel the Amish to meet the educational demands that apply to everyone else. But the statutes in these states rarely empower public authorities to close substandard schools; the only means of enforcement is to prosecute, under compulsory attendance laws, parents who send their children to these schools. When Amish parents are fined, jailed, or deprived of their property, those who have acted against them are blistered by angry protests from people sympathetic to the Amish, as in Iowa, and nasty publicity results. Elected officials soon find it morally or politically prudent to arrange a truce.

The Ohio situation illustrates the impasse that usually results from attempts to impose customary educational standards on the Amish. Officials of Ohio's Department of Education insist that virtually all Amish schools in the state are operating in defiance of the statutes, but these officials are painfully aware of popular support for the Amish and despair of enforcing the law without authority to close the schools rather than prosecuting the parents.

Until exemptions were provided for Amish schools in Iowa, Pennsylvania's attitude was clearly the most liberal of all. Long ago, after several embarrassing confrontations had occurred, George Leader, then governor, arranged a reinterpretation of the school code to legitimize the Amish educational pattern. Since that time, Amish elementary schools have been required to maintain school days and terms of standard length and to file adequate attendance reports, but practically no other stipulations are made — teachers, for instance, need not be state-certified. Children who complete the eighth grade and are at least fourteen years old may enter the Amish "school-work program" in "vocational high schools" until they reach the legal school-leaving age of sixteen. In this program, students perform farm and household duties under parental guidance and attend classes for a few hours each week. Many educators feel, however, that Pennsylvania has thus abdicated its responsibility to see that all future citizens receive an adequate education.

In a few areas, as in school districts immediately west of Hazleton, Iowa, a third policy has been adopted with some success. The Amish are provided with small public schools in their rural settlements rather than being assigned to consolidated schools in neighboring towns. (In a few instances the Hutterite colonies in Montana enjoy the same privilege.) The boards of these public schools seek teachers sympathetic to the Amish position and in numerous other ways ensure that the religious sensibilities of pupils and parents are not offended. The arrangement provides Amish youngsters with state-certified teachers and sometimes with more modern curricula and facilities than are found in private Amish schools.

Some legal scholars see such an explicit concession to a particular religious group as an establishment of religion, forbidden by the First Amendment. But the approach may be constitutional if viewed, not as a set of exceptions for a single sect, but as simply one application among many of a universally valid principle. To be effective, educational programs must be fitted to the cultures of the pupils served, whether these pupils come from Amish, Hutterite, Puerto Rican Catholic, upper-class WASP, or lowerclass Negro backgrounds. However, some Amish groups balk at a compromise of this type. Not only does it expose the young to teachers with alien values, but, unlike schools in the days before school district reorganization, the schools in question are governed by boards rarely drawn from the immediate communities.

Public school officers, and even the courts, are often guilty of simplistic comparisons between public and Amish schools. In Ohio's Hershberger case, for instance, advantages unique to the public school were emphasized; advantages unique to Amish education were brushed aside. What happened within the four walls of the public schoolhouse was compared merely with what happened within the four walls of the Amish schoolhouse, and the fact that Amish children are educated largely outside school walls was deemed irrelevant. The Amish community assigns only limited functions to formal instruction, requiring the school merely to teach the three R's. Yet away from the schoolhouse, each child undertakes a series of tasks under parental tutelage. Kitchens, stables, markets, and fields — not classrooms — are the principal educational facilities.

Many public educators would be elated if their programs were as successful in preparing students for productive community life as the Amish system seems to be. In fact, while some public schoolmen strive to outlaw the Amish approach, others are being forced to emulate many of its features. As tax-supported education struggles with the dropout and potential dropout, it is introducing sizable components outside school walls, as in the Job Corps and many other work-study programs. Investigations of teaching and learning indicate that much more differentiation of instruction is necessary, and schools are being criticized justly for their standardization and lack of adaptability.

Furthermore, serious attitudinal and cognitive consequences might ensue if Amish children were suddenly bussed into unaccustomed surroundings to be taught by teachers unsympathetic toward Amish customs, to associate with peers who maintain an incompatible life outlook, and to study subjects in which they have little or no interest. The practice implies the same blind application of inappropriate treatments to which the culturally deprived in the great cities have been subjected for so many years. There is no basis in educational theory, research, or experience for insisting, as critics of Amish education frequently do, that the within-four-walls approach of the typical public school is the only way adequately to educate the nation's future citizens. At times a nonpublic school that provides a particular group of students with a thoroughly appropriate preparation for the adult life they will lead may differ so fundamentally from nearby public schools that the notion of parity is farcical. When are oranges and orangutangs equivalent?

But even if the prevailing approach to regulation of nonpublic schools is ill-conceived, some kind of control may be needed. The most common rationale for this control inheres in the view that the state must, as a means of self-protection, require for all children an education essential to good citizenship. The state courts have defended this concept in many compulsory-attendance cases, holding that an education is not so much a right guaranteed the individual as a duty imposed on him for the public good.

Assuming the state must protect itself, one consideration is basic: Does the Amish educational approach represent anything more than the reasonable discretion of parents? Does it preclude anything plainly essential to good citizenship or include anything manifestly inimical to the general welfare? Since the recipients of Amish schooling function so well in the Amish communities and the larger society suffers no significant threat in the process, the answer has to be *no*. Unlike other rural youth, the Amish do not gravitate in large numbers to the cities, where their lack of a highly developed formal education might create serious problems. Individuals almost never leave the Old Order Amish culture for the nation's mainstream. The normal movement, accomplished over several generations, is from Old Order Amish to "Church Amish" to Amish Mennonite and then through a sequence of increasingly modern Mennonite persuasions. As some Mennonites put it, "We are all on the same train, but the Old Order Amish are in the last car." The existing evidence shows no trace of former Amishmen who are struggling unsuccessfully to adjust in the outside world, perhaps partly because they take so long to reach the head of the train and partly because of the habits of self-reliance, hard work, and frugality that are so central in the Amish and Mennonite cultures.

In most respects the Amish must be viewed as good citizens. Their aversion to political activity, social security, and military service is probably more than balanced by the thought-provoking dissent they contribute to our national dialogue. On the whole, it would be difficult to identify any other ethnic group that has done so little to burden society. If the Amish schools may be outlawed, why not the Amish communities? If it is permissible to live as an Amishman in the United States, why is it not equally permissible to prepare to live as an Amishman?

As a second basis for state intervention, it is maintained that every child should have access to the occupational and ideological options that a modern education makes available, regardless of parental preferences. One is inclined to by cynical, however, when many state authorities express this concern. There is something fishy about a legislator or schoolman who weeps over the limited opportunities of Amish youth and yet shows no pangs of conscience concerning the gross inequities that discriminate against the poor in public education. The state courts, moreover, have been too preoccupied with the self-protection prerogatives of the states to champion individual rights in education.

Nevertheless, the issue of freedom of choice must be taken seriously. With a typical Amish education, the individual would have difficulty moving into the more complex vocations. To expose the youngster to one life view exclusively during the formative years is virtually to coerce him into adopting that view. But while the public school may broaden horizons in the world of work, it is hardly a neutral forum for competing concepts in religion, politics, economics, and other controversial spheres. As a thousand battles in the courts and elsewhere have shown, attempts to make public education neutral in religion and in other ideological particulars have raised problems of the profoundest sort, and the eventual outcome of the efforts is very much in doubt.

Public schools — like Amish, Hutterite, Black Muslim, Lutheran, Catholic, Jewish, Greek Orthodox, and Seventh Day Adventist schools — seem inevitably the servants of their constituencies, reflecting the dominant values of the subcultures they serve. (Ask any pacifist who has attended a public school in wartime.) What agency of the state, then, may be trusted to select an educational format so superior or allegedly neutral that it may be imposed on every child? The destinies of the young will often be misguided by parents, but this state seems far less lethal than the alternative of giving government the ultimate power of indoctrination.

Furthermore, if the state legislatures are genuinely concerned about maximizing the choices available to Amish youth, appropriate steps can be taken that do not infringe the basic rights of parents and threaten to create a new collection of maladjusted, miseducated youngsters. To mention just one possibility: The state could provide special supplementary educational opportunities for defecting Amishmen who wish to acquire the skills and understandings they will need in the larger world. Such programs should represent no inordinate burden. Financially, the costs should be far less than those that would be incurred in educating all Amish children in public schools. Changes in occupation and way of life will be increasingly common in the future, and large numbers of citizens — not just a few erstwhile Amishmen — will require periodic retraining.

It is sometimes argued, finally, not that Amish education is a serious menace to the state or the child, but that the nation would be better off if all cultural backwaters, religious enclaves, and social classes were eliminated. Whites, according to this standpoint, must not be permitted to live entirely apart from Negroes. The wealthy must not be allowed to maintain a lofty isolation from the poor. Religious minorities must be brought into the mainstream of modern society. It is one thing, however, to forbid invidious distinctions in public functions and quite another to stifle self-determination in private affairs, when the individual infringes no rights of others.

To a large extent our form of government presupposes that rationality will win, in the long run, if the market of orthodox and unorthodox ideas is unrestricted. Over the centuries, important contributions have been made by groups that were at such marked variance with the established order as to need some degree of insulation to survive. In retrospect, the efforts of authorities to enforce, in private spheres, their concepts of the good tend to assume a bloody hue. In the words of the Supreme Court, "Those who begin coercive elimination of dissent soon find themselves exterminating dissenters. Compulsory unification of opinion achieves only the unanimity of the graveyard."

Appendix

The description of events in Iowa is based on a study of the relevant accounts in such newspapers as the Oelwein *Daily Register*, the *New York Times*, and the Chicago *Daily News*; on examination of the Iowa statutes; on analysis of a collection of pertinent documents courteously made available by Arthur Sensor, Superintendent of the Oelwein Community School District; on visits to the two Amish schools in question, located within the boundaries of the Oelwein district, to Prairie Grove School, Triumph School, and Perry School No. 1 in the Jesup Community School District, and to Schools No. 2 and No. 5 in the Wapsie Valley Community School District, all in Iowa; and upon 36½ hours of interviews held on three trips to Iowa (November 1, 1966; December 19–21; 1966; and March 16–21, 1967). After both of the first two trips, efforts were made to reconstruct the events in the controversy, and the following trip was planned in an effort to obtain the information that was still lacking. The 36 interviews, averaging slightly more than an hour each, were held with the following 28 people; with only two occasions as exceptions, the respondents were interviewed individually. In addition, a number of brief telephone interviews were used.

A. Five interviews with Arthur Sensor, Superintendent, Oelwein Community School District, Oelwein, Iowa

B. Two interviews each with:

1. Dan Borntreger, chairman of the Amish School Committee near Hazleton, Iowa

2. William Sindlinger, attorney for the Hazleton Amish, Cedar Falls, Iowa

3. Owen Snively, Principal, Hazelton Elementary School, Hazleton, Iowa

4. Abe Yoder, member of the Amish community and former teacher in an Amish school, Hazleton, Iowa

C. One interview each with:

1. C. J. Arthaud, president for 12 years and member for 14 years of the erstwhile Hazleton school board, Hazleton, Iowa

2. Fred Beier, Sheriff, Buchanan County, Independence, Iowa

3. Frank W. Brownell, member of the Oelwein school board before, during, and after the reorganization of 1962, Oelwein, Iowa

4. Orville Christophel, member of the Oelwein board before, during, and after the reorganization of 1962, Oelwein, Iowa

5. Rev. Richard Emery, member of the Oelwein school board since September, 1965, Oelwein, Iowa

6. Bruce B. Girton, member of the Oelwein school board before, during, and after the reorganization of 1962, Mason City, Iowa

7. Perry H. Grier, current Buchanan County Superintendent of Schools, Independence, Iowa

8. H. B. ("Herb") Hayes, Mayor, Hazleton, Iowa, from 1942 to 1963

9. Paul F. Johnston, State Superintendent of Public Instruction, Des Moines, Iowa

10. H. J. ("Buck") Kjar, member of the Oelwein school board since 1962 and previously chairman of the Hazleton Reorganization Committee, Hazleton, Iowa

11. Harlan Lemon, Buchanan County Attorney, Independence, Iowa

12. Ruth (Mrs. W. K.) Mattingly, teacher at Perry School No. 1, Jesup Community School District, Jesup, Iowa

13. Frank Z. Miller, member of the Oelwein school board since 1962, Oelwein, Iowa

14. Bishop John Nisley, Hazleton Amish Community, Hazleton, Iowa

15. Roger Northrup, Superintendent, Wapsie Valley Community School District, Fairbank, Iowa

16. Ellwood Sapp, Principal, Jesup Elementary School, Jesup, Iowa

17. Lawrence F. Scalise, Attorney General of the State of Iowa from 1964 to 1966, Des Moines, Iowa

18. Virgil (Mrs. Kenneth) Smith, member of the Oelwein school board before, during, and after the reorganization of 1962, Fayetteville, Iowa

19. Elda Struhbar, teacher at the North School, then functioning as a public school under the truce arrangement, Hazleton, Iowa

20. Charles Underwood, Superintendent, Jesup Community School District, Jesup, Iowa

21. Lewis A. Warren, Publisher, Oelwein *Daily Record*, Oelwein, Iowa

22. Fred Watts, Managing Editor, Oelwein *Daily Record*, Oelwein, Iowa

23. Minnie (Mrs. Anthony) Wengert, Justice of the Peace, Hazleton, Iowa

3 Franklin H. Littell

Sectarian Protestantism
and the Pursuit of Wisdom:
Must Technological Objectives Prevail?

There were two main groupings in sixteenth century Protestantism, constituting a division which still affects almost every problem which comes before the churches. In the days when professional theologians and church lawyers had a virtual monopoly of
religious conversation and decision in the state-churches, the confessional and liturgical divisions were foremost. Divisions into
Anglicanism, Lutheranism and Reformed (the latter two sub-
divided into several ethnic blocs) were still relevant. Little attention was paid to groups not legally privileged. Moreover, the
Continental Anabaptists of the sixteenth century were virtually
wiped out by persecutions, and the radical Puritans of seventeenth-century England survived without controlling public
policy; it was not until the emergence of the Free Churches
in eighteenth-century America and their predominance in the
nineteenth-century home and foreign missions that clear typo-
logical distinctions could be made and maintained. Entering the
twentieth century, in dealing with virtually every issue in inter-
Protestant affairs (and in most facing the Catholic-Protestant
dialogue as well), the lines of distinction fall between the teach-

The author is president of Iowa Wesleyan College.

ing of the conservative Reformers and the positions developed in the radical Reformation.

The distinction between the "churches" which emphasized *reformatio ecclesiae* and the "sects" which stressed *restitutio Christianismi* is the place to begin, even though in modern America many of the lines have begun to elide. For example, many traditions which once maintained state-churches and scorned religious voluntaryism as "enthusiasm" are now loyal defenders of religious liberty.[1] And some movements which began in criticism of the promiscuity of church membership in Christendom have, with affluence and great numbers of adherents, taken on many of the social characteristics of establishments. But "sectarian Protestantism" is still a viable, if somewhat pejorative, concept when attention is directed to major areas of discussion: the peace testimony, church discipline, church government based on consensus, the office-authority of clergy, the missionary obligation, the status of the laity, the education of the young.

The "Walled Cities" of the Restitution

The style of the radical Protestant groups, of which the Amish are a somewhat fossilized form, derives from their view of church history. Whereas the churches which followed the major Reformers were involved in a purification, a reform of doctrine and cultic practice — with little real break from the medieval parochial and territorial patterns, the "radical Reformation"[2] purposed a thorough-going restitution of the style and ordinances of the Early

1 Cf. "The American schema" ("The Declaration on Religious Freedom") which came out of Vatican II, to which American Catholics contributed so much; Walter M. Abbott, ed., *The Documents of Vatican II* (New York: Guild Press/American Press/Association Press, 1966), pp. 572–700.

2 The distinction between the radicals and the "magisterial Reformation" is definitively treated in George H. Williams, *The Radical Reformation* (Philadelphia: Westminster Press, 1962), Introduction; see also the writer's *The Origins of Sectarian Protestantism* (New York: Macmillan Co., 1964), PB edition, *passim*.

Church. To use the technical term, the radical Protestants were "primitivists"[3]: they divided history into a Golden Age (the Early Church), the period of the Fall of the Church ("the Constantinian era"), and a Restoration beginning with their own movements. They restored, so far as in them lay, the atmosphere and life of the church before "the fall." As they read the New Testament, this required separation from "the world" — including the world called "Christendom," where the automatic baptism of masses of infants could not hide an essential heathenism.

"Separation" was cultivated. They continued, so to speak, the walled-city strategy of the monastic movements of the Middle Ages, precisely at the moment of history when European nations were exploding outward and laying conquest the whole globe. In the very period of European history when Spain and Portugal, the Netherlands, Britain, France, and other "Christian" nations were founding empires of political and cultural and religious force around the world, following for three centuries "the great frontier,"[4] the sectarians were intensifying internal discipline. Only with the rise of modern missions did the sectarian Protestants enter, in their own way, upon global conquest.

For the restitutionists, the marks of the age were persecution and violence, and the most determined among them — Mennonites, Quakers, Amish, and the like — for generations followed the frontiers to find places where they might cultivate the separated life of the Christian community in peace. They became aliens and strangers in the land, even in areas where in late years they have been delivered from the hand of the persecutor. The place-names of the most vigorous groups show the constant migrations which the inner emigration occasioned: Pennsylvania, Danzig, Carpathia, the Volga basin, the Caucasus, Kansas, Alberta, and more recently Mexico and Paraguay. And now, of course, the industrial

---

3 Cf. "Primitivismus," in Franklin H. Littell and Hans Hermann Walz, eds., *Weltkirchenlexikon: Handbuch der Oekumene* (Stuttgart: Kreuz Verlag, 1960), col. 1182–87.

4 Cf. Walter Prescott Webb, *The Great Frontier* (Boston: Houghton Mifflin Co., 1952).

states — with their universal conscription, monolithic educational systems, and other instruments of bureaucratic control — have virtually filled the earth. There seems to be no hiding place left, no place of refuge where defenceless Christians can cultivate the life of simple obedience and hard work without being molested.

This is the historical occasion of the present conflicts, which would be much larger had not most of the Free Churches as well as establishments long since accommodated themselves to the spirit of the times. The Amish and Old Mennonites are carrying a testimony to the nature of the education once maintained by many more churches, and in the present conflict with bureaucratic state power they stand in the heritage of sectarian Protestantism — even if, by reason of historical change, some of the Free Churches have deserted them, even if some of their strongest support is coming from persons and groups of once hostile churchly tradition.

For the restitutionists, the high point of primitive virtue was the Church at Jerusalem. In that golden time, they believed, Christians lived together as brethren, sharing what they had and being blessed of the Spirit (Acts 4:31–35). Among some restitutionist groups, however — from the sixteenth century on — the recovery of Jerusalem has been blended with the recovery of the lost Eden. Restitution of the True Church pointed to reestablishment of Paradise. The "fall of the church," with the rise of private property and exploitation and violence, was confused with the "fall" which led to expulsion from the Garden. Religious restitutionism was blended, in short, with cultural and technological primitivism. This is of basic importance in attempting to understand the Amish, for example, where the restoration of the simple gospel without glosses is accompanied by hostility to technology. The austerity (*innerweltliche Askese*) of the spiritual life, with its rejection of speculative philosophy and sophisticated theological reasoning, is combined with opposition to the achievements of the artificer, the inventor, the scientist. Both formal theology and the manufacture of automobiles are considered, in sum, evidences of "worldly" cunning and products of the wisdom of this world.

From the beginning, sectarian Protestant education has tended to underscore the pursuit of wisdom and depreciate the technological. It is worth noting that, as recently as a century ago, some Methodists and Baptists were still challenging the utility of institutions of higher education. When the break came, they supported very generally the development of the Land Grant Colleges: the practical usefulness of agriculture and mechanical skills won them over, even while they still in considerable number rejected the "higher learning" and critical-analytical style of the universities. The sectarian Protestants wanted their children "educated for life" (and eternity), but they did not (then) want them exposed to the perils of classical (i.e., "pagan") philosophy. The Amish and Old Mennonites still stand on that ground. They are *not* opposed to education; the question for them is what the education shall consist of and what its goal shall be.

True education, for those of the Anabaptist-Mennonite line (and those who have been influenced by them before departing from the more stringent path), is devoted to the cultivation of simple living, humility (*Demut*), long-sufferingness (*Gelassenheit*). Their system of elementary education, which was developed very early, was aimed at producing young adults capable of participating whole-heartedly in the life of the Christian community. Across the generations they have centered school curriculum in reading, writing, arithmetic, and the Bible — the subjects in which a full and participating member of the community needs proficiency.[5] They have also treasured the use of the German language, for the spoken and memorized words are a large part of any group identity. Even the Mennonites of Iowa kept the Bible and German central to their school work until two factors changed the picture: (1) World War I, which worked so powerfully against community use of German among all groups of that ethnic descent — German Catholics and Lutherans as well as the Plain People;

5 Cf. "Education, Mennonite" and "Education Among the Mennonites in Russia," in *Mennonite Encyclopedia* (Scottdale, Pa.: Mennonite Publ. House, 1956) 2: 150–53 (M.S.H.); 153–57 (P.Br.).

(2) educated teachers began to teach High German, while the people spoke "Pennsylvania Dutch."[6] At that point *Techne* replaced utility, and instruction in German lost contact with the realities of community life and need.

There is one final factor to be mentioned in interpreting the alienation of such groups from the literary tradition prevailing in the age of science and industry, in their eyes so violent and power-conscious. For generations the Anabaptists and their descendants were persecuted, pillaged, and done to death by those wielding power. They naturally developed a healthy mistrust of those who built vast mountains of information and wrote the code books and pointed mankind toward ends of which they were profoundly suspicious. The sectarian Protestants have, often for good reasons, deeply doubted the literary artifacts of the prevailing culture — looking instead to persons in whom they could put trust. This point is evident even in the present court cases. Although those who have abandoned the church and pursued the world's *cursus honorum* have often shown high achievement, the relation of the communities as a whole to the prevailing school curricula is not unlike that of the Afro-Americans and other minorities who have not shared in the general social goals. Recent studies have shown that ghetto groups, whose culture is largely based on interpersonal relations and oral tradition, are at a distinct disadvantage when tested by standards developed for those thoroughly acclimated to the prevailing procedures. For the Amish, that disadvantage is not grounded in simple ineptitude, however; it roots in a basic psychological alienation and mistrust. Their inner emigration from the technology and violence of the age is so great that they are in our midst, not as citizens of peculiar views, but rather as aliens who want no part in the magistrate's office (*Obrigkeit*). It is the set of prevailing procedures and standards which must be challenged, if we are to get at the way in which the Amish case questions our present social and educational direction.

6 Melvin Gingerich, *The Mennonites in Iowa* (Iowa City: State Historical Society, 1939), chap. 25, "Schools and Education."

The Case of the Amish

The true name for the Amish is "Amish Mennonites." The movement became identifiable in separate congregations following the only serious division among the South German Anabaptists, a split led by Elder Jacob Amman among the Swiss and South German Brethren in 1693-97. The Amish Mennonites, who number less than 30,000 in the United States and less than 5,000 in Canada, first entered Pennsylvania *ca.* 1720; Ohio: 1807; Ontario: 1824; Indiana: 1842; Illinois: 1829; Kansas: 1888; South Dakota: 1874.[7] These dates are given to remind us that the Amish are among the "old settlers" in the New World. (Not too incidentally, there has never been in all of three centuries a Mennonite or Amish in prison for a felony — something which the government of a society might well consider in counting "social costs"!)

The original division occurred as a rigoristic reaction against apparent relaxations in the main Anabaptist-Mennonite movement, and the Amish have remained the most conservative of the whole family of Mennonite Churches since that time. The issues which they raise are known to all shades of the movement, however, and many of them recur on the much broader map of sectarian Protestantism as we scan four and a half centuries of restoration movements repeatedly attempting to recover the style and genius of the primitive church.

The Amish practice believers' baptism, repudiate the swearing of oaths and use of violence, practice mutual aid, strongly maintain New Testament ordinances in church government (including church discipline), cultivate the simple life, and proclaim the Simple Gospel. At the time of the original split, they condemned attendance at worship in the state-churches, restored regular use of a footwashing service, enforced a religious uniform dress, and practiced "shunning" (*Meidung*) toward those members who broke the rules. All of these ordinances are characteristic of move-

7 "Amish Division," pp. 90–92, and "Amish Mennonites," pp. 93–97, in Harold S. Bender *et al.*, eds., *The Mennonite Encyclopedia* (Scottdale, Pa.: Mennonite Publ. House, 1955), vol. 1.

ments bent on a return to the Early Church and its life, including making the counsels of perfection binding on all believers, and they have reappeared across the generations among Free Churches which have subsequently gained much larger followings: Quakers, Brethren, Baptists, Methodists, Disciples, Nazarenes, Church of God, Assemblies of God, etc. As a matter of fact, in the modern period many of the concepts and practices once confined exclusively to the Anabaptists and their radical Puritan and Free Church offspring have gained wide currency among confessions and communions which once whole-heartedly defended Christendom and denounced restitutionist thinking.[8]

At one major point only are the Amish Mennonites set apart by the vigor of their views, and it is this factor which throws them into conflict with an educational system which — particularly since the influence of the Gaither Report has been felt increasingly — is overwhelmingly committed to training in science. That factor is their technological primitivism. They have not only repudiated the glosses and human inventions which corrupted Christian doctrine and living following the "Fall of the Church" under Constantine: they also reject the whole world of the artificer, the inventor, the scientist whose Promethean cunning and will dominates modern civilization.

The issue is *not* opposition to education. As a matter of fact, the Anabaptists created the first system of universal education, three hundred years before the modern nation-states acknowledged the usefulness of an educated populace. In the Hutterite wing of the movement, a comprehensive system of elementary education was developed which began with the "Little School" of nursery and kindergarten (2–6 yrs.) and ran through the "Big School" (6–12 yrs.). (It is important to remember that male and female then generally assumed adult responsibility at 12–14 years, and so the duration of the schooling filled the pre-adult years.)

8 Cf. Michael Novak, "The Roman Church and the Free Churches," *Journal of Ecumenical Studies*, 2, no. 3 (1965): 426–47; Franklin H. Littell, "The Concerns of the Free Churches," in Hans Küng, ed., *Do We Know the Others?* (New York: Paulist Press, 1966), pp. 86–93.

The reason behind the founding of universal education is significant. Since the Anabaptist congregations were governed by the rules of the general priesthood, all must learn to read and write in order to help interpret the Scripture and guide the affairs of the church.

Beyond that, however, they did not go — nor do the Amish wish to go today. "Education beyond that was expressly declined as nonconducive to the fear of God — the highest goal of all Anabaptist education. That Hutterite education had a very high standard can still be seen from all their handwritten books, done with excellent penmanship, good spelling, skillful style, and as for contents, with excellent Bible knowledge and often deft arguments — things not so commonly found among people of the sixteenth and seventeenth centuries."[9] The education they cultivated was devoted to winning the good life and eternity. They avoided that training which seemed to produce only pride of place, enjoyment of power, and the skills of covert or overt violence. And this avoidance of technical education, combined with "shunning" of deviationists, practically fixes the limits of the Amish community today.[10]

Wisdom *vs.* the Scientific Method

The basic conflict lies not between the heart and the head, between ignorance and education, between irrationality and reason. Such generalizations are true only if the thinking life is confined to the intellectual enterprises which follow alienation and "the fall of man": analysis, critique, skepticism, tentativeness toward all fixed positions. But as long ago as the High Middle Ages educators already distinguished education devoted to wisdom (*Logos*) from training in skills (*Techne*), even though the distinction

9 Robert Friedmann, *Hutterite Studies*, edited by Harold S. Bender (Goshen, Ind.: Mennonite Historical Society, 1961), p. 138.
10 Cf. John A. Hostetler, *Amish Society* (Baltimore: Johns Hopkins Press, 1963), p. 144, n.12.

gained general importance only with the spread of learning following the invention of printing. The critical analytical method presupposes a basic disjarment between the thinker and his ground of being, both toward nature and toward the social matrix. That is its grandeur, its creative tension, and also the source of personal and social despair. Wisdom, however, relates to continuity and wholeness and ultimate coherence. Without a self-conscious awareness of the necessary dialectical tension between the quest for wisdom and scientific thought (*Techne, Wissenschaft*), the cunning artificer of structures becomes an idolater, a builder of Ziggurats to make heaven and earth stay put. Radical Protestants, as slowly as some of them move, are committed in principle to a continuing revelation of God's truth and to the style today called "the life of dialogue." They are pilgrims in the earth, not tower-builders; their "walled cities" are less representative of their basic faith than their missions and their social service (e.g., the Mennonite Central Committee).

Radical Protestant groups have for over four hundred years resisted as best they could the disintegrative and destructive bent of political machines increasingly devoted to the purely technological. Although generally pacifist themselves, they have noted that societies organized for defence against history, which merely tolerate historical events, which "obstinately adhere to an ahistorical position . . . are by that fact, exposed to the violent attacks of all revolutionary ideologies."[11] Opposed to violence and revolution themselves, they have nevertheless often been critical of those whose suppressive use of power in defence of fixed positions and frozen structures has occasioned social explosions. The fact that some sectarian Protestant groups move very slowly, and in a revolutionary age bear the outward appearance of social fossils, has blinded many scholars to the nature of the conflict between their beliefs and their assumptions of the society at large. In a time when "modern" and "modernity" are normative words, those

11 Mircea Eliade, *Cosmos and History* (New York: Harper & Row Torchbooks, 1959), p. 142.

who cultivate the dialogue with the past — sometimes to the virtual severance of dialogue with those happily flaunting the spirit of the time (*Zeitgeist*) — are denounced as "reactionaries" by (some) politicians and "culture lags" by (some) scholars. But, whereas those who greet with the greatest enthusiasm and defend with the mightiest force they can muster the latest tower they have built to reach unto the heavens — be it code book at law, ecclesiastical system in religion, or curricular requirements in the schools — the people of the separate congregations conceive themselves to be a "pilgrim people" with "no abiding city" in this world. Their claims for human ideas and achievements remain modest, and they are certain that God will call to account those who claim heavenly authority for earthly designs. To be specific, it is certainly no more difficult to discuss the ultimate ends of education with an Amish or Old Mennonite elder — even with the language difficulty — than it is to attempt a real dialogue with some of the ideologues running our present public instruction programs.

However slowly they move, the restitutionists do move. Their doctrine of the Spirit requires it, and their style of church government (e.g., "the sense of the meeting") implements it. They have de-sacralized the created order and shattered that monolith of Christendom which for over a millenium and a half maintained a stifling control over the minds and spirits of men. They found themselves in conflict long ago with those who defended with force the Christian Ziggurats. Today the conflict sharpens with those who strive to build statist closed systems. Both the old confessional schools of Europe, enforced by the sword, and the modern monolithic state systems, enforced by jailings and sheriff sales, have exacted their martyrdoms from the pilgrim people. Those who build the Ziggurats are, theologically speaking, idolaters. In terms of the practical denial of liberty, pluralism, and the dialogue, we can only lament that in their excessive zeal and arrogance the defenders of closed state systems have neglected the common sense of the Common Law. But first they abandoned its cornerstone in wisdom: they lost the wise awareness of what Walter

Bagehot, commentator on the evolution of the English constitutional tradition, called "the doubtfulness things are involved in."

Because they conceive of themselves as a pilgrim people, in a world in which final solutions are not to be achieved by cunning, Protestants of the type Ernst Troeltsch dubbed "sectarians" prefer a maximum of liberty and a pluralism of solutions in the political sphere. There is no record that such churches have ever exacted tax money to further their own cult or confession, have ever used violence to suppress the professions or practices of others, or would agree to a solution — highly speculative! — in which all persons were required to attend their worship and all children required to attend their schools. They prefer the life of dialogue, to practice what radical Puritans called "the principle of mutability" in public discussion and decision. "The principle of mutability," which was the despair of the followers of Archbishop Laud and others who were trying to build up the Christian Ziggurats again in seventeenth-century England, was very simply the sectarians' claims of the conscientious right to change their minds in the face of new and persuasive evidence. Those who purposed to issue doctrinal statements authoritative for all times and places, to anathematize any who should change one syllable or one punctuation mark, and to exact the death penalty of dissenters, found such dialogists puzzling and exasperating.

If a healthy dialogue is the oxygen in the lifeblood of the open society, if the pursuit of wisdom is at least as important to true education as the achievement of technological proficiency, there is one major dimension of the dialogue to which the most determined sectarian Protestant groups have given great attention: the dialogue with the past. The customs of the Amish, for example, document the great respect paid the testimony of those who have died in the faith. (And such are, as Peter Taylor Forsyth once pointed out, the majority of the faithful — in case "majority rule" is considered normative!)

In training for purely technical competence, several *desiderata* of true education fall away. For one thing, the importance of the style of life and example of the teacher is a minor matter. A thoroughly disreputable genius may possess precisely the intensely critical mind which points the way to mastery of a laboratory science or a major breakthrough in comparative linguistics. For another thing, the subject matter is controlling, rather than the interpersonal relations. In the beginnings of modern science, Francis Bacon and others spoke of the dialogue with the "Book of Nature." But the ocean of facts is infinite, and once the philosophical base is lost the novice may readily become that most fearsome of contemporary types: the competent practitioner who lacks a center as a person. "Science" is dependent upon books, the checking of sources, the analysis of differing reports and points of view. "Wisdom" is to a large extent preliterary. In point of fact, very sophisticated and viable cultures have flourished with little resource beyond the oral tradition. Third, since the twin population and information explosions have changed social patterns and specializations more radically than events of the previous three millenia, the development of competent technicians is largely cut off from study of the past. The whole view is needed for advance in the long haul, but at any given point able technicians can be produced who know nothing beyond the narrow confines of their specialties and their generation. There are more scientists living today than the total of scientists to be counted among the dead. Men and women can become extremely proficient practitioners of complicated science without having to study any thought not contemporaneous. In doing so, they may lose both personal center and historical continuity.

In terms of life values and ultimate meaning, however, the most spiritually impoverished person is the one totally dependent upon the merely contemporary. The most slavelike person may be an extremely competent technician within narrow limits, holding his retainer from a Stalin or a Hitler, a Mao or a Vorster, a Tito or a Franco, in total oblivion of the meaning of life or persons. It is the dialogue with the past, practiced in lively fashion, which holds in check the totalitarian ideologies and the accomplished new barbarians who implement them. Much, if not most, of that dialogue is of necessity preliterary.

The Oral Traditon

No part of their educational effort demonstrates more clearly the Amish Mennonites' attachment to the living dialogue which transcends the generations than their use of folksongs and hymns. To this day,

> . . . the singing of hymns is an integral part of the fortnightly meeting, and the time involved extends often beyond an hour's reach. A service is never dismissed without a final devotional act in song. An outsider finds it quite impossible to participate in the singing of the hymns, no matter how trained he may be, or how much he would like to share in the experience. It is difficult to their own congregation, incredible to those outside their group.[12]

A sociologist will readily perceive that in maintaining the wall of separation it is equally important that the singing should be impossible for an outsider and strengthening to the initiated. Most important of all, the singing of ancient hymns — like the repetition of traditional prayers and liturgical acts — is basic to their cultivation of the oral tradition. They have refused to update the hymnary, carefully reprinting traditional misprints and obscurities.[13] By such acts they fortify the group's resistance to change, as out-groupers have long observed. They also accomplish something else which reporters have often missed: they open the minds and spirits of the in-group to what Kierkegaard called "the thoughts that wound from behind." Their opposition to musical instruments, their standing in worship for the reading of the Luther Bible — whose High German is virtually unintelligible to them — is all of the same piece. The preference of many conservative groups for the King James Version has the same import. It is, of course, foolish to try to maintain the accuracy of the King

12 William I. Schreiber, "The Hymn of the Amish Ausbund in Philological and Literary Perspective," *Mennonite Quartery Review*, 36, no. 1 (1962): 36–60, 36.
13 *Ibid.*, no. 3, p. 36; p. 57.

James Version over the RSV; but there is no denying its musical superiority and greater serviceability to the community's cultivation of the hearing ear.

Conclusions reached by the critical and analytical — i.e., scientific — method have small part in Amish mentality. The reenactment of Biblical events and happenings in their own history, and the personal appropriation of group memory and group wisdom, make up the bread of the mind's life. Such a situation is "prescientific," but it is not anti-intellectual — once the impossible tenet has been abandoned that all intellectual effort must be controlled by the literary disciplines and the technical methods of critique, comparison, and analysis.

The concept of "oral tradition" is familiar to exegetes and church historians, who have been debating for decades the relations of the written Scriptures to that tradition of the forefathers which was memorized and transmitted orally. The problem is more complex than it seems, for the written *Torah* is memorized and used fully in debates, and for the oral *Torah* notes often in fact exist. But the distinction was made very early in the rabbinic schools between the two study disciplines — between "the reading" and "the repetition."[14] More fundamental is the distinction which was not made that early, for only with the printing of books did the critical analytical method come to be practiced on any general scale, between that type of knowledge which is primarily based on analytical study of sources and that type which is primarily a matter of memorization and reenactment.

The skeptical, critical-analytical pole of learning is often individualistic. Some philosophers have argued that it is of necessity a lonely path, although it is now generally recognized that teamwork plays a large role in scientific advance. The pole of learning which has to do with wisdom, with the reenactment of ultimate encounters, is supremely social. The tie to the community is primary: "The material is first committed to memory, and then an

14 Birger Gerhardsson, *Memory and Manuscript* (Uppsala: Almqvist & Wiksells, 1961), pp. 27–28.

attempt at understanding is undertaken."[15] Rhythm and cantillation are important in the material, and a certain style in the teacher: "There is no distinct boundary between these deliberate pedagogical measures and the teacher's way of life as a whole."[16] In training teachers for their schools, the Amish, like Jews and Christians of the early period, have preferred an apprentice system — very well developed — to formal attention to "teaching methods." Antiquity much preferred that which was taught from the lips of a living person and was skeptical of the written word. The same spirit prevails in much of sectarian Protestantism.

From the lips of a credible witness, and by the example of his life, the ultimate meanings could be learned — whether such witness had perished as a martyr in earlier years, leaving behind his prayers and sermons and letters, or taught the young as one among the living. For the wise, the truest accreditation of culture and education comes not from a skilled mechanic of learning methods but from a cultured and educated man. In sectarian Protestant belief, such a man is a Christian. The meaning of life, according to Menno Simons, a representative witness, is summed up in this: to be a faithful Christian. "Now this wisdom which effects such power and yields such fruits, I consider to be the very finest that can be named, even if it is taught and recovered by an ignorant teamster or hod carrier . . . I have preferred to be the fool of the world's learned men, in order that I might be found of God to be wise, rather than to be one of the most famous of the worldly wise, and at the last be a fool in God's sight."[17] On another occasion, Menno lamented:

> O Lord, the subtlety of the learned ones is great. Satan uses his wiles artfully. Some teach merely the doctrine and commandments of men, barren and corrupt trees.[18]

15 *Ibid.*, p. 127.
16 *Ibid.*, p. 186.
17 (Menno Simons) *The Complete Writings of Menno Simons*, translated by Leonard Verduin, edited by John C. Wenger (Scottdale, Pa.: Herald Press, 1956); "The Incarnation of Our Lord" (1554), pp. 791–92.
18 *Ibid.*, p. 68, "Meditation on the Twenty-Fifth Psalm" (*ca.* 1537).

And further his warning to the wise after this world seeks to turn them from their cunning designs to pure wisdom:

> Consider the end and ponder the outcome. You rely on human invention, but we rely on the Word and truth of God; you rely on the world, we on heaven; you rely on the present, we on the future; you rely on the emperor and force, we on Christ and His promise, until we all appear before Him who will come in the clouds of heaven to requite all flesh. Then you will see what you have lived for, who office you filled, what deeds you have done, for what hire you served, whose word you promoted, whose counsel you despised . . .[19]

There came in time to be a certain barrenness in this austere devotion to ultimate ends, coupled with resistance to human inventions and artifices. Cultural primitivism may be linked to religious primitivism, too. The Puritan resistance to sports and the theatre would be a case in point. And Amelia Mott Gummere, the Friend's scholar, elicits our sympathetic response in her discussion of the meaning of Quaker costume, at first a witness to "separation":

> The dress of the Quaker, when he first arose, was in cut and fashion simply the dress of everybody, with all extravagances left off . . .
> The climax, however, is reached, when we are told that a lowly mind would rather admire the wonderful hand of Providence in contemplating the necessary than the beautiful in nature, and the eye is not to be indulged in "great superfluity and too great nicety in gardens." In other words, the turnips and cabbages tend to keep the mind humble, but the rose and the lily may prove a snare![20]

Here, again, the historical setting is important. The customs against which sectarian Protestants bore testimony must be remembered for their case to be understood.

19 *Ibid.*, pp. 211–12; "Foundation of Christian Doctrine" (1534).
20 Amelia Mott Gummere, *The Quaker: A Study in Costume* (Philadelphia: Ferris & Leach, 1901), pp. 17, 24.

> The gentleman of fashion in 1695 wore his hair long under
> a broad plumed hat. The jeweled sword at his side dangled
> from an embroidered scarf; enormous coat cuffs concealed
> his hands, when they were not thrust into a large muff.
> The large bordered hat was turned up at three sides, and
> until 1710 kept the adornment of plumes. . . . Both sexes
> wore small looking-glasses. Men even wore them in their
> hats.[21]

The Anabaptist, Quaker, Moravian, early-Methodist witness was
all of a piece — even though separate manifestations of it sometimes diverted attention from that center. They were cultural
primitivists — suspecting artifice, show, glosses, conspicuous consumption, rubrics, code books, hierarchies, elaborate regulations,
and violence. They made man the measure and treasured interpersonal relations beyond externalities and artifacts and things.
They developed primarily that education which built up the
church, which linked in living fashion all the generations bound
together in the Communion of Saints.

The sectarian Protestants have also contributed mightily to the
liberty, dignity, and integrity of the human person which is — according to Pope John XXIII's "Mater et Magistra" — slowly evolving in the present age. When Jakob Huter rebuffed the Moravian
lords for abusing the consciences of the faithful Christians, when
William Penn addressed the King of England as "James Stuart"
(and accorded him the same respect he showed a farmer or a
wheelwright), they were guided by the text, "God is no respecter
of persons" (Acts 10:34). But their forthrightness helped to lay the
foundations for self-government and popular sovereignty. Even
the "walled cities" had their effect in reshaping the general land-
scape of the modern age, especially when some groups like the
Quakers carried the lessons of the Church Meeting into the Town
Meeting.

The pursuit of wisdom has also had its visible fruits, as has devotion to science. Most of us are doubtless convinced that both

21 *Ibid.*, p. 63.

poles should be maintained, that both emphases are essential to the achievement of the good life for a growing number of people. But who is so bold as to say that the depreciation of the technological is more dangerous to the future of the human race than the neglect of wisdom? Who will deny that for the present, at least, the twin poles of learning are best secured by avoiding an educational monolith, by providing for effective dissent from a single set of scientific goals? Considering the special arrangements made in this land of liberty by the Internal Revenue Service, the Selective Service System and the Social Security System, one can only view with dismay the ideological zeal of a Department of Public Instruction that knows no modesty, no self-examination. One is moved to exclaim, in the words of Oliver Cromwell to a zealot of his own day, a zealot whose rage was destructive of the public dialogue: "In the bowels of Christ, man! Did it never occur to you that you might be mistaken?" It is theoretically possible to have a technically far advanced society, led exclusively by Ph.D.'s — all of them *Barbari*. But there can be no true culture without cultivation of the oral tradition and the pursuit of wisdom.

In point of fact, technological and cultural primitivism are both unnecessary appendages to the religious motif of sectarian Protestantism. Their concern is the pursuit of wisdom, and the dialogue with the past which is essential to it. But charity must compel the conclusion among the balanced and sober-minded that there are more destructive forces at work in this age than the idiosyncrasies of dissenters. Of the various freedoms Americans use and abuse these days, love of bonnets and buggies seems one of the more harmless. But the central concern — the commitment to the wise and ultimately meaningful life — is today in short supply. We could do worse than to learn from the Amish, rather than to coerce them into our own undisciplined and violent arts. At the very least, if we still respect industry and mutual aid and religious liberty, we shall treat our strangers in the land more creatively than would the school bureaucrats of Siberia or Spain!

Contemporary Conflicts

Against the Amish the charge is frequently made that they keep their children from enjoying the benefits of our larger society, that they wrongly withhold them from advance in the scientific age. The more zealous administrators propose to force their compliance through jailings and other harrassment. The answer to this statist ideology is given by the late Bishop of Berlin, in a fine book he wrote after a long life of conflict with statism, a book which discussed the necessary opposition of Christian views of education to Nazi and Communist claims and practices. In a society which treasures liberty and maintains an openness of dialogue, no single group of persons is given the unchecked authority to define ultimate ends. Why are the employees of a Department of Public Instruction better situated to define the good of the children than those most directly involved by love and sacrifice? Parents and cobelievers have at least a neglected authority: love. In my judgment, the fact that such a monolithic claim can be advanced at all by state bureaus shows how desperately we have been infected by the totalitarian views, how little we love liberty when it is the liberty *of others* at stake.

Both types of totalitarianism claim that the state has the right to educate the youth, whereas Protestant and Catholic and Jewish beliefs are agreed that ultimate responsibility rests with the parents. The teacher and school are, in truth, both historically and in principle an extension of the parental and family stewardship. The fact that there are orphans, wards of the courts, or that some parents neglect their responsibilities, does not change the norms whatsoever. In such cases of necessity the courts and schools are acting *in statu parentis*; but the landmark itself is unmoved. Bishop Dibelius summed the matter up very neatly, in disposing of the totalitarian error: "The responsibility for the children is not a question between the parents and departments of education, but between the parents and God."[22]

There is another issue, even more critical in the present contro-

22 Otto Dibelius, *Grenzen des Staates* (Tübingen: Furche-Verlag, 1949), p. 95.

versy. That issue is the disastrous alienation of the public school systems, in many areas, from the colleges and universities — the traditional centers of humanism and personalism. The substantial contribution of such alienation to the rise of Nazism and the corrupt use of the schools in the Third Reich was discussed brilliantly in a book by the late Werner Richter. Richter was an officer in the Prussian Ministry of Education under Becker, a refugee in the United States for some years (teaching at Elmhurst College), and the most important returnee to work with the recovery of German university life after World War II. His discussion of the descent of the German public schools into mere technical training, of the separation of the public school teachers from the humanistic tradition of the universities, and of the way in which their technical training in teaching methods and political accommodations to the state bureaucrats prepared the teachers to be zealous supporters for Nazism in the purge of higher education comes hair-raisingly close to what the power drive of some Departments of Public Instruction may ultimately mean in this country too.

It is bad enough to have the universities so far gone in the abandonment of reasonable discourse and concern for persons. There, if he struggles hard enough, an able student may still get an education, may still achieve some wisdom as well as technical proficiency in preparation for his part in the world's work. Nevertheless, we are beginning to see the appearance in quantity of the same personality type which marked the decline of the academic communities in the Weimar Republic. As Richter described it, "A new type of student came into being — a smooth-tongued plausible, shrewd, arrogant, and often licentious busybody and go-between — who was superior to many an impractical professor not only in power but also in adaptability and cunning."[23] More serious by far, however, is the way in which the separation

23 Werner Richter, *Re-Educating Germany* (Chicago: University of Chicago Press, 1945), p. 73. (Richter was at one time *Rektor* at the University of Bonn, Chairman of the *National RektorenKonferenz*, president of the *Deutscher Akademischer Austauschdienst*, president of the *Alexander von Humboldt Stiftung*, and chairman of the German Fulbright Commission.)

of persons training to be school teachers from the humanistic tradition, and their almost single devotion in the teachers colleges and schools of education to teaching methods (*techne!*) rather than cultivation of the love of culture and learning, prepared them for the political game. To quote Richter on German education, "This meant that a type of teacher came into prominence which had previously played no part at all."[24] Both students and teachers were corrupted.

A fatal wedge was thus driven between the common schools and the universities, and it was ruthlessly exploited by the politicians of both state and education. As rapidly as the Nazis took over the *Länder*, they eliminated the university men from the education departments and finally from the leadership of the universities themselves, and replaced them with products of the teachers colleges. Technicians in teaching methods and manipulation of persons, possessed of what Richter calls "the despotism of the garrison mind," lacking that center which wisdom alone can give, they were just what the police state needed to run the schools.

It would be hyperbole indeed to claim that things have gone so far here in America. But the signs are there, and some of the statist doctrine is widely used to justify, for example, cruelty and denial of liberty to the Amish in Iowa. Before any further power and authority is granted to such a state Department of Public Instruction, two things must be achieved: one, a return to a sound doctrine of the teacher's stewardship in relation to parents and families; two, a recovery of balance in the training of teachers and in the programs of the schools, encompassing both the pursuit of wisdom and the achievement of technical proficiency.

The Amish and other sectarian Protestants are not about to blow up the world, even though they may slow up its vaunted onrush of progress a bit. On the other hand, the most dangerous man in the modern world — whether he fancies himself a nuclear physicist or a "human engineer" — is, as Mr. Justice Jackson said at the Nürnberg Trials, the technically competent barbarian.

24 *Ibid.*, p. 97.

4 Jules Henry

Is Education Possible?
Are We Qualified To
Enlighten Dissenters?

I write this paper when a continuing world crisis has erupted in an expanding war in Southeast Asia; when the extreme vulnerability of our economic system has appeared once again in a loss of purchasing power, a projected business slowdown, and an expanding deficit in our balance of payments; when the prestige of the United States is low, though its power is vast; when our Negroes' thrust toward equality threatens entrenched white status; when our cities are becoming too oppressive to live in; and when the defeat of school bond issues, refusals to increase local school taxes, a great scarcity of teachers, and a savage fiscal attack on the University of California testify to the continued reluctance of Americans to recognize their educational obligations.

Crisis and calm, feelings of vulnerability and strength, determine how one thinks about education and what one does about it. The word *education*, however, is so abused by the bureaucracies which have taken possession of it that it is easier to discuss our problem in terms of the idea of enlightenment. This automatically takes our problem out of the colleges of education and casts

The author is professor of sociology and anthropology at Washington University.

the discussion in a framework in which all efforts to understand may be examined.

Enlightenment, the process of testing the assumptions of a culture, usually leads to such questions as, "Is our form of political economy the best and the only moral one?" "Does my life have meaning?" "Is goodness always rewarded?" "Is our form of marriage really the best?" "Are whites really the superior race?" "Is it right to be rich when others are poor?" and so on. There is no enlightenment unless the conventional answers to these questions, and many others like them, are constantly examined, and there can be no education unless there is enlightenment. Any so-called educational endeavor that does not do this is doing no more than tooling up for conventional occupations.

The question then arises: In our present world situation is enlightenment possible? Since 1917 almost a third of the earth's surface and a third of its people have come under political economies radically different from our own. These are the peoples who have already become socialist; meanwhile, other millions want it. The emergence of a new socialist humanity has been accompanied by the disappearance or extreme weakening of many capitalist powers, to the degree that, feeling beleaguered amidst the diminishing strength of its allies, America, according to Secretary of Defense Robert MacNamara, "has devoted a higher proportion of its gross national product to its military establishment than any other major free-world nation. This was true even before our increased expenditures in Southeast Asia.

"We have had, over the last few years, as many men in uniform as all the nations of Western Europe combined — even though they have a population half again greater than our own."[1]

The rise of socialism and the doubling of the number of violent revolutions since 1958 (also according to Mr. MacNamara) have left the United States with such an extreme feeling of vulnerability that one wonders whether it can tolerate enlightenment, for

1. From the text of Mr. McNamara's address before the American Society of Newspaper Editors, as reported in *The New York Times*, May 19, 1966.

enlightenment always involves a reexamination of basic assumptions about political economy.

Since 1939 the central position of armaments in the American economy — the fact that the arms industries are its "balance wheel," as one Presidential commission put it; the fact that the *balance wheel* has become the *pivotal gear*, growing in importance each decade with our fear — has been taken for granted, because the fear has become domesticated. We are like those Africans among whom schistosomiasis is endemic, so that they think bloody urine is normal; or like the Kaingáng Indians, whose teeth are so rotten, they wondered whether mine were real.

When we ask, therefore, under what conditions enlightenment is possible, and realize that it seems possible only when fears are few, while our own are numerous, we must wonder about our own possibilities.

With such general considerations in view, I shall examine the problem under the following headings: Political Economy, The Gross National Product, War, The Historic Necessity of Stupidity, The Occupational System, Leisure, Vulnerability, and Narrowness.

Political Economy

The citizens of any society must be taught to believe that their form of political economy is the only satisfactory one. In our own society this is accomplished not only through verbal depreciation of other types of political economy but, especially in the lower grades of school, by presenting in educational materials the idea that decent human existence occurs in our type of political economy only. Elementary arithmetic, even the new mathematics, are presented in narrow middle-class settings. All of this restricts the possibilities of enlightenment.

Gross National Product

At no point may anything be taught that might interfere with the gross national product. This means not only that materials suggesting the possibility of an austere life, or one dedicated to *materially unproductive* activity, must be excluded from, or muted in, curricula but also that people must be portrayed as spenders. Clothes designers must surely have been employed to develop illustrations for current elementary school readers, for when the *Dick and Jane* series tells about the activities of the same family in a succession of stories, the entire family is wearing a different and attractive set of clothes in each story.

War

School does not interfere with the idea that all wars fought by the United States are just. Nothing must be presented that suggests that we could have done anything to avoid them, or that war is an unthinkable solution to contemporary problems. Pious sighs over the horrors of war have always been permitted, and sundry generals have been quoted, but little insight is given into war's causes, into American responsibility, into the general human responsibility for entertaining the possibility of war, or into the possibility that our citizens might have the right to reject the bellicosity of its statemen. Since the most important thing for a child to learn is that the United States must always have freedom to choose war when it pleases, nothing can be taught to dim this view. We cannot, for example, teach that violence is the last resort of even madmen, that a population has a right to voice its fierce objection to war, or that hostility in the face of the possibility of universal bloodshed is unconscionable.

Education for docility is the first necessity of a civilization oriented toward war, and a danger of enlightenment is that it undermines docility and replaces it with courage. One of the many paradoxes of modern warfare is that it exploits docility to train killers.

The Historic Necessity of Stupidity

Throughout history, whether among the so-called civilized, or so-called primitive, people have had to be taught to be stupid. For to permit the mind to expand to its outermost capabilities results in a challenge to traditional ways. Hence the paradox that, while man is intelligent he must also be trained to be stupid, and that a certain amount of intellectual sabotage must be introduced into all educational systems. It is better to have a somewhat stupid population than one trained beyond the capacities of the culture to absorb intelligence. It is clear that teachers with incisive minds, willing to take their students along all possible logical pathways, willing to entertain all intelligent questions, are a danger to any system. Hence, all educational systems must train people to be unintelligent within the limits of the culture's ability to survive. That is to say, there seems to be a cutting point where, if a people are too stupid, the culture will fall apart, and where the culture will fall apart if they are too intelligent. The cutting point is where the upward curve of intellect meets the downward curve of culturally necessary stupidity.

Common controversies in education revolve not so much around what students should know, and how they should learn, but how stupid we can permit them to be without wrecking the country and the world. In education for stupidity a nice line has to be drawn between teaching the child how to make obvious inferences and letting him make inferences that are too far-reaching for comfort; between training him to see the validity or the truth of a proposition in plane geometry and teaching him to perceive the fraudulence of a proposition in advertising, political economy, international relations, and so on. Teaching a child to think has obvious perils and for this reason has always been a delusive goal of education in our culture. Nobody can be taught to think, for example, where private enterprise, war, or the gross national product might be threatened.

Socialist countries, of course, have *their* forms of socially necessary stupidity. The fruit of stupidity is invulnerability, for when one has been rendered too stupid to penetrate an issue, he can only follow the crowd, and the crowd always follows what is popular and what it thinks is safe, even though it often leads to perdition. In any culture stupidity pays off in the social and political areas over the short run. This being the case there can be little inducement to being intelligent because intelligence leads to separation from the crowd and the crowd wants only to be safe from criticism and to have a good time.

This situation confronts the teacher at the college level in the "stone wall" effect: students who will not discuss, who will not object, who will not examine, and who are likely to become withdrawn and morose if forced to these by a determined teacher. What most of us encounter in the university are rows of moving hands that obediently write down whatever is said; and one need not worry about voicing the most radical opinions because they merely go into the notebook, along with algae, ions, historic places, dates and names, equations, and the dates of the next test.

Some might argue that, since in the present stage of evolution man is unable to develop a social system that will not make millions miserable, organized society would be impossible if everybody were smart, because they would see through all shams; and social organization is impossible without sham. Others might argue that if the scales were lifted from the eyes of all, the hands of all might be against all, for each would see that the other is a liar. Some might urge that since man is incapable of constructing a system without massive flaws it is better for children to be unable to perceive them.

However, I see no evidence that nature has set a certain pace on the clock of evolution, so that our brains will be regulated until such time as, having constructed a utopia, men may look the truth in the eye without murdering their neighbors. This being the case I see no choice but to seek enlightenment and introduce it into education.

The Occupational System

The occupational system in any culture has inexorable requirements because jobs must be filled if the culture is to survive, and in our culture the fundamental outlines of the occupational system are congruent with the economic system and with the requirement of the gross national product. The occupational system is a fixed reality, like the sky, and this is true the world over.

It follows that our educational system cannot enlighten regarding the possibilities of the soul, but must train children to fit the available jobs and teach students resignation to the occupational categories of the census bureau.

Children must be taught to accept the idea of fixed occupational niches and be so instructed that the freshman's question, "Philosophy is interesting, but what can you do with it?" will never become absurd. The question, "What am I doing with my life?" is the enemy of the question, "What job can I get?" The occupational system requires that the question, "Is this what I really want to do?" should not rise into consciousness, for it is an iron law of culture that to the degree that education touches on occupation at all it just should not permit the question to exist. Culture as a system of thought must exclude dialectical opposites, for when these are permitted to enter consciousness they shake a culture to its foundations. The dialectic, however, is a magic quern that grinds out its contradictions no matter where it is; so that socialist countries, where the quern presumably came to rest forever, now have to cope with it too.

Leisure

Nowadays, since there is much talk about leisure, it is necessary to say a few words about this tired subject. For the average person, leisure is the time left to him after he has stopped working for pay. That is to say, for the overwhelming bulk of the labor force, from lathe operators, chippers, riveters, and truck drivers to switchboard operators, secretaries, nurses, teachers, doctors, and so on, the main issue is what to do with themselves when they are not getting paid for doing it, or not learning a trade, as in school.

It is obvious that no use of this time can be tolerated that will interfere with our political economy, the gross national product, or with stupidity, and that, therefore, there can be no education for enlightenment after hours. Fishing, boating, bowling, cabinet-making, sex, and fixing up the basement can be engaged in because they help maximize the gross national product, but painting and reading not only make very minor contributions, as compared to the others, but too much reading of philosophy, history, etc., can be threatening to the system, for they bring enlightenment.

People who have been through our educational system, however, will not use their leisure for anything but fun and games. It must be borne in mind that an educational system that trains people for enlightening activities during leisure would threaten the occupational and even the class structure. If too many people, on the basis of leisure-time learning, were to start changing their occupations, considerable instability would be introduced into the occupational structure and hence into the class system. Hence there is a fundamental contradiction between the idea of productive leisure on the one hand and the maintenance of our present political economy on the other.

Vulnerability

There is no more vulnerable white-collar group than educators. For the most part without unions, subject to the whims of principals, superintendents, boards of education, and local parent organizations, elementary and high school teachers stand unprotected at the bottom of one of the most extended pyramids of power in the country. Hence they are in no position, even should they desire, to teach anything that might challenge the cultural features of which I have spoken. What I have said applies equally to so-called higher education, for there we see that educators are, on the whole, untroubled by problems of academic freedom, because, having come through the mill, they have divested themselves of dangerous thoughts, so that they have, on the whole, no freedom to worry about. They are self-imprisoned without knowing it. What would they teach that is unconventional? In my own discipline there are some brave men who have spoken in public against the war in Vietnam, but anthropology as an academic discipline is more innocent of dangerous thoughts than the late Pope John. What has become invulnerable also becomes rigid, because life has become safe. Thus invulnerable people are frozen, no longer because of fear alone, but because, by the miracle of the dialectic, they have come to feel so protected. Why venture out? Since invulnerability is thus a self-reinforcing system, it acts as an immovable obstacle to enlightenment.

Narrowness

Education must be narrow. It must not ask questions like, "Does life have meaning?" "What is meaning?" "What is the purpose of social life?" What is the place in life of compassion, solicitude, wisdom?" "Is there a *world* history?" "Is one country's richness a function of another's poverty?" "Is my country best?"

It is clear that broadening the questions asked would also question our political economy as presently constituted. A general examination of the question of meaning in life by the whole population would immediately drive the Dow Jones index through the bottom, because people interested in the question would not play the market.

Public Education and Public Anxiety

It is now necessary to ask: What has been the consequence of these conditions for education in the United States, and what is the feeling of educators and of the general public about education? Since the public press is about the best indicator, I am going to try to weave together, from the threads of opinion that have come to us over the years from *The New York Times* — a rather good reflector of educated public attitude — the pattern of public anxiety about education in the United States.

Fear

On June 5, 1962, T. M. Stinnett of the National Education Association said, according to an article in *The New York Times* of June 6, that "education in the United States is dominated by fear rather than by the power of constructive imagination." Nearly two years later, however (February 20, 1964), James B. Conant accused the National Education Association of being dominated by fear, claiming that its close link with state education departments made adequate accreditation activities impossible. On July 25, 1965, *The New York Times*, reporting on the White House Conference on Education, said the conference was failing because of educators' reluctance to deal with "explosive questions." Thus, though it is clear that a segment of national opinion believes that in this country education is dominated by fear, the fear is viewed differently, depending on who speaks. Education insiders, like Mr. Stinnett, talk as though the major source of fear is outside the system, while others believe that educators are afraid of one another. Mr. Stinnett said that

> "fear of the nation's own potentials has impelled us to worship excellence in education for the wrong reasons. . . ." As a result of fear instilled by "the defense industry-military establishment . . ." money for education "can only be voted in the sacred name of national defense. . . ." Mr. Stinnett warned that "niggardly" support for education as a defense necessity "is a dangerous departure from our educational history and tradition and emphasis upon the individual."
>
> "It is wrong," he said, "because history teaches well that a nation which conceives of the individual as a tool, a weapon, a resource, is likely to end up by treating him as such and no more."

Thus Mr. Stinnett places the blame where educators have traditionally placed it, on those evil others who are coercing us and ruining our children. Mr. Conant, on the other hand, as an outsider, blames the educational system itself because it is dominated by its own internal organizer, the NEA. One is prone to say of such polemics that they are a good sign because opinion is being freely expressed. This expression, however, is a symptom of a vast anxiety that has seized education in this country; an anxiety so immense as to make one wonder whether it is not a sickness. In the presence of extreme anxiety a person either runs without knowing where he is going or when to stop, or he freezes in an attitude of resistiveness, or he explodes. It is likely that all three processes can be documented in American education today.

Textbooks

On February 14, 1960, *The New York Times* reported that "Dr. Albert Alexander, textbook analyst for the New York City Board of Education, charges that there is 'a gray flannel cover' on *the American history textbook* . . . [that] they are 'strangely dull, lifeless, and bear striking resemblances to each other. . . .' "

> They are devoid of any historical opinion or interpretation by the author. Issues are artificially balanced in order to please partisans on every side of each controversy. They are "critical of neither the past nor the present."
> Authors bow to pedagogical rather than historical standards . . .
> . . . publications are prepared which are acceptable to all markets . . .
> . . . Mr. Alexander points out that the textbook publishers, whose industry has an estimated annual sales total of $300-million, have a business investment to protect.

The opinion of the textbook industry, meanwhile, clarifies even further the subject of history and its relation to social change:

> Dr. Austin J. McCaffrey, executive secretary of the American Textbook Publishers Institute, said . . . [that the textbook] "must never become a vehicle for social change . . ."

It is not difficult to understand why the textbook industry should take this position, for in 1962 there were "172 textbook companies competing for a total annual business of about $366,600,000. Of this, the elementary and high school business . . . account for about $232,000,000." The article reporting this (*The New York Times*, February 19, 1962) recites some of the previous criticism of textbooks, and then goes on to relate that

> . . . publishers say *they* are being held responsible for the lack of courage of their customers — school boards and educators . . .

> Lee C. Deighten, vice president of the Macmillan Company, said books are adopted because they have more colored pictures than competing books, because of the color of the paper, the depth of the margins, the attractiveness of the covers, the strength of the binding. At one point, said another publisher, books with nylon binding were turned down by the cotton-producing South.
>
> . . . the professional educators are resisting change partly because long practice has entrenched existing books and methods.

Thus while industry tries to protect its investment, and educators try to protect themselves, the pot calls the kettle black and the helpless children fall into the fires of controversy: fear and finance come together to form the indigestible American textbook. Meanwhile, emphasis on pedagogical technique rather than on subject matter does not equip the teacher to tell the difference between a good book and a bad one. The ignorant teacher is the ideal vehicle for communicating the vacuous message of the textbooks.

English

Beginning March 13, 1960 (June 21, 1960; January 8, 1962; November 27, 1963; December 30, 1963) a series of articles appeared in *The Times* examining *the teaching of English.* The National Education Association discovered in March, 1960, that gifted students were behind in English although they might be getting A's in everything else. Meanwhile a New York City study revealed that 10 per cent of the applicants for teaching jobs "have not mastered the ability to meet a minimum standard of acceptability" in writing correct English. In February, 1962, the National Council of Teachers of English reported that "70 per cent of colleges and universities had to provide remedial work in English and that 150,000 students failed college entrance tests in English in 1960." In 1963 Francis Keppel was warned that "the teaching of English is so poor it has reached a desperate point that threatens the nation's educational system." At that time a new "study showed that many high school teachers rated themselves as unqualified" to teach English. "In one category the figure was 90 per cent."

Taxation

Nationwide failure of efforts to raise adequate money for public education is documented monotonously in my clipping file. Americans fight expenditures for education with great ferocity and determination because, naturally, they add to the tax burden. Taxes interfere with expenditures for egoistic consumption — for more and better food, fancier houses, bigger and more luxurious cars, swimming pools, vacations, hunting gear, fishing tackle, skin-diving outfits, skiing, golfing, barbecue pits, liquor, fancy house-and-porch furnishings, bigger hi-fi sets that play the same garbage only louder, cameras, tape recorders, motor boats, and so on. Thus the drive for a high-and-luxurious standard of living interferes with taxes for education. Yet that is not quite the whole story of the death of the school bond issue, the demise of the school-tax increase; for, in an indirect way, these deaths are linked to the culture of death — the culture of war. As expenditures for war increase, tax burdens grow heavy. But as taxes to support war remain high, and as the desire to have a good time and raise one's standard of living increases, something has to give; and one of the things that gives is expenditure for education. So the failure of the tax increase in a small town in Arkansas is one of many such failures brought about by the emphasis on war and the American commitment to fun and good living.

Since it is now clear that the race to the moon is not quite separate from the race to war, I shall include here penetrating remarks on the relation between the space race and education made by Warren Weaver, one of the discoverers of information theory, the mathematical underpinning of automation. In an article in *The New York Times* of January 1, 1965, he said that with the $30 billion we are to spend in getting to the moon by 1970:

> We could give every teacher in the U.S. a 10 percent raise a year for 10 years; endow 200 small colleges with $10 mil-

lion each; finance the education through graduate school of 50,000 scientists at $4,000-a-year; build 10 new medical schools at $200 million each; build and endow complete universities for more than 50 developing countries; create three new Rockefeller Foundations worth $500 million each.

The Role of Big Business

As anxiety about education grew, Big Business, always ready to lend a hand, for a price, stepped boldly into the education scene. On January 9, 1961, the education combine that calls itself The Grolier Society Incorporated bought a full-page ad in *The New York Times*, proclaiming the *astounding new teaching machine available for home use*. A month later *The New York Times* did a full story on the "knowledge industry" in the financial section. Across the top of pictures of an acre of desks and chairs for schools at American Seating Company, of a new school in San Angelo, Texas, and of a speech laboratory, runs the caption "The Education Market, Already Large, Is Prepared for Its Biggest Period of Growth." Under the pictures another caption burbles "Behind the 3 R's: Heavy Spending," and we learn that business expects school construction alone to rise above $3.5 billion in 1961, as some of America's biggest corporate giants get into the multi-billion dollar knowledge industry. As *The Times* reported on November 20, 1965:

> Among those that in recent years have moved into the field are the Xerox Corporation, which last May acquired the Wesleyan University Press; Dow Jones & Co., Inc., with a burgeoning book division; the Cox Broadcasting Company of Atlanta; International Business Machines Corporation, Westinghouse Electric Company, Litten Industries, Columbia Broadcasting System and Radio Corporation of America. . . .

The article states that Time, Inc., and General Electric are also moving in. The 1961 article carried a similar list of blue-chip companies coming into education from other spheres; and on May 14, 1961, in the financial section, *The New York Times* ran an article entitled "Wall Street Studies Teaching Devices," in which investors were given a good hard look at the education line. Incidentally, Grolier, which in its ad refers to itself as The Grolier *Society*, Inc., is called simply Grolier, Inc., in the financial section of *The Times*. On December 16, 1963, *The Times* reported a working relationship between Dr. Omar K. Moore of Rutgers University[2] and the Thomas A. Edison Research Laboratory to develop electric typewriters for teaching children to read.

Since the growth of population has made the task of educating students by conventional means seem hopeless, business, urged on by the higher academia, has stepped in with an offer to transform children into *thought* machines with instant *knowledge* machines, and according to *The New York Times* (December 16, 1963) Professor Omar Moore, with the aid of his machine, will have them reading, writing, and taking dictation by the time they are two years old. Meanwhile anybody who knows something about the history of education is aware that in eighteenth-century England some children of upper-class parents were already writing Greek and Latin verses at three — without electric typewriters, *but with the aid of their parents and tutors.*

On January 1, 1961, in an article reporting a study done at Teachers College by Robert Thorndike and Elizabeth Hagen, *The Times* stated that "mentally superior" teachers leave the profession to take other jobs at more pay. While the article does not state specifically that the men studied left teaching for business, business certainly seems one likely choice, along with government. However, the dedication of these people to teaching was still very great, for they said that

> higher salaries would attract men back into education. But they also stressed the need for improved conditions such as smaller classes, better equipment and materials, and fewer nonteaching duties.

2 Professor Moore is now at the University of Pittsburgh and is co-inventor of a teaching machine costing $35,000. See *The New York Times*, October 29, 1966.

Higher salaries from nonpublic schools will also have the effect of draining away many of the best-equipped teachers and students from the public schools, if they continue to be starved. As pressures increase from all sources we confront the possibility that public schools, in some areas, may simply become residuals — institutions for children whose parents do not have the money or do not want to send their children to nonpublic schools, and for teachers who couldn't make the grade into nonpublic schools.

Reading

While many teachers were found to be poor English scholars, while the pressures grew to create a new race of scientists, while schools were being starved and teachers were leaving, millions of children were discovered to be years behind in reading. Hundreds of millions of dollars were therefore required for remedial reading classes, and the incidence of school failure and juvenile delinquency referable to reading failure was mounting. (*The Times*, April 15, 1961: "10,000 in 7th Grade Found 4 Years Behind in Reading.") This led John Theobald, former superintendent of education in New York City, to say to the Board of Estimates, "We have only two alternatives, either you give us the money we need or we will go back to 100 per cent promotion and say, 'To hell with education, we don't need it.'"

John F. Kennedy on Education

The national anxiety about education received expression in John F. Kennedy's famous speech on October 18, 1961, at the University of North Carolina. Interestingly enough, that speech, though devoted entirely to education, was reported in *The New York Times* on the following day under the totally irrelevant headline: President Warns of Long Struggle With Communism." I do not blame this on the caption-writer's failure to read the speech, but rather on his understanding of the fear-ridden mind of the American people, that will lead them to read an article on communism but turn in apathy from one on education. In this speech, great as it was, however, the late President undercut his very message by the following statement:

> Those of you who regard my profession of political life
> with some disdain should remember that it made it pos-
> sible for me to move from being an obscure lieutenant in
> the United States Navy to Commander in Chief in fourteen
> years *with very little technical competence*. [Italics supplied.]

Thus Mr. Kennedy, in the very act of emphasizing the critical
connection between politics and education, points out that you
can move to the highest position in the land with "very little
technical competence." Meanwhile, I prefer to emphasize the
crucial importance at all times of the politically educated mind.
As Mr. Kennedy put it in the same speech:

> I want to emphasize, in the great concentration which we
> now place upon scientists and engineers, how much we still
> need the men and women educated in the liberal tradition,
> willing to take the long look, undisturbed by prejudices and
> slogans of the moment, who attempt to make an honest
> judgement on difficult events.

Thus the late President, an intellectual himself, in his one speech
exclusively on education, does not stress anxiety stemming from
the enemy without, but his anxiety lest there not be enough people
educated well enough in the liberal tradition, the tradition that
will enable them to give cool judgments under stress. I submit
that, apart from the need to instill in our people from childhood
the love of knowledge for its own sake, the fundamental task of
the educational process is, as Mr. Kennedy stated it — to provide
minds, which, "undisturbed by prejudices and slogans of the
moment . . . attempt to make an honest judgement on difficult
events." My anxiety for my country, for myself and for mankind,
is that no education in the world is dedicated to the formation of
this kind of intelligence.

Thus year in, year out, *The New York Times* conscientiously
documents the anxiety, incompetence, and confusion in American education. Whether we deal with teaching English, science,

mathematics or communism; whether with desegregation, drop-outs, the race to Harvard or school counseling; press reports, mostly based on careful studies, document the rush from pillar to post. And the direct observation my students and I have done in classrooms over many years, and are still doing, shows nothing different.

Conclusion

American education is bleak; so bleak indeed that, on the whole, educators, having long ago abandoned the ideal of enlightenment, concentrate on tooling up. Feeble, neo-idealistic gestures in the direction of curriculum revision are merely tinkering with a machine whose basic drive must be — and has been through all history — the maintenance of a steady state. In our culture curriculum-tinkering very soon comes face to face with the factors constricting education — political economy, the gross national product, war, the historic necessity of stupidity, the occupational system, and vulnerability. All educational systems aim at a steady state — a condition in which, on the one hand, the system tirelessly corrects deviations from the prescriptions of the culture, while on the other the corrections become part of the psychoneurological equipment of the child and ultimately of the adult. Every educational system has different steady-state mechanisms; ours is unique in the degree to which it is selective. That is to say, the corrective devices operate uncompromisingly in the area of political economy but are much more flexible in science. All thinking that deviates from the traditional prescriptions of the former are rigorously controlled through instruction, beginning in the family and going on through school, while much more inventiveness is permitted in the sciences, beginning with the pseudo-science phantasies for small children on TV and going on through school. Yet, even in science, novelty is controlled, by the very nature of the disciplines themselves, and when novelty appears, it is immediately channeled into the political economy. That is to say, invention in science is guided by the theoretical structure of the disciplines, in the first place; and when an invention actually emerges, it is taken up by the structure of the economy and used in industry, which includes warfare.

All steady-state systems of culture are designed to develop a kind of equilibrium between, on the one hand, a spontaneity adequate to prevent a person's going to pieces when confronted with any novelty at all, and, on the other, a spontaneity so unfettered that he will propose new solutions to all problems. Adequacy in any educational system, therefore, means a nice balance between adaptation to what must continue and freezing so that what exists cannot possibly continue.

In closing I shall quote from *The Children's Charter*, a document distributed nowadays by the U.S. Children's Bureau but formulated at the White House Conference on Child Health and Protection in 1930. Article 10 reads as follows:

> For every child an education which, through the discovery and development of his individual abilities, prepares him for life; and through training and vocational guidance prepares him for a living which will yield him the maximum of satisfaction.

Article 18 says,

> To supplement the home and the school in the training of youth, and to return to them those interests of which modern life tends to cheat children. . . .

Article 10 contains a fundamental contradiction, for if there is a true interest in discovering a child's "individual abilities" this has to take place outside the categories of vocational guidance, for vocations, after all, are laid down by culture; categories negate individual abilities. But it is Article 18 that is particularly relevant, for since modern life does indeed tend to cheat children, no one with compassion and insight can introduce his own children to it without sorrow. Whenever he does, an enlightened person must feel that he is looking down the barrel of the absurd, for, on the one hand, it seems to him that this may be the only way in which he can raise their standard of living — the metaphysical Absolute of contemporary existence — while, on the other, he knows that he is introducing them to a life that will ultimately cheat them.

5 John Elson

State Regulation of Nonpublic Schools: The Legal Framework

The state cannot insure an adequate education for all children without setting instructional requirements for nonpublic schools. Nonpublic schools cannot fulfill their distinctive educational goals if these requirements preclude them from independently determining their own basic programs. Sharp controversy has arisen over how the state legislature should accommodate these conflicting needs for mandatory standards and decision-making discretion. One critic warns that the widespread lack of effective regulation seriously endangers large numbers of children, while another notes that many laws now threaten the purpose of nonpublic schools.[1] To illuminate the important issues underlying this debate, problems in the legislative enactment, judicial review, and state administration of nonpublic school laws will be explored.

The author is a member of the Illinois Bar and was a National Defense Education Act Fellow at the University of Chicago at the time of the conference.

1 Stolee, "Nonpublic Schools; What Must They Teach?" 92 *School and Society* 274 (1964); Erickson, "On the Role of Nonpublic Schools," 69 *School Review* 338 (1961).

Legislative Enactment of Nonpublic School Controls

There are five predominant policies behind nonpublic school regulation: (1) to reinforce school attendance requirements, (2) to prevent the teaching of socially dangerous ideas, (3) to promote cultural unity, (4) to provide criteria for choosing quality nonpublic schooling, and (5) to protect the public from dangerous business, health, and building practices.

Legislatures most commonly regulate nonpublic schools in order to reinforce the school attendance requirements which seek to guarantee to each child an education sufficient both for his own welfare and for the maintenance of a knowledgeable, politically responsible citizenry.[2] If the allowable alternatives to public schools were not of a certain minimum standard, these goals could be frustrated by anyone who would gather children under the name of school.

Forty-one state legislatures, which have enacted some type of compulsory standard for nonpublic school instruction, apparently accept this assumption.[3] Only six of these states, Alabama, Nebraska, North Carolina, Michigan, Iowa, and Washington, explicitly demand certification of nonpublic school teachers.[4] Of the thirty-one states regulating curricula ten specifically define required courses, while twenty-one demand various measures of equivalence between nonpublic and public school instruction.[5] Methods of enforcement also vary among the states; fourteen states can close schools violating state regulations, while seven-

2 In re Shin, 16 Cal. Rptr. 165 (1961); Knox v. O'Brien, 72 A.2d 389 (N.J. Super., 1950).

3 Cf. Stolee, "Nonpublic Schools," *supra* note 1, and Stolee, "Legal Control by the States Over the Areas of Instruction in Private Elementary and Secondary Schools," unpublished Ph.D. dissertation, University of Minnesota, 1963.

4 Code of Ala., Tit. 52 § 299 (1940); Rev. Stat. Neb. § 79–1233 (1958); Gen. Stat. N. Car. § 115–256 (1955); Mich. Stat. Anno. § 15.1923 (1921); Ia. Code Anno. § 299.1 (1953); Rev. Code Wash. Anno. § 28.67.010 (1964).

5 Stolee, "Legal Control," *supra* note 3.

teen states, having no such direct sanctions, enforce compulsory attendance laws against the students or their parents to prevent attendance at the substandard schools.[6]

The demand for nonpublic school regulation is likely to strengthen with the growing amount of federal and state aid received by public schools. As public school expenditures increasingly exceed those of nonpublic schools, the quality of education in the average public school can be expected to exceed that of the average nonpublic school.[7] One result of this could be more direct governmental supervision of nonpublic schools to insure that the education the nonpublic school child receives will not put him too far below the level of the public school child.

The other result could be an increase in nonpublic school aid. It is likely that this also will result in more governmental supervision of nonpublic schools, primarily for three reasons: the reluctance of governmental agencies and tax payers to give money to private bodies without any public controls, the possibility that publicly supported nonpublic schools will be subjected to the restrictions of the Fourteenth Amendment against discriminatory admissions practices, and the state and federal constitutional prohibitions against the use of public funds for religious purposes. To assure that the increased appropriations be used for general welfare or child-benefit purposes and not for religious functions, the state might find it necessary to expand its supervision of nonpublic schools.[8]

6 *Ibid.*

7 It is true that nonpublic schools, with their freedom to develop their own programs and choose their students and teachers, may in many instances provide instruction superior to that of much wealthier public schools. Yet, it is a reasonable assumption that public or private schools with comparatively high expenditures over time will more often than not develop better educational programs than schools with significantly less money to spend.

8 See Everson v. Board of Education, 330 U.S. 1 (1947) (statute authorizing local school districts to provide transportation of children to and from parochial schools held constitutional; state not prohibited from "extending its general state law benefits to all its citizens without regard to their religious belief."); and see Cochran v. Louisiana State Board of Education, 281 U.S. 370 (1930) (statute providing for the issuance of school books free

A second motive for nonpublic school regulation is to prevent the promulgation of ideas dangerous to the public order. Courts will uphold laws of this kind as long as the prohibition is not so broad that it violates the right of free speech.[9] Examples are New Hampshire's statute prohibiting teachers from advocating "Communism as a political doctrine or any doctrine including overthrow by force of the United States or this State" and Nebraska's law prohibiting "instruction subversive to American institutions and republican form of government or good citizenship."[10]

Fear for the public safety also has motivated several legislatures to try to promote cultural unity among people of diverse backgrounds by requiring their nonpublic schools to teach subjects deemed necessary for democratic citizenship. After World War I this justification was behind the passage of laws restricting foreign language instruction. According to the Nebraska Supreme Court, objections to the military draft

> demonstrated that there were local foci of alien enemy sentiment and that, where such instances occurred, the education given by private or parochial schools in that community was usually found to be that which had been given mainly in a foreign language.
>
> In 1919 the Legislatures of Iowa, Kansas, Maine, Arkansas, Indiana, Washington, Wisconsin and New Hampshire

of cost to public and nonpublic school students held constitutional; "The schools . . . are not the beneficiaries of these appropriations. . . . The school children and the state alone are the beneficiaries").

9 See Adler v. Board of Education, 342 U.S. 396, 403 (1952); but see, Keyishian v. Board of Regents, 17 L.ed2d 629 (1967) (loyalty statute upheld in Adler found unconstitutional: "We emphasize once again that 'precision of regulation must be the touchstone in an area so closely touching our most precious freedoms. . . . Because First Amendment freedoms need breathing space to survive, government may regulate in the area only with narrow specificity. . . .' When one must guess what conduct or utterance may lose him his position one necessarily will 'steer far wider of the unlawful zone. . . .' The danger of that chilling effect upon the exercise of vital First Amendment rights must be guarded against by sensitive tools which inform teachers what is being sanctioned," at p. 641.)

10 N.H. Rev. Stat. § 191.1 (1955); Rev. Stat. Neb. § 79-1705 (1958).

passed measures more or less drastic with regard to compulsory education in English and to prohibition of the use of foreign language in elementary schools.[11]

The United States Supreme Court, however, did not find the goal of national unity a necessarily valid basis for regulation. Finding that "no sudden emergency has arisen which renders knowledge by a child of some language other than English so clearly harmful as to justify its inhibition with the consequent infringement of rights long freely enjoyed," the Court in 1923 held unconstitutional the Nebraska law prohibiting foreign language instruction before the eighth grade.[12]

Three years later, in *Pierce* v. *Society of Sisters,* the Court found unconstitutional an Oregon law which would have prohibited children from attending any nonpublic school.[13] Strictly qualifying the cultural unity policy, the Court said: "The fundamental theory of liberty upon which all governments in this Union repose excludes any general power in the State to standardize its children by forcing them to accept instruction from public teachers only."[14] The Court affirmed this position in 1927 when it struck down an act of the Territory of Hawaii, the declared purpose of which was "to fully and effectually regulate the conducting of foreign language schools . . . in order that the Americanism of the pupils may be promoted. . . ."[15] Despite the Court's appreciation of "the grave problems incident to the large alien population of the Hawaiian Islands," it concluded that the regulations were "part of a deliberate plan to bring foreign language schools under a strict governmental control for which the record discloses no adequate reason."

It is important to note that in these three cases the Supreme

11 Nebraska District of Evangelical Lutheran Synod v. McKelvie, 175 N.W. 531, 533 (1919). (Holding overruled by U.S. Supreme Court in Meyer v. Nebraska, *infra* note 12.)
12 Meyer v. Nebraska, 262 U.S. 396, 403 (1923).
13 Pierce v. Society of Sisters, 268 U.S. 510 (1925).
14 *Ibid.,* at p. 535.
15 Farrington v. Tokushige, 273 U.S. 284, 293 (1925).

Court did not deny to the states the right to regulate nonpublic schools. "The power of the state to compel attendance at some school and to make reasonable regulations for all schools . . . is not questioned" and has never been questioned by the Court.[16] Instead, the Court established specific restrictions on how states could foster national unity through limiting an individual's freedom to educate his child according to his beliefs.[17]

After the decline of the rabid nativism of the 1920's the goal of national unity was no longer an important impetus behind nonpublic school regulation. Yet the allegation that nonpublic schools are divisive, or, in James Conant's words, that they endanger the "democratic unity provided by our public schools," is to some still an important reason for regulating nonpublic schools.[18]

Parents' need for valid criteria by which to choose quality private schooling has motivated several legislatures to set up voluntary procedures for nonpublic school accreditation.[19] Also backing such legislation were people wanting to protect the reputations of good nonpublic schools from compromise by "individuals lacking professional pride and willing to commercialize education."[20]

As a prerequisite for accreditation most statutes and state departments require that petitioning schools meet state public school standards. Only Iowa and Florida prescribe in any detail proce-

16 *Meyer, supra* note 12 at p. 402.

17 Cf. Pfeffer, *Church, State and Freedom* (Boston, 1953), pp. 509–19.

18 Conant, "Private and Parochial Schools," 49 *Nation's Schools*, 48, 49 (1952); "The greater the proportion of our youth who attend independent schools, the greater the threat to our democratic unity." p. 49. Cf. Greeley and Rossi, *The Education of Catholic Americans* (Chicago, 1966), which indicates that Catholic schools do not have a divisive influence.

19 Cf. Fla. State. Anno. § 247.01 (1959): "It is declared to be in the interest of and essential to the public health, education and welfare that the state create the means whereby minimum satisfactory educational standards may be established so that schools desiring to meet these standards may be identified. The purpose of this identification is to enable the selection of such schools by the citizens of this state thereby assuring themselves of a minimum satisfactory education."

20 Sherman, "Should Private Schools Be Subjected to Limited State Controls?" 50 *School and Society* 367 (1939).

dural safeguards for schools attempting to gain accreditation.[21] These safeguards include publication of accreditation standards, granting of accreditation whenever standards are met, notification of a school's particular disqualifying failure, a hearing after refusal or revocation of accreditation, and the right to judicial review of an adverse agency decision.

Whether a school could appeal without a statutory grant of the specific right of appeal is unclear. Under most state administrative procedure acts anyone "aggrieved by a final agency decision in a contested case is entitled to judicial review," and under common law courts will review when anyone alleges denial of any right conferred by a statute.[22] However, a New York court refused to hear an appeal from a refusal of accreditation, finding no right denied nor coercion applied. In denying accreditation the department of education is not, said the court,

> branding plaintiff's school as inferior or nonconforming. If conceivably some parents might misinterpret the absence of a Department of Education certificate as evidence of inferiority when in fact, it is no such thing, defendants cannot be held legally responsible for this false conclusion.[23]

The court here ignores the primary purpose of granting accreditation — to provide a valid standard for differentiating between the superior and inferior schools. Unless, as reported by a few state departments, voluntary accreditation makes no difference to nonpublic schools, wrongful denial of accredited status deprives a school of an important interest conferred by statute, which deserves protection by judicial review.[24]

21 Ia. Code Anno. § 257.25; Fla. Stat. Anno. §§ 247.17, 247.20.
22 Revised Model State Administrative Procedure Act, § 15a; Vernon's Anno. Mo. Stat., § 536.100 (1945); Dismuke v. United States, 297 U.S. 167 (1936); state administrative procedure acts are discussed further, *supra* pp. 33–34.
23 Jokinen v. Allen, 182 N.Y.S.2d 166 (1958).
24 Questionnaires from Tenn., Fla., and Ore. Questionnaires were solicited from all state departments of education in the preparation of this paper. Hereafter, these sources are identifid simply as "Conference Questionnaire."

A fifth policy behind regulation is based on the rationale that governmental controls in the form of business, building, health, and zoning regulations are as necessary for the public protection from actions of nonpublic schools as they are for its protection from any private business. Courts will find these regulations valid only if they are reasonably related to the protection of the public welfare.[25]

A typical nonpublic school business regulation is a California requirement that private trade schools must post bond.[26] This regulation was found to be reasonably related to the valid legislative purpose of protecting students from losing their tuition to "fly-by-night schools" that do not give the promised instruction.[27] However, laws regulating trade school tuition and advance payments were struck down by South Dakota and New York courts because their relation to the public interest was not deemed sufficient to justify their infringement of the individual's freedom to contract.[28]

A corollary to the policy of protecting students from fraudulent trade schools is that of protecting the public from students trained in those schools. To a New York court the need for state regulation of private schools "is obvious lest untrained and improperly prepared technicians be foisted upon an unsuspecting public."[29]

Although nonpublic school business, health, and building regulations are rarely invalidated by the courts, zoning regulations have been troublesome. In a leading Kentucky case an act permitting voters to exclude private trade schools from their precincts was held to exceed the police powers of the state because such schools promoted the public welfare.[30] Other courts, however, have held exclusion of schools from residential districts to

25 Nebbia v. New York, 291 U.S. 502 (1933).

26 Cal. B. & P.C.A., § 7398.

27 Olson v. Glens Falls Insurance Co., 5 Cal. Rptr 233 (1960).

28 State v. Nuss, 114 N.W.2d 633 (S.D., 1962); Grow Systems School v. Board of Regents, 98 N.Y.S.2d 834 (1950).

29 Grow Systems School, *supra* note 28.

30 Columbia Trust v. Lincoln Institute, 129 S.W. 113 (Ky., 1910).

be sufficiently in the public interest.[31] The Wisconsin Supreme Court, following this line of authority, held in 1954 that a community could ban nonpublic schools from a district while permitting public schools.[32] It justified the distinction on the grounds that nonpublic schools do not compensate the community for the disadvantages of their presence as much as public schools, which have features equally objectionable to a residential community but serve the people within that community without discrimination. A year later, the California Supreme Court found that a similar ordinance arbitrarily discriminated against private schools.[33]

A final rationale for increased nonpublic school regulation stems from the desire to limit unreasonable discrimination, racial and otherwise, in nonpublic school admissions. This rationale, too complex to be treated adequately within the bounds of the present paper, is examined by Norman Dorsen in chapter 6.

Most people would now agree that at least a few of the above policies justify some form of nonpublic school regulation. Probably the only noted critic who would now be for complete immunity from all state instructional requirements is Paul Goodman. Believing the compulsory educational system to be a trap that subdues vitality and generates cynicism and defeatism, he might view regulation of nonpublic schools as an attempt to close the few remaining avenues of escape from the public school mold.[34] The majority of nonpublic school officials, however, would not join in arguments against all forms of state regulation. Their once preponderant view of even minimal controls as ultimately destined to crush their independence declined in the 1920's and is no longer widely held.[35]

31 Yanow v. Seven Oak Park Inc., 94 A.2d 482 (N.J., 1953).
32 State v. Sinor, 65 N.W. 2d 43 (1954).
33 Roman Catholic Welfare Corp. v. City of Piedmont, 289 P.2d 438 (Cal., 1955).
34 Goodman, *Compulsory Mis-education* (New York, 1966).
35 Cf. Beck, *Lutheran Elementary Schools in the United States* (2d ed. 1965), p. 260; McLaughlin, *A History of State Legislation Affecting Private*

Yet, anxiety is felt by those who see a trend developing toward more rigid regulation of nonpublic schools.[36] The critics do not quarrel with such comparatively narrow purposes of nonpublic school laws as protection of the public from fraud, health hazards, subversive teaching, or even national disunity. Rather, the controversy is focused on the laws intended to implement the compulsory attendance policy of securing to each child an education sufficient for his own welfare and the welfare of the state.

Critics fear that controls enacted to achieve this open-ended purpose will force nonpublic schools to become more and more like public schools and thereby reduce or eliminate their usefulness. They feel that distinctive values are lost when nonpublic schools must teach subjects like state resources or alcohol education and their teachers, even those having Ph.D.'s or the experience of a Toscanini, must take a stipulated set of Education courses. It is also feared that the flexibility of many nonpublic schools in conforming their programs to their students' individual needs will be impaired by broad rules designed to assure equal treatment for all. Some educators look to the courts to check this extension of public controls.

Judicial Review of Nonpublic School Controls

Although the constitutional limits of nonpublic school regulations are vague, a general judicial approach to the subject can be derived from settled constitutional doctrines. This analysis indicates that federal and most state courts will invalidate a state statute on an educational matter only if, without any justification, it seriously infringes on a right guaranteed by the Fourteenth Amendment.

It is commonly said that the state's power over nonpublic schools

Elementary and Secondary Schools in the United States 1810–1945 (Washington, D.C., 1946).
36 Erickson, "Nonpublic Schools," *supra* note 1.

"is subject to the same limitations as exist in the case of private property or rights generally."[37] "Under our form of government," observed the Supreme Court, "the use of property and the making of contracts are normally matters of private and not of public concern. The general rule is that both shall be free of governmental interference."[38] This freedom is protected against state action by the Fourteenth Amendment's guarantee that "no State shall . . . deprive any person of life, liberty or property, without due process of law. . . ." The Amendment however, does "not prohibit governmental regulation for the public welfare."[39] Rather, "the guarantee of due process demands only that the law shall not be unreasonable, arbitrary, or capricious, and that the means selected shall have a real and substantial relation to the object sought to be attained."[40] Individual liberty is never infringed by a "regulation which is reasonable in relation to its subject and is adopted in the interests of the community. . . ."[41]

State controls over nonpublic schools, thus, must in theory evidence a definite relation to the public welfare. State courts differ widely on what degree of public benefit must be shown to validate nonpublic school regulations. North Carolina strictly limits private school controls to instances in which "there is a manifest present need which effects the health, morals, or safety of the public generally. . . ."[42] But a New York Court found the state's right to regulate nonpublic schools inherent in the function of education, stating it to be "an indisputable fact that all schools, public or private, are affected with a public interest and hence subject to reasonable regulation under the police powers of the state."[43] Under this more common view, state courts will pre-

37 47 *Am. Jur., Schools,* § 221 (1943).
38 Nebbia, *supra* note 25 at p. 523.
39 *Ibid.* at p. 525.
40 *Ibid.*
41 West Coast Hotel Co. v. Parish, 300 U.S. 379 (1937).
42 State v. Williams, 117 S.E. 2d 443 (N.C., 1960).
43 Packer Collegiate Institute v. University of State of New York, 76 N.Y.S. 2d 499, rv'd. on other grounds, 81 N.E. 2d 80 (N.Y., 1948).

sume a nonpublic school regulation to be in the public interest and will not strike it down unless it is clearly unreasonable, regardless of whether it fulfills a "manifest present need."

Since the 1930's an even broader presumption of validity has been accorded state regulatory legislation by the United States Supreme Court. In the 1937 *Carolene Products* case the Court ruled that "[judicial] inquiries, where the legislative judgment is drawn in question must be restricted to the issue whether any state of facts either known or which could reasonably be assumed affords support for it."[44] In the 1952 *Daybrite Lighting* case the legislative discretion was given its widest scope: "Our recent decisions make it plain that we do not sit as a superlegislature to weigh the wisdom of legislation nor to decide whether the policy it expresses offends public welfare."[45]

This sweeping presumption of legislative reasonableness does not immunize all types of regulatory measures, for also since the 1930's the Supreme Court has viewed less expansively the state's discretion to restrict political and religious liberties guaranteed by the First and Fourteenth Amendments. The Court said in *West Virginia State Board of Education* v. *Barnette*:

> The right of a State to regulate, for example, a public utility may well include, so far as the due process test is concerned, power to impose all of the restrictions which a legislature may have a "rational basis" for adopting. But freedoms of speech, of press and of assembly, and of worship may not be infringed on such slender grounds. They are susceptible of restriction only to prevent grave and immediate danger to interests which the state may lawfully protect. . . ."[46]

In weighing the interests for and against a contested regulation the court demands that the scales fall decisively on the side of public necessity to justify any infringement of religious or politi-

44 United States v. Carolene Products Co., 304 U.S. 144, 154 (1938).
45 Day-Brite Lighting Inc. v. Missouri, 342 U.S. 421, 423 (1952).
46 West Virginia State Board of Education v. Barnette, 319 U.S. 624 (1942). See also Sherbert v. Verner, 347 U.S. 398, 406 (1963).

cal liberties.[47] In *Barnette* the public necessity of expelling students for refusing to salute the flag was held insufficient to justify the denial of religious liberty; "neither our domestic tranquility in peace nor our martial effort in war depend on compelling little children to participate in a ceremony which ends in nothing for them but a fear of spiritual condemnation."[48]

Illustrative of cases in the state courts in which the public interest in compulsory education was held to outweigh the individual's interest in religious freedom is *Commonwealth* v. *Beiler*, affirming the conviction of Amish parents for violation of the compulsory attendance law.[49] Although education past the eighth grade was shown to violate profound tenets of Amish faith and was alleged to threaten the existence of their religious community, the court found no substantial First Amendment question, observing; "there is no interference with religious liberty where the State reasonably restricts parental control, or compels parents to perform their natural and civic obligation to educate their children." Similar is *Commonwealth* v. *Bey*, affirming the conviction of Mohammedan parents for not sending their children to school on Friday, their Sabbath.[50] Pfeffer argues against both the result in the above cases and the weight of state judicial authority on two grounds: first, the religious liberty of the few parents who object to higher education outweighs the state's interest in compelling secondary schooling, and, second, alternative methods of education would satisfy the attendance policy without violating religious principles.[51]

Even under its restrictive view of legislative power in *Barnette*, it is doubtful that the Supreme Court would protect religious liberty to the extent Pfeffer advocates. Implicit in the Barnette "grave and immediate danger" test is the starting premise stated

47 Cf. Feiner v. New York, 340 U.S. 315 (1951), concurring opinion of Frankfurter, J.
48 Barnette, *supra* note 46, concurring opinion of Black and Douglas, J.J., p. 643.
49 Commonwealth v. Beiler, 79 A.2d 134 (Pa., 1951).
50 Commonwealth v. Bey, 70 A.2d 693 (1950).
51 Pfeffer, *supra* note 17, pp. 594–97.

by the Court in *Prince* v. *Massachusetts* that "neither rights of religion nor rights of parenthood are beyond limitation. . . . Its [the state's] authority is not nullified merely because the parent grounds his claim to control the child's course of conduct on religious conscience."[52]

Courts clearly cannot strike down all laws that interfere with all expressions of religion. The conflict can be resolved in favor of the right of free exercise of religion only when such a holding will not jeopardize an essential legislative policy. "Legislation intended to facilitate the opportunity of children to get a secular education . . . " is unquestionably in furtherance of an essential policy.[53] How necessary to this policy's success a particular nonpublic school law must be in order to override the First Amendment attack depends on the facts of each case. However, a few generalizations about the Court's probable line of reasoning may be useful.

State court holdings and Supreme Court dicta establish that claims of religious liberty cannot limit the state's authority to require school attendance.[54] Insuring that all children receive an education is clearly a vital interest of the state. It is also hardly open to dispute that some specifications of the type and quality of schooling offered are imperative if the compulsory attendance law is to be effective. Were the Court to invalidate these reinforcing rules, it would undermine, along with the compulsory attendance law, the state's entire policy of maintaining educational standards.[55] Because of the interdependence of instructional regulations and because of the expertise necessary to forge them into an effective statutory framework, the Court would be extremely reluctant to interfere with the legislative choice of particular instructional requirements. Judges have no special competence in the field of school administration, and the social costs of frustrating the legislative purpose are high. Even when an instructional

52 Prince v. Massachusetts, 321 U.S. 158, 166 (1944).
53 Everson, *supra* note 8 at p. 7.
54 Prince, *supra* note 52, at p. 166; People v. Donner, 302 N.Y. 857 (1951).
55 Cf. *supra* p. 104.

prescription directly conflicts with claimed First Amendment rights, it is doubtful that the Court would demand a greater showing of necessity to sustain the law than that it significantly advances the purposes of the compulsory attendance law. Where the state policy, as here, is an essential one, the Court could not be expected to reverse a rational legislative choice of a particular means of implementation because better ways of accommodating all interests occur to the Court.

In view of a widespread assumption that a need exists for high academic standards, it should not be difficult to show that a nonpublic school regulation significantly promotes the policy behind the compulsory attendance law. Most of the rules, as noted above, require that nonpublic schools meet the minimum criteria deemed necessary for the education of public school children. Although the Court could find that these criteria do not significantly advance the purpose of maintaining educational standards, such holdings would be exceptional and probably limited to obvious discriminations against nonpublic school religious interests, as, for instance, a law prohibiting any student in a school building from fastening his clothes with hooks instead of buttons.

In most controversies over nonpublic school laws it is unlikely that the Court would have to decide whether a law positively furthers the state's educational policy, since only the exceptional litigant can legitimately claim substantial infringement of First Amendment rights of religious liberty and free speech. The majority of disputes in this area concern economic or pedagogical issues that threaten remotely, if at all, religious or political interests. Unless a significant First Amendment question can be shown, the Court will accord the legislature the wide latitude afforded by the "rational basis" test, which requires no showing of positive social benefit to balance a showing of individual harm.

Despite the liberality of the "rational basis" test where First Amendment questions are not involved, the Supreme Court may yet find a nonpublic school regulation unconstitutional because it is not sufficiently related to any public benefit. For example, it might well find unjustifiable a law requiring all schools to teach beauty culture not less than two hours a day. However, the only laws now governing nonpublic schools that might give the Court difficulties under the "rational basis" test are those requiring nonpublic school instruction to be equivalent to public school instruction. The 1962 case of *Meyerkorth* v. *Nebraska* illustrates a state supreme court's unsatisfactory disposition of a constitutional attack on such a law.[56]

The Code sections in question provided that nonpublic schools "shall be graded the same and shall have courses of study for each grade conducted therein, substantially the same as those given in the public schools where the children attending would attend in the absence of such private, denominational or parochial schools," and that all nonpublic school teachers have certicates entitling them "to teach corresponding courses or classes in public schools. . . ."[57] The complainants argued that these provisions "have no relevance to the interests of the state in children not educated in public tax-supported schools." The state's interference with nonpublic school children, they maintained, must be limited to ascertaining "if they know the language of their country, understand its government, and are able to participate in the democratic process." The precedent cited to support this principle was a 1919 decision in which the same court said:

> The state should control the education of its citizens far enough to see that it is given in the language of their country and to insure that they understand the nature of the government under which they live and are competent to take part in it. Further than this, education should be left to the fullest freedom of the individual.[58]

Surprisingly, instead of expanding this statement of the state's limited authority to control education, the court treated it as binding. Yet, the court did not attempt to reconcile its earlier narrow limitation of the state's power of control with the broader equivalency and teacher certification laws. Rather, it dismissed this cru-

56 Meyerkorth v. State, 115 N.W. 2d 585 (Neb., 1962).
57 Neb. §§ 79–1701, 79–1702 R.R.S. 1943.
58 Nebraska District v. McKelvie, *supra* note 11, at p. 533.

cial problem by generally referring to its 1919 decision as supporting the state's position, without apparent recognition of any conflict in doctrine.

The United States Supreme Court, though not bound by the 1919 Nebraska precedent, would have more trouble than the present Nebraska court in justifying the equivalency requirement. Supporting its doubts would be a recent North Carolina Supreme Court decision emphasizing the need to protect nonpublic school diversity:

> Standardization and regimentation in the field of learning is contrary to the American concept of individual liberty. It would be difficult to over-estimate the contribution of private institutions of learning to the initiative, progress and individualism of our people. Regulation should never be resorted to unless the need is compellingly apparent.[59]

Most important, the Court would be reminded of its own denial in *Pierce* of the state's power "to standardize its children" and in *Farrington* v. *Tokushige* of its guarantee of "reasonable choice and discretion in respect of teachers, curriculum and textbooks."[60] It is dubious whether the Court's policy opposing standardization of children and advocating preservation of reasonable discretion in the choice of education can have any substance if the legislature can require nonpublic schools to teach "substantially the same" courses as public schools.

Yet the Court would be even less willing here than in contests over religious liberties to interfere with the expertise of the legislature in deciding how to regulate the standards of compulsory education. The intent and effect of the equivalency requirement is to guarantee to all children a substantially similar level of education. Were the Court to find this law unconstitutional because it is not rationally related to a valid public purpose it would seem to contradict its thirty-year-old policy of giving legislatures wide discretion to make laws for the general welfare. The Court might well believe that this method of maintaining satisfactory stand-

59 State v. Williams, *supra* note 42, at p. 450.
60 Pierce, *supra* note 13; Farrington, *supra* note 15, at p. 293.

ards is outweighed by the countervailing interest in allowing non-public schools more freedom to develop their own standards. It is highly improbable, however, that the Court would find the equivalency requirement so devoid of relevance to the essential goal the state is trying to achieve that it would make this judgment for the legislature.

In view of this judicial deference to the legislative judgment, the critics who look to courts to strike down laws seriously restricting nonpublic school diversity would be better advised to seek such protection from the legislators. Unfortunately, in debating what should be the role of legislative controls, many critics have overlooked the real function of the legislature. It is a remedial agency that reacts to specific problems. While thoughtful observers argue the theoretical merits of policies of strict, permissive, or no controls, the legislators consider regulatory policies if and when they are responsive to some particular exigency.

Conditions potentially dangerous to the public welfare, such as large numbers of militant aliens sympathetic to the wartime enemy, numerous profit-hungry proprietory schools, or the existence of fire-hazards in many nonpublic school buildings are likely to stimulate the enactment of strict controls. But if a state's nonpublic schools are heavily endowed college preparatory schools, or affiliated with major religious groups, or accredited by responsible associations, then a legislature is unlikely to feel a need to interfere. Thus, the wisdom of a particular state's regulatory policies can be determined only in the terms of the social problems created by nonpublic schools in that state. Useful observation of the effectiveness of the implementation of those policies, however, can be drawn from a general study of the statutes and their methods of administration.

State Administration of Nonpublic School Controls

Nonpublic school laws vary widely in the degree to which they specify substantive standards and enforcement procedures. One of the few examples of detailed statutory prescription is the California Education Code which requires instruction in the subjects of public safety and accident prevention, physical education, fire prevention, the effects of alcohol and narcotics, and others.[61]

Illustrative of statutes granting wide discretion in the implementation of legislative policy is the Nebraska provision empowering the State Board of Education to "establish standards and procedures for classifying, approving and accrediting schools, including the establishment of minimum standards and procedures for approving the opening of new schools, the continued legal operation of all schools. . . ."[62]

Most nonpublic school statutes fall between these extremes in prescribing substantive standards that still require the exercise of considerable discretion in their implementation. An example of this approach is the Ohio code, which defines the criteria the State Board of Education must use in determining the minimum nonpublic school standards that will satisfy students' compulsory attendance requirements. It states that the Board's standards "shall provide adequately for: a curriculum sufficient to meet the needs of pupils in every community . . . efficient and effective instructional materials and equipment . . . the proper organization and administration and supervision of each school. . . ."[63] It concludes: "In the formulation and administration of such standards for non-tax supported schools the board shall also consider the particular needs, methods and objectives of said schools, provided they do not conflict with the provision of a general education of a high quality. . . ."

The legislative goal in requiring administrators to follow specific statutory standards is to insure that they will carry out the legislative intent. Many courts will invalidate statutes lacking sufficiently definite standards to guide agency rule-making.[64] The New York Court of Appeals observed that "it would be intolerable for the Legislature to hand over to any official or group of

61 Cal. Ed. C.A. §§ 8001, 8159, 8156, 8157, 8051, 8052, 7852.
62 Rev. State Neb. § 79–328 (1958).
63 Ohio Rev. Stat. § 3301.07 (D) (1964).
64 American Power and Light Co. v. S.E.C., 329 U.S. 90, 104–6 (1946);
High School Board v. Board of Education, 122 N.E. 2d 192 (Ohio, 1953).

officials an unlimited, unrestrained, undefined power to make such regulations as he or they should desire and to grant or refuse licenses to such schools, depending on their compliance with such regulations." [65]

Yet, despite their lengthy specifications, the Ohio statutory standards have apparently not provided adequate guidance. The Ohio Department of Education reports that its authority over nonpublic schools needs statutory clarification, that it enforces nonobjective laws less rigorously than objective ones because of difficulties in interpretation, and that it needs a greater delegation of authority over nonpublic schools to fulfill the legislative policy.[66] Not only has the Ohio statute failed to guide administrators in fulfilling legislative intent, it also has failed to stop them from trying to exceed that intent. For, in its efforts to close down Amish schools, the Ohio Department of Education has attempted to create and enforce prohibitions that go beyond what both the legislature and state supreme court have deemed to be legal regulations.[67]

The most common and troublesome instructional standard requires nonpublic schools to have courses of instruction equivalent to those in public schools. Typical expressions of this standard provide that nonpublic school instruction shall "be equivalent to that provided in the public schools," teach "subjects comparable to those taught in the public schools," and equal "in thoroughness and efficiency and in the progress made therein that in the public schools . . ." [68]

Considerable discretion is necessary to implement these mandates, since their language gives little indication of how the legislature wants them construed. One administrator might reasonably find that failure to provide courses in home economics violates the equivalency standard, while another might just as reasonably

65 Packer Collegiate Institute v. University of State of New York, 81 N.E. 2d 80 (N.Y., 1948).

66 Conference Questionnaire (Ohio).

67 State v. Glick, 175 N.E. 2d 68 (Ohio, 1961).

68 N.J.S.A. § 18;1422 (1940); Mich. Stat. Anno. § 15.3732 (1921); Anno. Laws Mass. ch. 76 § 1 (1950).

find nonequivalency only when nonpublic school instruction is virtually without educational value.

Because of this ambiguity, courts are often called on to resolve disputes over how the equivalency requirements should be interpreted.[69] One court said equivalency in this context means "equal in worth or value, force, power, effect, import and the like." Such a statement gives a judge or administrator no more certain basis for applying a standard than does the single term "equivalent."[70] As a result of this uncertainty many courts will presume the state school official has used his professional expertise properly and affirm his decision without a close analysis of the particular circumstances.[71] Such narrow judicial review can be dangerous where enforcement is by local school officials, who are often influenced by personal animosities, loyalties, or local pressures to the disregard of objective educational issues.[72] Judicial reluctance to review state department decisions would seem more justified, since state officials are more often above local embroilments, have knowledge of statewide school conditions, and have co-workers to discuss and check their work.

Statutory vagueness may result not only in administrative and judicial confusion but also in the failure even to attempt implementation of statutory purposes. The seriousness of this problem is evidenced by the report that fifteen states take no steps to enforce statutory instructional requirements.[73] The Michigan nonpublic school laws exemplify how statutory ambiguity can result in nonimplementation of legislative intentions.

The Michigan Superintendent of Public Instruction is granted "supervision of all the private, denominational and parochial

69 People v. Levison, 90 N.E. 2d 213 (Ill., 1950); Knox v. O'Brien, *supra* note 2; State v. Pilkington, 310 S.W. 2d 304 (Mo., 1958); State v. Vaughn, 207 A.2d 737 (N.J., 1916); State v. Superior Court, 346 P.2d 999 (Wash., 1959); Wright v. State, 209 P. 179 (Okla., 1922).

70 Knox v. O'Brien, *supra* note 2.

71 State v. Hershberger, 144 N.E. 2d 693 (Ohio, 1955).

72 Donald A. Erickson, "Showdown at an Amish Schoolhouse," chapter 2 above.

73 Stolee, "Nonpublic Schools," *supra* note 1.

schools of this state in such matters and manner as is hereinafter provided. . . ."[74] The statute specifies the purpose of this delegation of authority: "It is the intent of this act that the sanitary conditions of such schools, the course of study therein and the qualifications of the teachers thereof shall be of the same standard as provided by the general school laws of the state."[75] It then requires that all nonpublic school teachers be certified, that nonpublic schools in violation of state law shall be closed, and, finally, that nonpublic schools must both teach "subjects comparable to those taught in the public schools" and comply with all provisions of the act, in order that their students may comply with the compulsory attendance requirement.[76] Despite the twice-stated statutory intention that nonpublic schools have curriculum standards equivalent to public schools, the Michigan Department of Education reported that its grant of power is too vague to permit regular enforcement of the equivalent instruction requirement.[77]

Legislatures could vastly improve nonpublic school regulation if they would define specifically the regulatory purpose and all the precise standards and procedures to be used in fulfilling that purpose. However, few legislatures even attempt to eliminate vagueness through detailed statutory definition, and none has ever succeeded.

Inept draftsmanship and political opposition often contribute to this failure. But the primary and unavoidable reason is that legislatures cannot possibly foresee and stipulate all the detailed, changing circumstances which a good administrator must consider in effectuating legislative policy. Just as the Internal Revenue Code cannot specify every type of personal gain that is taxable, so a school code cannot specify every type of instruction that meets a mandatory minimum level.

In applying a statutory mandate to dissimilar situations, individual judgment must have leeway to avoid inappropiate im-

74 Mich. Stat. Anno. § 15.1921 (1929).
75 Mich. Stat. Anno. § 15.1925 (1929).
76 Mich Stat. Anno. §§ 15.1923, 15.1924, 15.3732.
77 Conference Questionnaire (Mich.).

plementation of legislative policy. An especially wide grant of discretion would seem necessary for effective regulation of nonpublic schools since the variations in both the educational approaches of nonpublic schools and the character of the communities they serve defy sound classification by statutory formula. One questions the fairness and social value of statutes that prescribe the same compulsory standards for an Amish school, a Montessori school, and a mission school, or for an Exeter, a military academy, and a special school for slow learners and problem children.[78]

The legislature, unlike an administrative agency, cannot devote sufficient time to the study of all the regulatory problems raised by these different types of schools and the communities they serve. Nor has it time to work out detailed solutions and review them in the light of changing circumstances. Unlike an administrative agency, it cannot develop increasingly better regulations through the accumulation of specialized knowledge in its rule-making and rule-enforcing functions. Only a department of education vested with ample discretion to make and enforce rules can reconcile legislative policy with the problems and purposes of each type of nonpublic school.

This approach is subject to the criticism that the result of giving any agency discretion to make and enforce its own rules will be sweeping and harsh controls exercised by administrators who want maximum extension of their jurisdiction. Evidence indicates, however, that this is not the most likely result.

The Nebraska State Department of education, which has extensive discretionary authority, reports that if a nonpublic school's deviations from regulations are based on what it considers a well-established philosophy of education it will consider such schools as maintaining an accredited program.[79] The Hawaii Department of Education, which also has wide discretionary authority, reports that it is not as concerned with the imposition of its po-

78 Cf. Erickson, "The Plain People vs. The Common Schools," *Saturday Review*, November 19, 1966, pp. 85–87, 102–3.
79 Conference Questionnaire (Neb.).

tentially severe controls on nonpublic schools accredited by regional associations as with their application to unaccredited schools.[80] The Kansas State Department, in certifying nonpublic schools for compliance with the compulsory attendance law, will permit them to have classes with as many as forty students, while the public school maximum is thirty.[81] The Washington State Department, recognizing a desperate teacher shortage in the state's nonpublic schools, grants exceptions from the department's teacher certification requirements to nonpublic school teachers advancing towards the necessary degree.[82] Finally, the Connecticut State Department, while seeking authority to set minimum nonpublic school standards, reports that it "has no desire to regulate beyond the necessities of public protection, it will not dictate or criticize the philosophies peculiar to the good institutions, and it has no intention of imposing supervision or curtailing institutional autonomy."[83]

The argument against expanding agency discretion does recognize, however, that the dangers from abuse of discretion vary in proportion to the degree of delegation of rule-making and rule-enforcing power. Although the inability of many state departments to impose serious restrictions may allow nonpublic schools to continue substandard teaching, it also prevents the departments from imposing harsh requirements not contemplated by the legislature. Perhaps in states where substandard nonpublic schools are not considered a danger, a lax system of enforcement is the best way to protect the independent role of the nonpublic school without completely abdicating state control in the face of extreme deficiencies. Where substandard nonpublic schools do jeopardize the welfare of society, however, there is an urgent need for ways to compel their compliance with instructional standards without subjecting them to unreasonable administrative demands.

80 Conference Questionnaire (Haw.).
81 Letter from Kansas Dept. of Educ., December 7, 1962, quoted in Stolee, "Legal Controls," *supra* note 3, at p. 370.
82 Conference Questionnaire (Wash.).
83 Conference Questionnaire (Conn.).

Many state courts, it has been noted, attempt to curb administrative abuse of power by requiring all statutes delegating rule-making authority to specify standards for the agency to follow. The requirement has largely been futile and has been abandoned by several state courts.[84] The inescapable difficulty in using statutory standards to check agency power is that standards effective in curbing abuse preclude needed discretionary authority, while standards allowing sufficient discretion are too vague and general to prevent abuse.

The real need in regulatory statutes, Professor Davis has noted, "is usually not for standards, but for safeguards."[85] Many state departments have asserted their need for more rule-making and rule-enforcement authority over nonpublic schools.[86] However, if they do not convince their legislatures that effective safeguards will prevent abuse of this discretion their repeated failures to attain more authority are likely to continue.

In fifteen states administrative procedure acts have been enacted to provide safeguards for the rule-making and adjudicating functions.[87] Two provisions are usually considered of greatest importance: first, that all interested parties after notice of rule-making be given reasonable opportunity to present their own views to the rule-making officials; and second, that parties contesting enforcement of rules against them be given a hearing in which they can present evidence and arguments on all issues involved.[88]

Many more safeguards of greater stringency must bind all exercises of agency authority in order to provide complete immunity from administrative abuse of discretion. Yet, as most leg-

84 Butler v. United Cerebral Palsy of Northern Ky., 352 S.W. 2d 203 (Ky., 1961).
85 K. C. Davis, *Administrative Law Treatise*, § 22.11, p. 125.
86 Conference Questionnaires (Conn., Ohio, Fla., Minn., Wisc., Ind., Wyo., and Utah).
87 Ind., Mass., Mich., Pa., Va., Wisc., Calif., Ill., Mo., N. Car., N. Dak., Ohio, Ga., Okla., W. Va. Cf. Davis, *Treatise, supra* note 83, at §1.04, pp. 19–20.
88 Mich. Stat. Anno. § 3.560 (7a) (1964) and § 3.560 (21.4) (1953).

islatures recognize, comprehensive procedural safeguards, though theoretically sound, are apt to suffocate independent judgment when it is most needed for fair and efficient administration. The proper balance between discretion and safeguards cannot be found in general theories of administration but must be sought in terms of the particular functions of each agency.

Administrative determinations are based either on issues of policy and law that depend on general knowledge and principles or on issues of specific facts about specific parties that must be resolved on their individual grounds. The former type of determination, common to agency rule-making, requires different procedural safeguards from the latter type, which is common to agency adjudication.

For example, when the Federal Aviation Agency makes a rule for pilot health standards, the rule is based on general information that is available to and concerns all the affected parties equally. A hearing in which all parties are allowed to present unrestricted oral or written arguments is sufficient procedure for making a well-informed decision. The requirements of a trial type of hearing, including compliance with the judicial rules for admission of evidence, cross-examination, and rebuttal, would demand much more time and would not present the issues as well as straightforward arguments by the parties. Formal trial type of procedures, however, would be appropriate for a National Labor Relations Board adjudication to determine whether acts alleged to be an unfair labor practice actually happened. Here, the decision depends on illuminating specific issues of fact peculiar to the activities of the individual parties, the exact function for which trial procedures are designed.

In regulating nonpublic schools state departments of education engage in both types of determinations, making rules on the basis of broad issues of policy and law and enforcing them against individual parties on the basis of particular facts. When these parties contest enforcement there is rarely any reason why they should be denied the basic safeguards of a judicial trial, including the right to specific notice of the charges; sufficient time to prepare a defense; opportunity to present evidence, to cross-examine witnesses, and to have a determination based on the record of the proceedings. There would seem to be no major problem in securing these safeguards. They are required by both appellate courts and many regulatory or administrative procedure acts and are readily obtainable on the initiative of counsel. Administrators should not be reluctant to accord these safeguards since they are helpful in illuminating the facts necessary for a correct decision.

The crux of the problem lies in providing safeguards against abuse of an agency's power to make comprehensive rules. The inescapable dilemma in this attempt is that on the one hand, the rule-making discretion needed to implement legislative policy is undermined by inflexible procedural safeguards, while, on the other hand, if that discretion is not safeguarded the administrator can largely pursue his own policy, regardless of legislative intent.

It is true that the rule-making discretion of any agency is never complete. The legislature can always revoke its grant of authority and funds. Legislative committees, especially those controlling appropriations, can be highly effective in both preventing deviations from statutory policy and working with administrators to better understand and satisfy community needs.

A more available check than the legislature on rule-making discretion is the court, which will strike down rules which are not within the granted power, not issued according to proper procedure, or unreasonable.[89] Although judges may exercise wide discretion in determining reasonableness, they cannot be expected to provide consistent protection against unwise or unfair rules. The Court, Mr. Justice Cardozo said, "is not at liberty to substitute its own discretion for that of administrative officers who have kept within the bounds of their administrative powers. . . . [E]rror or unwisdom is not equivalent to abuse."[90]

Although the success of legislative policy often depends on enlightened rule-making, there are no safeguards that can guar-

89 Davis, *Administrative Law; Cases-Text-Problems*, 1965, p. 111.
90 American Telephone and Telegraph Co. v. United States, 299 U.S. 232 (1936).

antee the making of wise rules. However, certain procedures, such as the requirement of an open hearing, can promote sound rule-making. The hearing requirement is based on the assumption that through exchanging ideas with all the regulated parties the rule-maker can more fully understand the position of those parties and, consequently, write wiser and fairer rules. It is an attempt to put into practice the salutary jurisprudential principal that decisions can be made in the public interest only to the extent that all the interests affected are first fully considered.[91]

For reasons peculiar to the field of education the policy of considering all views before making rules is vital to effective nonpublic school regulation. The constant intellectual ferment in educational thought precludes the possibility that anyone can make rules to meet all school situations solely on the basis of his own belief in certain enduring principles of sound education. Traditional theories are being supplemented, amended, or discredited so rapidly that unswerving reliance on long-accepted, unreexamined ideas inevitably sacrifices the best for the easiest solutions.

Equally as important as willingness to consider different ideas is the predisposition to consider ideas from different people. More than in most areas of governmental regulation, in education valuable insights are not limited to persons with professional qualifications. They can come from anyone of intelligence, seriously concerned with educational problems, especially if they are his own.

The harm resulting from a rule-maker's refusal seriously to consider challenging ideas from different sources is aggravated where the conflict between regulator and regulated stems from differences in cultural attitudes towards the proper social function of nonpublic schools. It seems a reasonable probability that where the two antagonistic parties join in a good-faith discussion of the reasons behind their respective positions, mutual under-

91 Stone, "The Twentieth Century Administrative Explosion and After," 52 U. Cal. L.R. 513, 532.

standing will be promoted and will contribute to improved rule-making and rule-abiding.

Lack of communication is not always a serious problem. Many state departments of education reported having open and friendly relations with officials of the major nonpublic school organizations, such as the Catholic and Lutheran Churches.[92] Yet, also frequently reported were either no communication or strained relations with the smaller unconventional religious groups and the unaffiliated independent schools.[93]

The bare hearing requirement is clearly insufficient to bring these small but important nonpublic school groups into communication with the rule-makers. Hearings are often cumbersome, costly, and excessively time-consuming. Successful interchange with nonpublic groups requires a department of education to try a wide variety of tactics.

The most effective procedure for this purpose is to draft tentative rules and then submit them to the interested parties for written comments. A department of education can also sponsor periodic statewide nonpublic school conventions or hold smaller, more specialized conferences. Space in its bulletin or journal can be devoted to views of nonpublic school officials. It can initiate informal contacts through questionnaires, telephone calls, or personal consultations. The industry-committee system used by the War Production Board and Office of Price Administration during World War II could be effectively adapted to nonpublic school regulation. Such advisory committees made up of professional educators, religious leaders, and community spokesmen of various types could be the source of valuable ideas in proposing and reviewing rules governing nonpublic schools. The agency could also promote consideration of divergent views by employing people with diverse school backgrounds. Finally, inviting detailed criticism of the statutory scheme and agency practices by various

92 Conference Questionnaires (Conn., Haw., Ohio, N. Mex., Me., Mich., Wisc., N. Dak., S. Dak., Ida., Wash., Ind., Utah, Neb., Ia.).
93 Conference Questionnaires (Haw., N. Mex., Ohio., Me., Mich., Fla., Kan., Wash., Mont., Ia.).

nonagency experts could facilitate periodic reevaluation of the department's success in regulating nonpublic schools.

Although these tactics could stimulate illuminating exchanges of ideas, the legislature would be ill-advised to require an agency to use them. Their success depends on the administrator's personal judgment of the type of issue involved, the proper timing, the dispositions of the parties, and the agency's past experiences. A statute cannot tell an administrator the proper time to hold a conference or consult outside advisors. It cannot estimate which problems could be best solved by soliciting suggestions from knowledgeable parties. The simple requirement of holding a hearing before rule-making, Professor Davis points out, can cause much wasted effort when the rules being made concern minor matters such as parking in the agency lot or amending printers' errors in published regulations.[94]

The costs in administrative efficiency must, thus, be carefully measured before binding agency discretion by procedural requirements. But even if the legislature is willing to sacrifice administrative efficiency for procedural protections, it has been noted that there are no safeguards that can require agencies to make wise and fair rules. Legislative oversight in the present condition of most state legislatures is virtually nonexistent. Judicial review is almost always available, but judges are usually reluctant to substitute their own ideas of wisdom and fairness for those of the agencies.

For wise and fair treatment under statutes delegating broad rule-making powers nonpublic schools must rely primarily on the intelligence and goodwill of government officials. Even assuming a high-caliber staff, it may be argued with some force that agency fair-mindedness is a product of happenstance, the luck to have a particular person in a particular position, and therefore cannot be depended upon for real protection. However, on deeper analysis it is apparent that government fairness in making and enforcing regulations originates in popular respect for the educational competence and social contributions of nonpublic schools. With-

94 Davis, *Treatise, supra* note 87, at pp. 125–26.

out the support of public opinion, as it is reflected in the attitude of state offiicials, the only substantial protection against harsh nonpublic school controls is the defeat of the legislation authorizing the controls. In view of the harm done children educated in substandard nonpublic schools, this decision to preclude effective regulation is a difficult one to make. It would be far better for government and nonpublic school officials to avoid such an impasse by entering into a continuing dialogue to find common bases for constructive work together and practical methods for cooperative settlement of differences.

Summary

Nonpublic school regulations are intended to promote five main policies. First and most important, minimum curriculum and teacher certification laws are enacted to make school attendance requirements effective. Second, statutes more common in recent years are designed to prevent the teaching of ideas considered socially dangerous. Third, regulations are intended to promote cultural unity, although this concept is less popular since the 1920's and is now apparent in only a few states. Fourth, voluntary accreditation statutes are enacted to provide criteria by which to choose quality nonpublic schooling. Finally, in all states, laws applicable to nonpublic schools as well as to any private business are designed to protect the public from dangerous business, health, and building practices.

Federal and most state courts profess extreme reluctance to hold statutes governing educational matters unconstitutional unless they directly conflict with significant First Amendment interests. Even then, however, it can be expected that if the contested statute advances a valid educational objective, courts would not hold it unconstitutional despite their realization of better ways to reconcile the state policy with First Amendment liberties. Thus, although Supreme Court dicta from the 1920's deny to the states the power to eliminate reasonable choice in education, under the Court's present view a law requiring nonpublic school instruction to be equivalent to public school instruction would probably be held constitutional.

A wide delegation of discretionary authority is needed in the regulation of nonpublic schools, because the problems encountered are highly specialized, highly dissimilar, and in a field of study that is in constant flux. Safeguards against abuse of this discretion may be provided in administrative adjudication by certain judicial trial type of procedures and in administrative rule-making by methods designed to promote exchanges of ideas between administrators and parties being regulated. The conflict between an effective delegation of administrative discretion and the maintenance of safeguards to prevent abuse of that discretion can be successfully resolved only when the nonpublic school supporter respects the state's role of maintaining educational standards and the citizen respects the nonpublic school's role of providing an educational alternative to the public schools.

6 Norman Dorsen

Racial Discrimination
in "Private" Schools

The national struggle to secure equal rights for black Americans persists unabated and perhaps intensified as the thirteenth year since the Supreme Court decision in *Brown* v. *Board of Education*[1] draws to a close. Conflict rages in the streets and in the courts, and it touches all aspects of civic life. The docket of the Supreme Court may not be the surest touchstone to the problems of the nation, but it is not by chance that within the past few months the Court has been called upon to act on important cases stemming from many types of racial discrimination, including voting, education, housing and physical violence.[2]

It is folly, in my view, to try to identify a single key to racial discrimination. Equality is indivisible, and the American dilemma will not be resolved until all channels of opportunity are cleared for citizens irrespective of their origins, beliefs, and color. It does

The author is professor of law and director of the Arthur Garfield Hays Civil Liberties Program, New York University School of Law.
1 347 U.S. 483 (1954), 349 U.S. 294 (1955).
2 See, e.g., Katzenbach v. Morgan, 384 U.S. 641 (1966) (voting); Bd. of Supervisors of Prince Edward County v. Griffin, 385 U.S. 960 (1966) (education); Reitman v. Mulkey, 387 U.S. 369 (1967) (housing); United States v. Price, 383 U.S. 787 (1966) (physical violence).

not seem inconsistent with this unitary view to focus special attention on the blight of segregated education. This condition led to the massive legal and public effort culminating in the Brown case, and success in that litigation opened the modern era of race relations. Ever since, a high proportion of civil rights energy has been expended in trying to fulfill the noble promises of that decision.

The record is not uplifting. In the 1965–66 school year but 6 per cent of Negro children in the Deep South attended public school with white children, and although the record is improving only a small percentage of black children in the South receive an integrated education.[3] In the North, too, there is a severe problem of racial isolation, and there the problem is getting worse rather than better. The figures are that 72 per cent of all Negro first graders in the North attend schools that have a majority of Negroes, and in some cities there is virtually total segregation. For example, in Buffalo 77 per cent of Negro children attend elementary schools that are more than 90 per cent Negro, while 81 per cent of the white children are in almost all-white schools. In Gary, Indiana, the figures are 90 per cent and 75 per cent, respectively. The evidence shows that this pattern does not vary much, whether one considers a large Northern city or a small one, or whether the Negro proportion of the population is large or small.[4]

The legal war to rectify this sad condition is being pressed on many fronts. In the South, the United States Court of Appeals for the Fifth Circuit recently ruled that the Constitution requires all school grades, including kindergarten, to be desegregrated by

3 Statistics recently released by the Southern Education Reporting Service show that 16 per cent of the 3,000,000 Negro students in the South are now attending desegregated schools. This figure includes an additional 305,000 pupils in such schools for the first time in 1966–67. See *New York Times,* April 3, 1967.

4 Racial Isolation in the Public Schools, A Report of the United States Commission on Civil Rights 2–10 (1967). See also Coleman *et al., Equality of Educational Opportunity (1966),* a study conducted pursuant to Title IV of the Civil Rights Act of 1964.

the 1967–68 school year.[5] If the past is any guide, however, there will be many cases of tokenism and even of outright defiance of this decision, and it would be foolish to conclude that the battle is won. In the North the legal situation is more complex, reflecting the fact that segregated housing patterns and historic school district lines are often the cause of segregation. Civil rights leaders are currently trying to induce school boards to eliminate this "de facto segregation" by redrawing district lines and locating new schools at points which would lead to an integrated student body.[6] If board action is not forthcoming, the next step is litigation, but the prospect for success in the courts is at best uncertain.[7]

It is against this background of a still unfulfilled constitutional promise that the situation of the nonpublic school must be considered. My broad thesis is that a great opportunity awaits the nonpublic school, that these institutions have a chance to prove to the nation that the quality education for which they are known can be sustained, and indeed enhanced, with an integrated student body. If this opportunity is grasped, these schools will both improve their moral position and provide the kind of education that will be most relevant for national leaders of the next century.

In this paper I shall discuss four other subjects. First, the role that independent, largely nonsectarian schools have played in the general southern resistance to *Brown* v. *Board of Education*. Second, the judicial power under the Constitution to force nonpublic schools to integrate racially. Third, some legal problems a nonpublic school could confront that wants to accept Negroes

5 United States v. Jefferson County Board of Education, 372 F.2d 836 (5th Cir. 1966), aff'd en banc, 380 F.2d 385 (1967), cert. den., 389 U.S. 840 (1967).

6 There has been some success in this effort. See Note, "Racial Imbalance in the Public Schools: Constitutional Dimensions and Judicial Response," 18 *Vand. L. Rev.* 1290, n. 180 at 1319–1321 (1965).

7 See, e.g., Bell v. School City of Gary, Indiana, 324 F.2d 209 (7th Cir. 1963), cert. den. 377 U.S. 924 (1964). But see Barksdale v. Springfield School Committee, 237 F.Supp. 543 (D. Mass. 1965), rev'd on other grounds, 348 F.2d 261 (1st Cir. 1965).

for the first time. And, finally, the special situation of church-related schools.

I

First the South. The "massive resistance" of that region to integrated public education is well known, as is the fact that the means chosen to assure the perpetuation of lily-white schools ran the gamut from pure violence to sophisticated constitutional arguments of "interposition" and "nullification". Less well known is the fact that "private" schools were and are being used as an important instrument of state policy to achieve the same end.

Most southern states, at one time or another, provided for the closing of public schools when these were under court order to integrate and simultaneously passed laws making available state funds to white parents who wanted to send their children to segregated private institutions. The state aid took many forms, including scholarships, tuition grants, and tax credits for private donations to the schools.[8] Thus, Alabama provided for grants or loans to persons for "educational purposes," while authorizing payments to parents who desired their children to attend schools "provided for their own race."[9] Georgia provided for suspension of state funds to closed schools and allowed the governor to make grants to school boards in districts where schools were closed, in the same amount as when the public schools were open; the state also provided for grants of state and local funds directly to parents of a child going to a nonsectarian nonpublic school.[10]

8 For a rundown of the pertinent statutory provisions, see 2 Emerson, Haber and Dorsen, *Political and Civil Rights in the United States, 1652–1654 and 1659–1662* (3d ed. 1967). See also Leeson, "Private Schools Continue to Increase in the South," *Southern Education Report*, Vol. 2, No. 4, pp. 22–25 (November, 1966).

9 Ala. Acts 1956, Spec. Sess., Act No. 82, p. 119, 1 *Race Rel. L. Rep.* 417 (1956). See also Ala. Acts 1959, Act No. 652, p. 1576, and Ala. Acts 1959, 2d Spec. Sess., Act. No. 127, p. 378, 4 *Race Rel. L. Rep.* 1056 (1959).

10 Ga. Acts 1959, No. 8, p. 18, 4 *Race Rel. L. Rep.* 180 (1959), Ga. Acts 1961, No. 13, p. 31, 6 *Race Rel.. L. Rep.* 289 (1961), Ga. Acts 1961, No. 14, p. 35, 6 *Race Rel. L. Rep.* 280 (1961).

The net effect, of course, was the use of public moneys for segregated and ostensibly "private" education.

These efforts to circumvent the command of the Constitution naturally found their way into court. The judicial experience of Virginia and Louisiana is particularly instructive.

In Virginia the controversy centered on the school system of Prince Edward County, which was brought into litigation as far back as 1951 and was one of the constituent cases handed down with *Brown* v. *Board of Education*. Efforts to desegregate following *Brown* met with resistance from the white community, and in 1956 the Virginia Consitution was amended to permit the General Assembly or local governing bodies to appropriate funds to assist students to go to nonsectarian nonpublic schools. The Assembly responded promptly by enacting legislation to close any public schools where white and colored children were enrolled together, to cut off funds to such schools, and to pay tuition grants to children choosing to enter the new independent schools.[11] This legislation was struck down in 1959 by the Supreme Court of Virginia as inconsistent with the state constitutional requirement of compulsory public education.[12] The General Assembly then enacted a new tuition grant program and made school attendance a matter of local option by repealing the state's compulsory attendance laws. A federal court immediately ruled that this plan was invalid and ordered the Prince Edward County schools to open as integrated institutions.[13] But the supervisors of the county refused to levy school taxes. As a result the county's public schools did not reopen in the fall of 1959, although the public schools of every other county in Virginia continued to operate. At the same time a private group, the Prince Edward School Foundation, was formed to operate independent schools for white children, who were aided by the tuition grants.

This scheme continued for five long years, during most of

11 Va. Code, § 22–188.3 *et seq*; § 51–111.38:1.
12 Harrison v. Day, 200 Va. 439, 406 S.E.2d 636 (1959).
13 Allen v. County School Board of Prince Edward County, 266 F.2d 507 (4th Cir. 1959).

which the Negro children of Prince Edward County received no formal education at all. Eventually, in May, 1964, the Supreme Court ruled that the school children of the county were deprived of equal protection of the laws, because they were treated differently from the school children of all other Virginia counties.[14] In ordering the reopening of public schools in the county, the Court said:

> Prince Edward children must go to a private school or none at all; all other Virginia children can go to public schools. Closing Prince Edward's schools bears more heavily on Negro children in Prince Edward County since white children there have accredited private schools which they can attend. . . . [T]he result is that Prince Edward County school children, if they go to school in their own county, must go to racially segregated schools which, although designated as private, are beneficiaries of county and state support.
>
> A State, of course, has a wide discretion in deciding whether laws shall operate statewide or shall operate only in certain counties. . . . But the record in the present case could not be clearer that Prince Edward's public schools were closed and private schools operated in their place with state and county assistance, for one reason, and one reason only: to ensure, through measures taken by the county and the State, that white and colored children in Prince Edward County would not, under any circumstances, go to the same school. Whatever nonracial grounds might support a State's allowing a county to abandon public schools, the object must be a constitutional one, and grounds of race and opposition to desegregation do not qualify as constitutional.[15]

The decision had a profound impact on every southern state that had authorized the closing of public schools. But it remained for litigation arising in Louisiana to administer the coup de grace

14 Griffin v. County School Board of Prince Edward County, 377 U.S. 218 (1964).
15 *Id*. at 230–31.

to "private" school programs transparently designed to avoid integration.

There are two cases. First, in 1961 a federal court invalidated a 1958 Louisiana statute which provided a way by which public schools under desegregation orders could be changed to "private" schools operated in the same way, in the same buildings, with the same furnishings, with the same money, and under the same supervision as the public schools.[16] Louisiana was not through yet. Its legislature immediately enacted a simpler plan to replace the 1958 law. The new act did away with provisions for closing public schools; it provided for payments to be made to students and parents rather than directly to the "private" schools, and it transferred administration of the program from the State Board of Education to the Financial Assistance Commission.[17]

In August, 1966, a federal court in the case of *Poindexter* v. *Louisiana Financial Assistance Comm'n*.[18] dashed the hopes of any who thought that this version of the "private" school technique would succeed. Terming the tuition grant program merely "a refined, sophisticated substitute" for the earlier program, the court struck it down, using these reasons: In the first place, public payment of tuition grants was state action under the Fourteenth Amendment. Second, the funds provided a "stimulus" in the founding of the "quasi-public" segregated schools and were used to support these schools. Third, the court noted the Negro plaintiffs' allegation that these state-supported schools deprive them of equal protection rights not only because they were denied admission to these schools but because the very existence of a second and "quasi-public" school system endangers bona fide public schools and damages Negro pupils. The reason for this is that it drains teachers, students, and funds into a competitive system and puts the stamp of state approval on Negro inferiority,

16 Hall v. St. Helena Parish School Board, 197 F.Supp. 649 (E.D. La. 1961), aff'd 368 U.S. 515 (1962).
17 Act 147 of 1962, La. Rev. Stat. 17:2959.
18 258 F.Supp. 158 (E.D. La. 1966).

perpetuating the humiliation of Negroes implicit in segregated education.

A vital aspect of this decision is the test used by the court to determine when a "private" school comes within the ban of the Constitution. It referred to an earlier decision by another federal court that held segregated nonpublic schools invalid under the Fourteenth Amendment if they are "predominantly maintained" by the state.[19] The earlier ruling was based in part on §401(c) of the Civil Rights Act of 1964, which defines "public school" as any school "operated wholly or predominantly from and through the use of governmental funds."[20] Despite this statutory language, the court in Poindexter rejected the test of whether nonpublic schools are "predominantly maintained" by the state. It instead held that *"any amount* of state support to help found segregated schools or to help maintain such schools is sufficient to give standing to Negro school children."[21]

The importance of this holding should not be underestimated. If not disturbed by a higher court, it could mark the end of circumvention of the Brown decision by southern states through the use of phony "private" schools. Second, the decision could have important ramifications for independent schools in all parts of the nation. These will be explored shortly.

II

I turn now to the general problem of civil rights in "private" schools: that is, to the issue uncomplicated by, or perhaps I should say unsimplified by, public payments as an inducement to maintain the races in separate institutions. But I shall exclude from consideration, for the present, problems especially perti-

19 Griffin v. State Board of Education, 239 F.Supp. 560, 565–66 (E.D. Va. 1965), cert. den. 385 U.S. 960 (1966). This case is a later version of the Virginia School Closing Litigation, discussed at pages 139–40 of the text.
20 42 U.S.C. § 2000(c.)
21 258 F.Supp. at 164.

nent to integration in elementary and secondary church-related schools.

The private school tradition is strong in certain parts of the country, and there is evidence that it is growing stronger. Nevertheless, I have been able to obtain no accurate count of the number of pupils enrolled in such schools. Apart from my own research, the National Association of Independent Schools, which has 780 member institutions with about a quarter of a million pupils, has informed me that no reliable figures exist for the total national enrollment in independent secondary or elementary schools.

In connection with the enrollment of Negro students we are fortunate, however, to have available the results of a survey conducted earlier this winter by NAIS. Of the 780 member schools, 740 responded to a questionnaire, and 462 (over 62 per cent) reported at least one Negro enrolled this year. Several of these schools had several Negro pupils; 239 schools reported five or more and 109 reported ten or more. All told there were 3,720 Negro students, $1\frac{1}{2}$ per cent of the total student population, in NAIS member schools.[22]

This figure of $1\frac{1}{2}$ per cent plainly means that there is some way to go before racial balance is achieved in independent schools. Since NAIS members include some of the most enlightened schools in the country, I do not think it unfair to add that it would not surprise me to learn — if comprehensive figures were available — that Negro enrollment in *all* independent elementary schools fell below $1\frac{1}{2}$ per cent. This is not racial balance.

What is to be done? At once I reject one possible answer — nothing. Needless to say, my conclusion reflects not only a personal preference but, more important, the fact that the nation as a whole has made a profound commitment to remedy its great and long-standing debt to the Negro people. The independent schools must do their share, along with all other public and private institutions.

22 National Association of Independent Schools, *Summary Report on Enrollment of Negro Students* (March, 1967).

We therefore must inspect potential solutions under existing law. First to be considered are the Fair Educational Practices Acts. Six states have enacted such a statute — Indiana, Massachusetts, New Jersey, New York, Pennsylvania, and Washington. These laws are enforced by administrative commissions, and each is part of omnibus state antidiscrimination legislation which also prohibits discrimination in private employment, housing and accommodations.[23] Typical provisions of such laws are found in the recently promulgated Model Anti-Discrimination Act of the Commissioners on Uniform State Laws. The Model provides in section 502 that it is a discriminatory practice for a private or public educational institution:

> (1) to exclude, expel, limit, or otherwise discriminate against an individual seeking admission as a student or an individual enrolled as a student, in the terms, conditions, and privileges of the institution, because of race, color, religion, or national origin; or
> (2) to make or use a written or oral inquiry or form of application for admission that elicits or attempts to elicit information, or to make or keep a record, concerning the race, color, religion, or national origin of an applicant for admission, except as permitted by regulations of the Commission; or
> (3) to print or publish or cause to be printed or published a catalogue or other notice or advertisement indicating a preference, limitation, specification, or discrimination based on the race, color, religion, or national origin of an applicant for admission.

Such a statute is comprehensive in its prohibitions. Further, there is little question about its constitutionality,[24] or of the

23 Citations to these statutes can be found in 2 Emerson, Haber and Dorsen, *Political and Civil Rights in the United States 1793* (3d ed. 1967).

24 There is no record of a state fair educational practice act being invalidated on federal or state constitutional grounds, and such an argument appears far-fetched. See Fox, "Discrimination and Antidiscrimination in Massachusetts Law," 44 *B.U. L. Rev.* 30, 71 (1964). See generally Note, "Fair

fact that the legislature and especially the administrative agency can be flexible in establishing and carrying out the enforcement process. Why, then, are not such laws an ideal solution to racial discrimination in independent schools?

The answer is a practical one. Despite the early high hopes for antidiscrimination commissions, more than two decades of experience reveals that they promise more than they deliver. Timid administrators, niggardly budgets, and insufficient statutory powers all have played a part.[25] While critics have focused on the failures of enforcement against discrimination in employment, it is fair to say that the six education laws have hardly been implemented at all.[26] Whatever the reasons, and whatever their potential, the fact is that they have become something of a dead letter except to the extent that they exercise a salutary if vague influence on the policies of school administrators. Fair education laws thus do not appear to be a promising solution, at least for the present.

There is a second statutory alternative. Several states include "private" schools in their laws prohibiting discrimination in public accommodations. Thus, the Pennsylvania Public Accommodations Act[27] covers "kindergartens, primary and secondary schools, high schools, academic, colleges and universities, extension courses, and all educational institutions under the supervision of this Commonwealth." There is an exception in the statute for places of public accommodation that are "in their nature distinctly private," and this provision is currently in litigation in the latest instalment of the Girard College Case, about which I shall have more to say later. The important point now is that these general public accommodations laws, which can be found

Education Practices Acts: A Solution to Discrimination?" 64 *Harv. L.* 307 (1950).

25 See the criticisms contained in Symposium, Fair Employment Practices Acts, 14 Buffalo L. Rev. 1 (1964).

26 The annual reports of the antidiscrimination commissions in states having fair educational practices acts bear this out.

27 Act of May 19, 1887, P.L. 130, § 1, as amended, 18 P.S. § 4654.

in several states,[28] have never proved a satisfactory vehicle for desegregation of "private" schools, or for that matter of anything else. They are, assuredly, not the answer here.

This brings us to the Federal Constitution. The Fourteenth Amendment in its terms prohibits arbitrary action by the "state." Can this provision be interpreted to ban racial discrimination by independent schools? In my view the Fourteenth Amendment *can* properly be interpreted by courts to reach this result, and I suggest that nonpublic school administrators should immediately act on the implications of this fact, *before* courts are called upon to render decision.

Two constitutional theories support this conclusion. The first has been partially developed above in the context of the southern problem. It will be recalled that in the Louisiana Poindexter case Judge Wisdom stated that "any amount of state support to help found segregated schools or to help maintain such schools is sufficient to give standing to Negro school children." This line of reasoning traces back to the important Little Rock case, where the Supreme Court said:

> State support of segregated schools through any arrangement, management, funds, or property cannot be squared with the [Fourteenth] Amendment's command that no State shall deny to any person within its jurisdiction the equal protection of the laws.[29]

This theory of "state support" has been applied in the analogous area of discrimination by private hospitals. In 1963, a Federal Court of Appeals ruled that a so-called "private" hospital which received a portion of its funds from the federal government was subject to the constitutional requirement of equal protection.[30] The Supreme Court declined to review the decision, and it has been accepted ever since.

28 For example, Illinois and Minnesota.
29 Cooper v. Aaron, 358 U.S. 1, 4 (1958).
30 Simkins v. Moses H. Cone Memorial Hospital, 323 F.2d 959 (4th Cir. 1963), cert. den. 376 U.S. 938 (1964).

The "support" necessary to fulfill the constitutional test of the Poindexter case can be found in the financial aid now provided "private" schools through many federal programs, including the National School Lunch Act, the National Defense Education Act, the Economic Opportunity Act of 1964, and particularly the Elementary and Secondary Education Act of 1965.[31] Likewise, at least in some jurisdictions there is much state aid to independent schools. If the test is "any support", there would seem ample basis for a judicial decision that "private" schools are subject to the Fourteenth Amendment.

The second route to the same result is premised on the theory, now well established in its general outline, that where private individuals are allowed to perform a function ordinarily undertaken by the state, they are to be treated as agents of the state for constitutional purposes, and their discriminatory acts therefore prohibited. This theory has been applied where private bodies conducted a primary election, administered a company town, or operated a park.[32] Its potential application to an elementary or secondary school is obvious. At least one federal judge, J. Skelly Wright, has made the point forcefully. In a desegregation case involving Tulane University, a "private" institution, he said:

> . . . one may question whether any school or college can ever be so "private" as to escape the reach of the Fourteenth Amendment. . . . [I]nstitutions of learning are not things of purely private concern. . . . Clearly the administrators of a private college are performing a public function. They do the work of the state, often in the place of the state. Does it not follow that they stand in the state's shoes? And, if so, are they not agents of the state, subject to the constraints on governmental action, to the same extent as private persons who govern a company town . . . or control a political party. . . . Reason and authority strongly suggest that

31 See Pfeffer, *Church, State and Freedom* 596–604 (Rev. ed. 1967).
32 See Terry v. Adams, 345 F.2d 461 (1953); Marsh v. Alabama, 326 U.S. 501 (1946); Evans v. Newton, 382 U.S. 296 (1966).

the Constitution never sanctions racial discrimination in our schools and colleges, no matter how "private" they may claim to be.[33]

Although Judge Wright's judgment in the Tulane case was vacated on a procedural ground,[34] the above language was not disapproved; moreover, since he spoke in 1962, additional judicial support for his views has appeared.[35]

In short, I believe that the "law" is there and waiting under which an enterprising court could rule that "private" schools are subject to the constitutional command to desegregate. Whether it will be so employed is perhaps less a legal than a political question, less a matter of principle than of timing. In this respect the issue resembles the already much-litigated question whether public school boards are under an affirmative obligation to eliminate segregation in schools under their jurisdiction, as distinguished from their established duty to refrain from causing such racial separateness.

What lesson should be drawn from this conclusion? Should civil rights lawyers immediately repair to the nearest courthouse and begin suits to force all independent schools in the nation to admit Negroes at once? I hardly think that is the answer, although one day it could come to pass. The vicissitudes and frustrations of litigation are amply illustrated by the Girard College case in Philadelphia. In February, 1954, two Negroes applied for admission and were rejected on the ground of race. Now, more than thirteen years and many judicial opinions later, there is still no final order requiring a nondiscriminatory admissions policy for this school.[36] No, the courts are not the preferable forum to integrate the nation's independent schools.

The right forum, it seems to me, is the offices and boardrooms of the schools themselves. In this forum administrators and direc-

33 See Guillory v. Administrators of Tulane Univ., 203 F.Supp. 855, 853–59 (E.D. La. 1962).
34 207 F.Supp. 554 (E.D. La. 1962), aff'd, 306 F.2d 489 (5th Cir. 1962).
35 See Evans v. Newton, *supra* note 31.
36 For a history of the case, see 11 *Race Rel. L. Rep.* 1696–1698 (1966).

tors can act without compulsion, with full regard to the particular problems of each school. They can fulfill their general obligations as citizens and their special obligation as educators by working toward the high civic goal of equal opportunity, and simultaneously they can fulfill their professional responsibilities to their institutions by achieving the goal without the embitterment or the expense or the loss of dignity that has characterized the Girard College litigation.

III

The next logical question is whether there is any legal impediment to voluntary integration by independent schools. We first note that the Supreme Court has come a long way since the Berea College case,[37] in which it upheld a Kentucky statute making it "unlawful for any person, . . . to operate any college, school or institution where persons of the white and Negro races are both received as pupils for instruction." Recent constitutional doctrine makes the Berea case an antique, a legal relic. State or local law is now powerless under the federal constitution to require racial separation.[38]

A more difficult issue is presented for schools that have accepted gifts whose terms specify an all-white student body. Girard College, for example, was established by a trust that specified that the school should be maintained for "poor, white, male orphans." Is there a legal means to avoid such anachronistic instruments? In the Girard case the Negro plaintiffs sought to *force* the unwilling school to accept a modification of the trust and admit children irrespective of race or color, in accordance with the grantor's alleged intent to benefit all the citizens of Philadelphia. That question has not yet been resolved, and it is important to see that it

37 Berea College v. Kentucky, 211 U.S. 45 (1908).
38 See, e.g., Gayle v. Browder, 352 U.S. 903 (1956) (statute requiring segregation on buses); Turner v. City of Memphis, 369 U.S. 350 (1962) (administrative regulation requiring segregation in airport restaurants); Johnson v. Virginia, 373 U.S. 61 (1963) (segregated courtroom seating).

involves a different situation from the one now being proposed, where a school administration *desires* to terminate a donor's limitation to white children.

Two recent cases suggest that success can be achieved by such a school but also that obdurate state officials can at least delay a favorable outcome. In 1964 Rice University of Houston, a private institution, brought an action in a Texas court against the Attorney General of Texas, seeking authority to ignore restrictions in its charter which prohibited it from admitting Negroes. The court, rather surprisingly, empaneled a jury, which made special findings of fact that the main purpose of the benefactor of the University was to create an educational institution of the first class; that the restrictions on admitting Negroes now render impracticable the development of the University as such an institution; and that it has now become impractical to carry out the intent of the benefactor. The court thereupon rendered a judgment authorizing the University to admit qualified applicants without regard to color or race.[39]

In this case not only did Rice University wish to eliminate the restriction, but the Attorney General had no apparent objection. In our second case, involving the Sweet Briar Institute of Virginia, a more complex situation is presented, largely because the state officials opposed the petition. After the Rice decision, Sweet Briar, which had been set up by a trust to carry on a school "for the education of white girls and young women," and had operated in that fashion for more than sixty years, brought suit in a Virginia court against the State Attorney General and the County Attorney to eliminate the restriction. A state judge refused to grant relief, ruling that the will was unambiguous and could not be modified under Virginia law.[40] Sweet Briar then went into Federal Court, and in April, 1966, a three-judge dis-

39 William Marsh Rice Univ. v. Carr, 9 *Race Rel. L. Rep.* 613 (Harris Cy. Tex. Dist. Ct. 1964), aff'd sub nom Coffee v. William Marsh Rice Univ., 408 S.W.2d 269 (Tex. Civ. App. 1966).

40 Sweet Briar Institute v. McClenny, 10 *Race Rel. L. Rep.* 1005 (Amherst Cy. Cir. Ct. 1965).

trict court decided to hear the complaint after Sweet Briar claimed it would suffer irreparable harm unless the racial restriction was removed because its ability to attract high-caliber faculty and students would be impaired and it would be ineligible to receive federal financial assistance under the Civil Rights Act of 1964.[41]

The case has become something of a labyrinth. Once the federal suit was begun, the state judge took no further action. But then the federal court also decided to abstain from further action. The federal court said that considerations of federalism required deference to the Virginia courts on an issue of Virginia law.[42] Rather than return to an unreceptive state court, counsel for Sweet Briar appealed the decision of the federal court. The Supreme Court found that abstention was inappropriate and remanded the case to the district court.[43]

However the litigation comes out, it is plain from the Rice University experience that if state officials do not obstruct willing school officials, integration can be achieved very easily. The Sweet Briar case disclosed some of the difficulties when state officials do stand in the way, but perhaps that case will be the precedent that clears the path for other institutions seeking to avoid racial restrictions imposed by donors from another era.

Having tried to do justice to some of the legal problems involved in the desegregation of independent schools, I should like to underscore the point that the future will be in the hands, not of the legislatures or the courts or the fair education commissions, but rather of the schools themselves. As the NAIS statistics show, many independent schools have already accepted this view. Further, as recounted in a recent study, vigorous and sensitive efforts are being made in many schools to recruit and smooth the way for Negro applicants to independent schools.[44] The vital ingredient is the will to achieve the end; once that is present, the prac-

41 Sweet Briar Institute v. Button, 11 *Race Rel. L. Rep.* 1176, 1177 (W.D. Va. 1966).
42 Sweet Briar Institute v. Button, 12 *Race Rel. L. Rep.* 85 (W.D. Va. 1966) (2–1 decision).
43 387 U.S. 423 (1967).
44 Mallery, *Negro Students in Independent Schools* (NAIS 1963).

tical problems — the admittedly difficult practical problems — can be solved, as scores of "private" schools have already demonstrated. But we should not kid ourselves on this question. The responsibility is the schools', and that is where it should be. John D. Verdery, headmaster of the Wooster School of Danbury, Connecticut, recognized this fact when he said:

> . . . another, more subtle argument is epitomized by the statement that "We would be glad to consider any qualified Negro, but none has ever applied." It took us some years to face the simple fact that Negro parents, like other parents, are not eager to place their children in an environment in which they are not really wanted. . . . It cannot be sheer coincidence that Wooster in fact did not have a single Negro applicant during the first thirty years of its existence, while it has had an average of five or six applicants a year since the first Negroes enrolled six years ago. Nor have all of these students been scholarship candidates by any means. This seems to me, in retrospect, to demolish completely all validity for the argument that it is wrong to go out and seek candidates. From a practical standpoint the institution that wants Negroes must at first *ask them to come*. If it has none, it is really quite fair to say that it simply does not want them. [Emphasis in original.] [45]

IV

We must now consider the integration of church-related schools, a matter of particular importance because some very difficult problems of policy and constitutional law are presented against a backdrop of a vast and increasing parochial school population. Church schools are now a formidable bloc in American education, and about 90 per cent of church education is Roman Catholic. From 25 per cent to 50 per cent of school-age children in Northern cities attend nonpublic (mostly Catholic) schools; for example,

45 *Id.* at 69.

in Philadelphia it is 40 per cent and in Pittsburgh 46 per cent.[46] All told, about 5.7 million students are enrolled in Catholic elementary and secondary schools; this is one out of every seven students in the nation, double the proportion of 25 years ago.[47]

It is thus plain that if American schools are to be integrated, church-related schools have a major part to play. It is also true that many parochial schools have taken strong steps to achieve racial balance.[48] Nevertheless, the fact that such schools attract a higher proportion of white than Negro students from public school systems tends to upset an already unbalanced racial situation, particularly in the central cities of the nation. The evidence is clear that parochial as well as other schools have a serious problem of racial imbalance.[49]

I should like to raise briefly two sets of questions; first, those that might arise if it is decided to coerce unwilling church schools to integrate, and second, those that would emerge if church schools themselves wish to improve racial balance.

First, coercion. This issue could arise in two ways: Either through legislation requiring all schools, including parochial schools, to refrain from racial discrimination, or through a court action based on the Fourteenth Amendment. The first route would most likely be in the context of a fair educational practice act, and the second route would presuppose all that we have discussed earlier regarding "state action" — the possibility that church

---

46 Cronin, "Negroes in Catholic Schools," *Commonweal Magazine*, Vol. 85, No. 1, pp. 13–14 (October 7, 1966).

47 "The Changing World of Catholic Education," *Columbia College Today*, Vol. 14, No. 1, p. 19 (Fall 1966).

48 Cognizant of the fact that parochial schools, like public schools, "reflect segregated housing patterns," the United States Catholic Conference, comprising all American Bishops, has called a nation-wide conference on "racial isolation." *New York Times*, March 27, 1967.

49 See, for example, the statistics contained in the 1964 Intercultural Survey of Roman Catholic elementary and secondary schools in Manhattan and the Bronx, New York City. See also the exchange in *The Catholic News*, August 18, 1966, and October 6, 1966, between Msgr. George A. Kelly and Mr. Aryeh Neier, executive director of the New York Civil Liberties Union.

schools, like other nonpublic schools, are subject to the Fourteenth Amendment because they receive financial aid from the government or because they perform a "public function" which makes them in effect agents of the state.

For purposes of simplicity, I shall consider the issue in the context of a legislative policy decision whether or not to include parochial schools in any general prohibition against racial discrimination. The specific question that emerges is whether it is an unwarranted interference with the autonomy of church schools, and perhaps a violation of their right to free exercise of religion, to require them to integrate against their will. For example, could a statute validly provide that it was unlawful for a parochial school to prefer applicants of the same religion? While I know of no directly applicable case,[50] it appears to me that such a statute would be gravely suspect from a constitutional standpoint, as well as unwise in policy.

But does this mean that a church school can not be ordered to end discrimination on *racial* grounds? The Commissioners on Uniform State Laws recently wrestled with that problem in the preparation of its Model Anti-Discrimination Act and concluded that there was no good reason to permit such discrimination unrelated to the religious purposes of the institution.[51] On the other hand, Title VII of the federal Civil Rights Act of 1964, which prohibits discrimination in *employment*, grants a total exemption for religious education institutions.[52] The Act does not deal with "private" education, but Title VII reflects a policy choice different from that of the Commissioners, and I should say different from my own.

The final question in this series will perhaps be of interest only to law professors who must strive each year to prepare imaginative examination questions. Suppose that a parochial school dis-

50 See generally the materials in Pfeffer, *Church, State and Freedom* 696–721 (Rev. ed. 1967); 1 Emerson, Haber and Dorsen, *Political and Civil Rights in the United States 1167–74* (3d ed. 1967).
51 Section 503(1).
52 Section 703(e), 42 U.S.C. § 2000e–2(e) (2).

criminates on the ground of race and does this because of some religious belief associated with the religion. Black Muslims might so exclude white children from their schools, and there may be white religious groups that exclude Negroes on doctrinal grounds. Should this be forbidden by the state, and if so is it an interference with religious freedom? I must confess I have not thought the problem through, but my tentative solution is to resolve the issue in favor of prohibiting the discrimination, even if it apparently flows from a bona fide religious belief, because of the opportunity for disingenuous racial exclusion that a contrary decision would permit.

Now to the second broad question. Suppose that a parochial school desires to integrate and achieve a healthy racial balance. What problems can be expected? For present purposes I put to one side strictly educational matters. Obviously, the church school can aggressively recruit Negro students, and indeed it can do so without problems of divided control that might plague a public institution. It can also arrange for redrawing of parochial school district lines and provide for bussing between, say, a predominantly white suburban school and a Negro neighborhood in the central city. It can even close some or all of the parochial schools in an area where this would lead to reduction of racial imbalance in the public schools. All these steps can be taken by the school system of a particular denomination, without difficulty, assuming the policy is accepted by the church leaders.[53]

But these efforts may be insufficient. There just may be too few Negroes of the same religious faith to achieve more than token integration. In response to this problem, a writer in Commonweal Magazine has recently proposed that public and parochial schools share their facilities so that children from the two systems could attend certain classes together, and thus to that extent eliminate racial isolation.[54]

Here we encounter an authentic consttiutional problem. "Shared time" programs have a long history, and it is much mooted

53 Cronin, *Negroes in Catholic Schools, supra* note 45 at 14–15.
54 *Id.* at 15.

whether the Establishment Clause of the First Amendment forbids children to divide their school day by taking such "neutral" subjects as languages, mathematics, and gymnasium in the public school and subjects with some religious orientation — literature, history, etc. — in the parochial school.

This is not the occasion to delve deeply into the controversy. Suffice it to say that strong arguments have been mounted on both sides. Shared time proponents say that it will break the deadlock on federal aid to public schools; will help breach the wall isolating the Catholic community and give it a greater stake in the public school system; and is consistent with church-state separation because the program provides assistance to the child and not to the parochial school. The other side argues that shared time will not solve the federal aid problem, nor will it in practice break down the isolation of Catholic children, because they will be a special and identifiable group within the public school. Moreover, there will be administrative havoc and added expense. Finally, it would be inconsistent with separation of church and state, first because it would involve aid to church schools, who would be saved considerable sums that would go into strictly religious aspects of education, and second, because it would involve church officials in the management of public schools, where their voices could have considerable influence.[55]

How the dispute will be resolved in the courts is yet unclear, although a leading authority has suggested that no doctrinaire answer will be forthcoming and that the result will depend on the precise form of a given shared time program.[56]

How does this controversy bear on our problem of civil rights? Presumably not at all if a particular shared-time program is upheld under the First Amendment; in that case it would be one further useful method of achieving racial balance in public and parochial schools.

55. See the thoughtful discussion in Pfeffer, *Church, State and Freedom* 571–79 (Rev. ed. 1967).
56 *Id*. at 578–79. See also the statement of the American Civil Liberties Union on shared time, issued April 4, 1965.

But what if a particular shared-time program ordinarily would violate the Establishment Clause? Might such a plan survive if its purpose is to achieve racial balance in the schools? In other words, would the command of the First Amendment be tempered in the interest of carrying out a mandate of the Fourteenth Amendment? Much would depend, of course, on the precise nature of the program. But in general my guess is that the constitutional balance is sufficiently close so that the use of shared time as a way of helping to eliminate racial isolation would be sympathetically received in the courts, especially if the Fourteenth Amendment is ever held to mean that schools have an affirmative duty to integrate.

Because I know of no precedent that would control the decision, I merely present the question as a final perplexing problem that our courts one day may have to answer.

Conclusion

I have attempted to analyze some diverse and difficult problems relating to racial discrimination in "private" schools, but the fundamental thought I should like to emphasize is that a great opportunity awaits the independent schools of this country. I only hope that they seize the occasion to make their institutions the proving grounds of the future in education rather than the battlegrounds.

7 Donald A. Erickson

Freedom's Two Educational Imperatives: A Proposal

It is timely, I believe, to discuss state regulation of nonpublic schools as this juncture. In a number of states, existing prescriptions seem ill-advised. In other states, fly-by-night schools are flourishing without governmental purview to protect pupils and parents. Several legislatures are considering changes in their mechanisms of control.

Guidelines for public education, too, may bear scrutiny. Some pedagogical approaches may have been institutionalized prematurely through legislation, state department criteria, accreditation standards, and school board decisions.

The subject of state regulation is complex. Perhaps the chapters in this volume will serve mainly to stimulate the prolonged attention that is needed. For my part, I shall leave unexamined several aspects of the problem, dealing only with what I consider to be the most important imperatives if control is to be beneficial and freedom is to be maintained. Finally, I shall make a few policy suggestions that seem to flow from the two imperatives.

I shall make no attempt to predict how the courts may rule on the issues. My concern is with the ethically and educationally advisable. Neither shall I try to specify the legal doctrines best suited to my suggestions. I leave these exercises to the attorneys.

The First Imperative

As the first and most basic imperative, *state regulation of non-public schools must encourage the pursuit of pluralistic goals.* Education, probably more akin to religion than most men realize, is not a process that leaves life aspirations and moral commitments unaffected. To the extent that schooling is efficacious, the power to choose the goals of learning is the power to manipulate society. According to the Supreme Court, "The fundamental theory of liberty upon which all governments in this Union repose excludes any general power of the State to standardize its children by forcing them to accept instruction from public teachers only."[1] But standardization may as readily be achieved by requiring nonpublic schools to serve the same ends as public schools. It think it a priceless principle that radically different educational purposes are not only tolerable but desirable in our democracy. The concept is perhaps not so crucial to the University of Chicago Lab Schools as to the Greek Orthodox day schools, and not so necessary to the Catholics as to the Hutterites, but I hope private educators will unite to preserve it.

The most fundamental yet most neglected question concerning state regulation of nonpublic schools is this: What disparate goals shall we allow and even encourage in education? At present, we are often deciding the issue by default, through a mechanistic application of narrowly drawn demands. If a public school is preparing pupils for life in a complex, urbanized world, and an Amish school is preparing its pupils for life in an Older Order community, we have no business judging the two programs in terms of identical criteria — that is, unless one of the objectives is taboo. If a comprehensive secondary school is attempting to move students of widely differing backgrounds and abilities toward some kind of productive adulthood, it may need a complex array of services, programs, and facilities. Students who don't know where they are going may require a great deal of counseling. Youngsters from disadvantaged backgrounds may get no-

1 Pierce v. Society of Sisters, 268 U.S. 510 (1925).

where without social workers. Boys and girls who cannot handle college preparatory work, or for other reasons are not destined for a higher education, deserve access to other areas of study, such as business education, industrial arts, and vocational agriculture. But it is ridiculous to insist, as several states have done, that the same gamut of services, programs, and facilities must be maintained in the independent academy, whose *raison d'être* is often to provide a specialized preparation for college for scholars of proven ability and motivation — unless, again, there is something abominable about that function. Public schools are generally committed to the Melting Pot philosophy, emphasizing commonality and a secularistic approach to ethical issues. Hebrew day schools, in contrast, aim to acquaint the child intimately with one of the nation's richest subcultures, stressing his ethnicity, his uniqueness, his religious underpinnings. So unless the State of New York maintains that only an emphasis on mass culture is tolerable, why should it withhold charters from high schools that teach the Talmud instead of American Literature in the morning hours, especially when students in these schools earn a vastly disproportionate share of academic honors? There is evidence to suggest, furthermore, that the subcultural orientation is psychologically preferable to the emphasis on the societal mainstream.[2] Membership in well-integrated subgroups may be necessary to full participation in the larger world.

One could cite many other instances of the disposition to discourage or prohibit the pursuit of diverse goals in education, not explicitly and deliberately, not as a consequence of discussion and

2 See evidence, for example, that Catholics who have attended their church's schools exclusively tend to outstrip other Catholics in academic achievement and occupational mobility. Andrew M. Greeley and Peter H. Rossi, *The Education of Catholic Americans* (Chicago: Aldine Publishing Company, 1966). Also see the findings of Morris Rosenberg, "The Dissonant Religious Context and Emotional Disturbance," in Louis Schneider, ed., *Religion, Culture, and Society: A Reader in the Sociology of Religion* (New York: John Wiley & Sons, 1964), pp. 549–559. I have discussed this question at somewhat greater length in "Contradictory Studies of Parochial Schooling: An Essay Review," *School Review*, 76 (Winter, 1967): 425–36.

debate, but through attention to false considerations. It was argued with disturbing monotony in Iowa, for instance, both in the legislature and on the street, that the Amish had no right to be exempted from any provisions of the school code. That is a pseudo-issue, serving only to obscure analysis. The place to begin is to discover whether the statutes themselves are defensible. If the Amish are entitled to rear their offspring to function in an Old Order community, rather than in Oelwein, Des Moines, or New York City, until recently Iowa's school laws were as inappropriate as the requirement that everyone leaving O'Hare Airport on a given date must take United Airlines Flight 295. Different destinations presuppose different travel plans, and different educational objectives presuppose different programs, personnel, and physical facilities. We must decide which goals are permissible.

A good many social scientists and commentators have lamented a trend toward conformity in our nation and the losses in identity that apparently result. But one sees little corresponding concern among educators and lawmakers regarding the pedagogical rigidity that often lies behind societal sameness. If we want an orchestration of diversity, we must train some people to play the exotic instruments. In the words of Dean M. Kelley:

> These self-sustaining, nonconforming communities are precious to our whole society. Not only are they a collective expression of the individual exercise of conscience, but they are a living reminder that human life can be organized around other values and at other tempos than those prevailing in our harried and neurotic urban mass society. We could not pay men and women to live out these arduous and alternative patterns of existence. If these fragile colonies of dissent must be crushed by the heedless onrush of the modern age, the loss to our culture will be tragic, and every citizen who cherishes the liberty to follow conscience will be poorer.[3]

3 Dean M. Kelley, "Is There Room for the Amish?" *Town and Country Church*, May–June, 1966, pp. 7–9, 13.

If divergent values are to be preserved, some institutions must have as their aim the production of Amishmen, others must accentuate the Hebraism of Jewish Americans, and a few must even be permitted to groom the academically apt for Ivy League colleges.

The chief enigma in this connection concerns the fact that the child does not choose for himself, particularly at the elementary level, the life orientation to which he will be molded. Given the power of culture, there is no method I know of to permit the young unbiased choice, *either in public or nonpublic institutions.* Schooling as we know it is rarely if ever neutral, a number of statements of the Supreme Court notwithstanding. If we move the youngster from Amish School No. 1 to the consolidated public school in town, we have not made him free to determine his own future. We have exchanged one set of constraints for another.

Since the life choices of humans are so largely determined by culture, the problem is one of deciding who shall choose, to the extent choice is possible, the influences by which the child shall be socialized. If the parent is not to decide whether his child shall be reared to become an Amishman, an orthodox Jew, or a member of a Harvard club, who is? The majority of the voters in Hazleton, Iowa, many of whom have demonstrated their prejudice toward the Plain People?[4] Public educators at state or local levels, who have frequently discriminated against minorities, both in the North and the South, when community pressures demanded it?[5] Legislatures, which have often passed laws condemned by the Supreme Court as travesties on human dignity? Parents are subject to error, but so are emissaries of the state. It is difficult to improve on the words of economist Robert Lowe in this regard:

4 See my case study on the Hazleton, Iowa, controversy, "Showdown at an Amish Schoolhouse," chapter 2.
5 Callahan argues that a major characteristic of public school administration is its vulnerability to citizen pressures. Raymond E. Callahan, *Education and the Cult of Efficiency* (Chicago: University of Chicago Press, 1962).

> Parents have one great superiority over the govern-
> ment. . . . Their faults are mainly the corrigible faults of
> ignorance, not of apathy and prejudice. They have and feel
> the greatest interest in doing that which is for the real bene-
> fit of their children. . . . They have the wish to arrive at a
> true conclusion, the data are before them, they must be the
> judges in the last resort; why should we shrink from mak-
> ing them judges at once? [6]

We are most inconsistent. Except in the most drastic cases, we
allow fathers and mothers to decide what clothing their children
shall wear, what shelter they shall enjoy, what neigborhood they
shall live in, what companions shall influence them, what praise
and punishment they shall receive, what food they shall eat, what
medical treatment they shall be given. Yet when parents want
to groom their offspring for adulthood in an Amish community,
one of the most tranquil existences known to the modern world,
we fine these parents, harass them, throw them in jail, and con-
fiscate their property. Yet, as I shall indicate in more detail later,
I am not advocating unlimited parental choice in schools functioning for compulsory attendance purposes.

Even if one wanted to obliterate dissent, he might be unwise
to force the assimilation of the young, as if they were so many
tomato plants in a hothouse. When individuals are alienated
from their origins and close-knit communities are disrupted, psychological malfunctions usually ensue. The problem, then, is to
change the subculture without demolishing it. To this end it

6 Quoted in E. G. West, "Private Versus Public Education: A Classical
Economic Dispute," *Journal of Political Economy*, 72 (October, 1964): 475.
As West points out, the question of parental ability to make wise choices
in education has been debated at length among economists. Adam Smith
was probably the most prominent proponent of parental choice, while John
Stuart Mill and his disciples argued the contrary view. For my own part,
I believe that most parents will make wise decisions *if they are provided
with the proper evidence*. As I argue in a later passage, it should be the
responsibility of the state to see that appropriate evidence is made available to parents.

may be more effective to reduce isolation by building trust than to assault the community's ramparts.

The Second Imperative

The second imperative is that *state regulation of nonpublic schools must encourage diverse approaches to the achievement of goals.* The reason is simple: as a field of study, education is in its infancy. Most current instructional procedures have about as much scientific evidence to support them as the home remedies and patent medicines of a century past. It is a time for exploration, not codification. The biggest danger is not that a few schools will depart from the orthodox, but that methodologies will become sacrosanct and compulsory, like the Copernican view of the solar system, before the evidence is in. A look at the school codes suggests that this premature crystallization of strategies is already well developed. Consider a few examples:

Scarcely any aspect of educational practice has drawn more censure from reputable scholars than the prevailing approach to teacher certification, mostly because the certificates must be earned by taking education courses widely acknowledged to be of questionable value in most institutions (please note that my own university is an exception). In a review of the relevant studies under the auspices of the American Educational Research Association, Reynard concludes that "values ascribed to most of the component parts and methods used in pre-service programs [for teachers] rest primarily on questionable theoretical foundations. Experimental evidence is needed if a sound base for teacher education is to be established."[7] Another reviewer calls for research to establish "the relationship of certification to the quality of teacher competence."[8] The connection has not been demonstrated.

7 Harold E. Reynard, "Pre-Service and In-Service Education of Teachers," *Review of Educational Research*, 33 (October, 1963): 378.
8 James C. Stone, "Teacher Certification, Supply and Demand," *ibid.*, p. 352. So far as I can determine, the study that comes closest to providing some empirical justification for teacher certification requirements is John R.

But let me speak more specifically of my own area, educational administration, where I have personally reviewed the recent findings. It is typical for the states to demand, as prerequisites for the certification of school administrators, several years of teaching experience and a strong dose of graduate courses in educational administration or supervision, or both. What is the evidence on these two points?

In the recent National Principalship Study at Harvard, neither type nor length of teaching experience distinguished principals who were well accepted by teachers.[9] The more extensive the teaching experience, the less the principal lived up to his own belief that he should support innovation in his school.[10] In a Mississippi investigation in 1966, a lengthy background of teaching

Beery, "Does Professional Preparation Make a Difference?" *Journal of Teacher Education*, 12 (December, 1962): 386–95. In Beery's study, beginning teachers who were fully certified seemed more effective in the classroom than beginning teachers who were provisionally certified. But only three counties in southeastern Florida were involved, rather than a representative national sample, and it appears likely that the fully certified teachers felt a stronger commitment to the teaching career than the provisionally certified. Given the present legal requirements, an individual who plans to make a career of public school teaching is well advised to complete his certification requirements, for otherwise he will be penalized financially. The Beery study provides no evidence concerning the relationships that would apply if certification were permissive rather than mandatory. Neither does it consider the potentially superior teachers who reject teaching as an occupation because they will not submit to the typically tedious prerequisites of certification.

9 Neal Gross and Robert E. Herriott, *Staff Leadership in Public Schools: A Sociological Inquiry* (New York: John Wiley & Sons, 1965). What I interpret as a measure of acceptance by teachers is identified by Gross and Herriott, inappropriately, in my view, as Executive Professional Leadership, a measure of the principal's attempts to lead his staff. But the distinction is unimportant to the point I am making here. Cf. Donald A. Erickson, "Essay Review: Some Misgivings Concerning a Study of Leadership," *Educational Administration Quarterly*, 1 (Autumn, 1965): 52–59.

10 Robert Dreeben and Neal Gross, *The Role Behavior of School Principals*, U.S. Office of Education Cooperative Research Project No. 853, Final Report No. 3 (Cambridge, Mass.: Graduate School of Education, Harvard University, 1965).

in the elementary grades showed some tendency to *disqualify* the individual for the administrative role. Years of elementary teaching were negatively associated with the disposition to entertain a broad range of decision alternatives and to consider the wider implications of choices.[11] In one of the best studies in this area in recent years, the evidence is even more startling. Considering several criteria of administrative effectiveness, several groups of raters, and several types of school districts, long teaching experience characterized the administrator who was "outstandingly unsuccessful as both a principal and a superintendent."[12]

I now turn, with obvious embarrassment, to the evidence on graduate training programs. In an extensive national study, years of formal preparation showed no relationship to estimated administrative effectiveness, and no impact on the performance of various leadership tasks.[13] In Harvard's National Principalship Study, the number of graduate courses in educational administration was *negatively* related to the principal's acceptance by teachers.[14] In the above-mentioned Mississippi investigation, courses in administration and supervision lacked any demonstrable effect whatsoever.[15] Knowledge of the content of administration courses was associated with certain decision-making styles, but the research worker failed to allow for the fact that those who master course content best are generally more intelligent to begin with. Furthermore, in a much superior investigation in

11 Elizabeth Martin Antley, "Creativity in Educational Administration," *Journal of Experimental Education*, 34 (Summer, 1966): 21–27. The relationships fall short of statistical significance, but since they are congruent with the tendency in other studies, they deserve consideration.

12 Edgar L. Morphet and William C. Schutz, *Procedures for Identifying Persons with Potential for Public School Administrative Positions* (U.S. Office of Education Cooperative Research Project No. 1076, Final Report: Berkeley: University of California, 1966).

13 John K. Hemphill, Daniel E. Griffiths, and Norman Frederiksen, *Administrative Performance and Personality: A Study of the Principal in a Simulated Elementary School* (New York: Bureau of Publications, Teachers College, Columbia University, 1962).

14 Gross and Herriott, *Staff Leadership in Public Schools.*

15 Antley, "Creativity in Educational Administration."

California, the same general type of technical knowledge showed no linkage with ratings of effectiveness.[16] The weight of evidence suggests, obviously, that most preparation programs for school administrators have very limited outcomes and may even create a trained incapacity for the job.

Such information is enough to make professors weep. But my purpose is not to disparage my field. I wish to emphasize that we are faced with uncertainty. We simply do not know the best way to prepare people to run schools. The rational response to this lack of knowledge is to say, "Gentlemen, we do not know. Let us experiment!" as Campbell, one of the first-rank scholars in this area, has done.[17]

But those who write the school codes are seldom troubled by such uncertainty. Setting rigid certification requirements, they have made the exploration Campbell urges illegal in many states. Neither are associations of professional educators much deterred by a dearth of evidence. In Iowa, they argued that half a century of educational progress would go down the drain if nonpublic schools were exempted from the demand for certified teachers. Not only is the connection between certification and effectiveness scientifically unestablished; only six states maintain such a requirement for nonpublic schools, and the bulk of the most renowned independent institutions are found in states that lack it. The main reason for the demand for certification is, obviously, that organized educators, like virtually every other organized occupational group, want to control access to their profession. It may be true, in addition, that in public schools, where large numbers of personnel must be processed, some fairly arbitrary guidelines are unavoidable. But why impose these questionable practices on nonpublic schools as well? There ought to be a few small pedagogical islands where it is possible to prepare and utilize personnel in new and imaginative ways.

16 Morphet and Schutz, *Procedures for Identifying Potential* . . . .
17 Roald F. Campbell, "Selection and Preparation of School Principals," in A. W. Reeves, John H. M. Andrews, and Fred Enns, eds., *The Canadian School Principal* (n.p.: McClelland and Steward Limited, 1962), pp. 41–51.

Certification requirements turned out to be a rather involved instance of the tendency to impose practices that are questionable. Let me cite a simpler example:

In one of the best surveys of city school systems thus far conducted, Havighurst protests the inclination to apply to slum children curricula and methods developed for the clean, inhibited offspring of the middle classes.[18] Now that it is no longer politically feasible simply to dump youths who do not respond to the standard within-four-walls-sitting-in-a-desk-staring-at-a-textbook approach, schools and the Job Corps are trying various combinations of work and cogitation, time on the job and time in school, practice and discussion. Some students are spending many "school" hours in nearby workaday enterprises, coupling on-the-job and in-the-school learning in unusual ways. But the Seventh Day Adventists introduced this tactic decades ago and, because it was unorthodox, encountered protests from state and local authorities. Educational leaders and the highest court in Kansas have recently refused to recognize the work-and-study mix of the Amish "vocational high school" as genuine education. To quote the court, "Sharon did not attend any school where the school month consisted of four weeks of five days each of six hours per day during which pupils were under the direct supervision of a teacher."[19] When the student is not in the schoolroom under the instructor's nose, Kansas insisted until recently that he is not learning in a manner worthy of legal recognition.[20]

18 Robert J. Havighurst, *The Public Schools of Chicago: A Survey for the Board of Education of the City of Chicago* (Chicago: The Board, 1964).
19 State v. Garber, 419 P. 2d 896 (Kansas, 1966). In March, 1968, the Kansas legislature passed an amendment which, in effect, legalized the Amish vocational high school.
20 Apparently a similar attitude characterizes officials in New York State. According to David A. Kennedy, Headmaster, DeVeaux School, Niagara Falls, N.Y., "The . . . case is that of an excellent day school which operates at both elementary and secondary levels but maintains a somewhat unique schedule because it is for professional children who are concurrently employed in the arts, acting, ballet, music, etc. The secondary school program is college preparatory, and many of its graduates go on to college. However,

Some Implications for Policy

On the positive side, what can be done to help ensure that state regulation of nonpublic schools will encourage the pursuit of pluralistic goals and promote diverse approaches to common objectives?

Let me begin by agreeing with John Elson on three points (chapter 5).[21] Since he argues them well, I shall assume they need little further support. First, if we place regulatory authority at the state level, we are less likely to encounter prejudice and bad faith than if we grant it to local officials.[22] Second, the chief state school officer needs a broad grant of power from the legislature so that he may deal flexibly with changing conditions and different kinds of nonpublic schools. Third, it is vital that educators acquaint themselves with nonpublic schools before undertaking to regulate them. The last point may bear particular emphasis. In correspondence undertaken in preparation for this paper, most complaints from nonpublic schoolmen came from states where officials apparently had not bothered to consult with spokesmen for nonpublic education before drafting the offending stipulations.

Given these three conditions — authority at the state level, broad administrative discretion, and a disposition to base demands on

the school has been unable to obtain accreditation from the Middle States Association of Colleges and Secondary Schools because it is not 'registered' by the New York State Department of Education. . . . The State Department refuses to 'register' this school because it cannot quite fulfill the 'book' requirement of a five-and-one-half hour school day and at least one full day of instruction each week for every student. The school cannot do this because of the professional obligations of most of the students. There is also some question of the degree of physical education classes held, although the school has a good program. It appears to us that this refusal evidences too inflexible an attitude in not being willing to make exceptions from 'the book' for a school which thereby suffers inability to obtain formal accreditation. The latter hurts its money-raising efforts as well as its relations with some colleges."

21 John Elson, "State Regulation of Nonpublic Schools: The Legal Framework," chapter 5.

22 Compare "Showdown at an Amish Schoolhouse," chapter 2.

knowledge — my primary suggestion is this: the chief state school officer should be forbidden by statute to conclude that any non-public school is substandard simply because it fails to comply with existing criteria. In questionable cases he should be required to determine whether his criteria are applicable to the school's basic goals. If his criteria are not appropriate, he should be directed to replace them with criteria that *are* appropriate — *unless the school's basic goals are unacceptable in a democracy.* Someone must rule explicitly, not merely by implication or default, on the acceptability of goals. We need a clear legal sanction of plurality in education.

To rule on the permissibility of goals will be a sensitive and difficult task. But it cannot be avoided. If it is not done openly and thoughtfully, it will be done inadvertently and by implication, as at present, without attention to the basic issues that are at stake. I am not sure what mechanism should be suggested for this purpose, but the following is a possibility: When the state superintendent thinks a school has aims that are repugnant to the general good, he could submit the issue to a special panel appointed by the governor or the state supreme court, a panel composed of men of acknowledged breadth and integrity from the state and elswhere. Moreover, the legislature might establish guidelines to assist in the panel's decisions.

To illustrate how the system might work, assume that two rural communities are created in the State of Lafayette, one by Amishmen from Ohio and the other by "Sons of Freedom" Doukhobors from British Columbia. Both communities establish their own schools. None of the schools seems acceptable in the light of existing state standards. Both the Amish and the Sons of Freedom claim they are preparing the young, not for life in the larger society, but simply to be Amishmen and Doukhobors. Lafayette's special panel, consulting the school code, finds a statement something like this:

> Nonpublic schools shall be permitted to function, within the meaning of the compulsory attendance law, primarily to

prepare children to participate in dissenting communities whose cultures have proven viable in the modern world, provided that these communities are not characterized by indigence, crime, anarchy, or subversive doctrines and are not seriously burdening the state with defectors who have difficulty adjusting to life in more complex settings.

The panel should have little trouble ruling that the Sons of Freedom may not maintain schools for the purposes avowed — not within the purview of the compulsory attendance law — for the sect has been a scourge to government for decades. The sect's communities are unstable and disorganized. Its adherents protest the statutes by blowing up bridges and burning buildings. Their dogmas are often seditious. They embarrass Canadian prime ministers by disrobing in front of the podium in political rallies. The panel's decision against the Sons of Freedom would not represent thought control. It would not prevent the Sons of Freedom from promoting their doctrines, particularly in classrooms not maintained for compulsory attendance purposes. It would, however, require that Doukhobor schools functioning in lieu of public schools for compulsory attendance purposes must provide children with the conceptual tools they must have to function in American society generally, since the Sons of Freedom communities do not represent a viable alternative.

The panel might lose more sleep deciding what to do with the Amish. But at least it would be unable to hide the decision beneath a plea for consistency or some pseudo-issue, and if it were well advised (in terms of my values, at least), it would rule that the Amish educational goal should be permitted and encouraged in a pluralistic society.

Given the panel's judgment, the state commissioner's task would be to establish a system of regulation appropriate to the goals of Amish schools, just as he had previously developed evaluative procedures fitted to other school types. In some cases, his best approach might be to let reputable schools regulate themselves, through their own accrediting mechanisms, for instance. Whatever criteria the state *does* adopt should concern the outcomes rather than the methods of instruction, and the central means of enforcement, though not necessarily the exclusive one, should be parental purview. To put the matter another way, the state should demand that Amish schools and all other nonpublic schools be informed and informative concerning the extent to which they are achieving the ends they avow, but the schools should have much freedom to test methodological alternatives. If parents are given systematic findings concerning the effectiveness of the schools they patronize, in most cases they will be far more rigorous than any state agency in demanding excellence. State regulation at present is often a matter of perfunctory compliance with technicalities. It seems unlikely, for example, that the two Amish schools in Iowa that were recently so much in the news were any better when they met the statutory demand for certified teachers, for many of the instructors they were able to import were probably not superior, and may even have been inferior, to bright Amish girls chosen to teach because they desired to do so and "had a way with children."[23] But show a parent he is paying for services inferior to those available elsewhere for the same money, and action usually follows.

Representatives of each type of nonpublic school should participate with state officials and consulting scholars in deciding what evaluative materials are to be provided to parents and governmental agencies. In the case of Amish schools, information should be published regularly concerning the accomplishments of the graduates in Old Order communities and elsewhere. What handicaps do these graduates feel? What successes have they experienced as farmers and housewives? What do they believe their school should have done for them that it did not do? The results of achievement tests in the basic skill subjects should probably be included. In the case of prep schools, comprehensive evidence should be made available concerning the colleges to which alumni gain admission and the success of these alumni in subsequent studies. Remedial schools should be required to produce data concerning the results they attain with students having specified problems. Catholic, Lutheran, and Seventh Day Adventist schools

23 *Ibid.*

might systematically compile facts of the type Greeley and Rossi gathered in their recent national study.[24]

With such intelligence at hand, the state could publish a handbook summarizing, chiefly for the use of parents, the success each school is experiencing in meeting the goals it has named. The schools could be separated into categories in terms of the types of students served and the objectives sought. On a scientific sampling basis, public officers could audit the materials from which the reports were derived as a means of ensuring accuracy. By disseminating such information, a state could bring enormous pressure to bear for the improvement of nonpublic education. I should not object, in fact, to giving state officials the authority to penalize nonpublic schools that continued to be significantly inferior to sister schools of the same variety. The combined demands of parents and government would operate, under these conditions, not to trammel originality in education, but to encourage it.

Many of these ideas are almost equally applicable to public schools. Much more than formerly, public education must adapt itself to the subcultures of the pupils served, not primarily in deference to the religious convictions of the parents, but because such adaptation is pedagogically essential. If schools are adapted for instructional rather than religious reasons, it seems to me that no constitutional issues arises. The child of the disadvantaged inner city requires a school designed for his particular needs. The Amish youngster is probably better served by a simple one- or two-room school in his community than by a large consolidated institution whose environs, programs, social structure, and physical characteristics all threaten his rootage in the Old Order community. I see no good reason why the simple rural schools for the Plain People should not be provided at times within the public sector.

But perhaps the state commissioner is a genuine humanitarian. He worries about the comparatively few individuals who defect from the Amish fold and seek to make their way in the urbanized world outside. They may need a somewhat more extensive

24 Greeley and Rossi, *Education of Catholic Americans.*

and elaborate education than the Old Order school has given them. In such a case, he could institute special instructional opportunities for ex-Amishmen who wished to acquire new skills and understandings.[25] Such programs would represent no inordinate burden to the state. Financially, the costs should be far less than those that would be incurred in educating all offspring of the Plain People in public schools. Changes in occupation and way of life will be increasingly common in the future, and large numbers of citizens — not just a few erstwhile Amishmen — will require periodic retraining. To provide this training is obviously preferable to curtailing religious freedom by outlawing Amish schools.

Finally, a suggestion to the nonpublic schools: If private educators wish to be consulted and understood, they must sometimes go out of their way to understand and accommodate public officers. The nonpublic schools can afford to comply on occasion with suggestions that seem unjustified, especially when the consequences are innocuous. The payoff in trust will justify the cost. One wonders, for instance, whether an extra coat of paint on Hazleton's Amish School No. 1 would have averted some of the local hostility, even if the paint was not as necessary as some people thought.[26] Often a tactful explanation of a prep school's approach to counseling goes further than a protest.

This has been a plea for conditions conducive to diversity in society generally and in education specifically — a defense of the unorthodox and experimental in the nation's schools. I have attempted to identify conditions that will protect liberties now seriously under attack in nonpublic institutions. The strongest arguments for freedom, I believe, are ethical, not pragmatic. But who knows, if the schools now branded as substandard and unacceptable are given leeway and encouragement, they may even teach us something about education.

25 I thought I had originated this idea until I noticed that Dean Kelley, too, had proposed it. He calls the approach a "Half-way House for Escaping Amishmen." Kelley, "Is There Room for the Amish?"
26 "Showdown at an Amish Schoolhouse," chapter 2 above.

8 William J. Sanders

Regulation of Nonpublic Schools as Seen by a State Commissioner

I hope, in this chapter, to deal with state regulation of nonpublic schools from the point of view of developments in a New England state. It must be remembered that Massachusetts Bay Colony was settled by dissenters and its sister colonies were settled by those who were dissident from the dissenters. Traditionally, strong central government, federal or state, has been held suspect in New England. "Home rule" is highly regarded, and many towns in Connecticut have special charters which exempt them, even in some educational matters, from the General Statutes of the state.

During the colonial and federal periods and later, there sprang up many church-sponsored colleges, as well as private academies also sponsored by churches or by Yankee philanthropists who had become rich through private enterprise. For years, most educated New Englanders were not aware that a first-class education could be got west of the Hudson River except, with some reservations, at Princeton. The father of public education in Connecticut, Henry Barnard, toward the middle of the nineteenth century, proposed the first public high school at Hartford as an institution that would be "good enough for the best and cheap enough for the poorest." He didn't say it would be free. He did not say it would replace private enterprise. He was simply ex-

The author is commissioner of education of the state of Connecticut.

tending educational opportunity to those who could not afford it under current conditions. He was not threatening the existing system. As a result of this early dedication and gratitude to private education, New England has been quite backward in providing public higher education. The prestige of private education remains very high. The private school is definitely preferred. Along with this preference there is a feeling that, like Caesar's wife, the private school is above suspicion; if it is regulated by the state, it would suffer in quality, it would decline to mediocrity. This feeling may not be logical, but it does not have to be logical to be effective. As a result, there is no *regulation* of private elementary and secondary education in the state. Anyone can start a school as long as the building is declared safe by the State Fire Marshall and has adequate toilets and sanitary drainage, as well as a safe water supply as determined by the Commissioner of Health. There is no state certification of teachers for such schools nor any requirement of a statement of financial responsibility. Since 1947, all degree-granting post-secondary institutions have been required to receive a license from the state. Significantly, this law was passed to control the new institutions opened to help World War II veterans take advantage of the G.I. Bill. Furthermore, since we are an industrial state, at about the same time a law was passed to require licensing by the state for private vocational industrial schools. Only in 1965 was this amended to cover other private occupational and correspondence schools. The purpose of the amendment was to protect students and industry from potentially fraudulent schools that appeared on the scene to teach data-processing, airline hostessing, modeling, office occupations, etc. Industry and labor in the state supported this move strongly. But there appeared to be no corresponding concern lest fraudulent secondary or elementary schools be established.

It is interesting that the Connecticut Association of Independent Schools, itself concerned about the rise of noncreditable institutions, introduced a licensing bill to the Connecticut 1967 General Assembly, a bill the Association asked the State Department of

Education to help design but, because of differences within the Association, withdrew. The parochial schools, for one group, did not wish to submit to state regulation on principle, nor, on principle, did some of the other member schools, and I hasten to add that they were schools, like the parochial schools, that had nothing to fear from regulation. They just could not swallow the idea of "losing their independence."

The State Department of Education does publish an approved list of schools. It approves, but does *not* accredit. Approval of nonpublic schools is on a voluntary basis. They can request an evaluation for the purpose of a listing in the state directory, and most of them, including those that oppose state licensing, are interested in listing. The parochial high schools seek such listing because it is required for participation in interscholastic athletic competition by the Association of Secondary Schools.

But these well-established schools are no problem; it is the fringe schools that are the issue, and they are growing in number for several reasons.

Parents are more affluent and more anxious. They can afford a good education for their children, and in New England they assume a private school is better than a public school. They are subject to anxiety; they are worried about their youngsters getting into college. But they know neither how to judge a school nor where to turn for advice. They patronize private pre-schools to give their children a good start and then feel they should send them to private elementary schools to prepare them to pass the examination for a private preparatory school, which in turn is expected to get them into a "good college."

Or they have a child who is a problem they cannot handle. There are some good schools for children with behavior problems, but they are expensive and limited in number and capacity. Marginal schools that are quite poor are appearing and offering to do the job. In desperation parents turn to them.

New schools are also appearing in the large cities to serve parents who are afraid to have their children in public schools enrolling Negroes in large numbers. There is a flight to private schools corresponding to the flight to the suburbs.

There is, in addition, the choice of the school based on religious convictions. These motives are not new. For years, nonpublic schools have served the religious convictions of parents. Indeed, they were started because the public schools at first did not exist and later could not handle the flood of immigrant children. Parochial schools performed a service in adapting these youngsters to American life.

Private schools have long flourished to serve those who wished their children to be educated with other children at their own social level. In the past many problem boys were sent to what are now prestigious schools. But the demand for private education has suddenly become enormous. Where there is little or no responsible supervision people may and do set up institutions that defraud parents and harm pupils.

It is contrary to the public interest that any youth be poorly educated by unfit persons, and the winds of change are blowing. Perhaps they will blow away mythical fear of central government control of the minds of children. Freedom of parents to choose a school other than public, freedom of religion, and the concept of free enterprise are not threatened by insistence that teachers be qualified personally and academically, that schools have adequate libraries and laboratories, that they be financially responsible, and that the educational programs offered be what they purport to be. Innovation and experimentation are not impeded by "rigid bureaucratic control" except in imagination. State departments of education are quite sensitive to the need for flexibility, innovation, and experimentation.

Furthermore, education is attracting much attention, and public policy, as it becomes incorporated in federal laws, appears to be losing patience with shoddy educational practices in the nonpublic as well as the public sector. The federal government is moving to strengthen the backbones of the states and get them to do what they have been failing to do because of apathy and penuriousness.

The G.I. Bill required that the institutions attended by veterans for collegiate or vocational training be approved by the states. This moved some states, such as Connecticut, to pass acts licensing and accrediting degree-granting institutions, and acts licensing nonpublic schools preparing for trades and industries. This was a revolutionary step which the state might not have taken had it not been prodded by Congress.

The National Defense Education Act of 1958, which provided matching grants for equipping and remodeling science, mathematics, and modern language laboratories in public schools, grants for improving guidance counseling and testing for the identification of able students, and partially cancelable college loans for the education of those preparing to teach in public schools, also provided funds for testing in nonpublic schools and *loans* for remodeling and equipping science, mathematics, and modern language laboratories. It has since been amended to include cancellation in part of loans for those who are preparing to teach in nonpublic schools. This was a dramatic shift in public policy on the part of Congress in recognizing the need for upgrading nonpublic schools as well as public schools.

Even more dramatic is the Elementary and Secondary Education Act of 1965, which provides for dual enrollment and the sharing of services with nonpublic schools in economically and culturally deprived areas. The law indicates grave national concern with educational opportunities afforded by public schools serving areas of poverty and also by nonpublic schools, particularly parochial schools, in such areas.

Title II of the Act makes available textbooks, instructional materials, and library books, to teachers and pupils in nonpublic schools. The language of Title III urges the participation of nonpublic schools in cooperative exemplary projects, such as model schools and educational service centers. Title IV invites them to participate, along with public schools, in regional laboratories.

Expenditure of funds for dual enrollment and ancillary services under the Act may be only for projects approved and evaluated by state departments of education. Books and instructional materials for nonpublic school pupils and teachers must be in accord with specifications set by state departments of education, and the exemplary centers or model schools established must be reviewed and given a priority by state departments of education. Here is explicit control; objections are not forthcoming from the nonpublic schools.

Parenthetically, attention should be called to the Higher Education Facilities Act of 1963, which authorized construction grants to nonpublic as well as public institutions of higher learning for instructional and library facilities. The Act clearly enunicates the policy that the nation cannot afford to have youth poorly educated because they choose to attend inadequate colleges. It is significant that institutions, to benefit, must be accredited by regional agencies, and so conformity to standards is required. The nonpublic institutions of higher learning *are* conforming.

Nursery schools in Connecticut, in league with the Association of Independent Schools, have long resisted licensing, yet at this moment the 1967 General Assembly has before it a bill to license day care centers and designate the State Board of Education as the licensing agent and give the Department *authority to prescribe the educational program* for day care centers. The bill was introduced by the community councils of the state in opposition to other bills that would place the licensing power in the Department of Health or the Department of Welfare. The Nursery School Association and the Association of Independent Schools do not object, because licensing by the state is a requirement of recent federal legislation if federal funds are to be captured.

The National Highway Safety Act requires driver education to be provided for all youth or else a percentage of federal highway funds will be withheld. Parochial schools are supporting a bill in the Connecticut General Assembly that will make them eligible to receive funds for driver education *if they follow the course prescribed by the state.* Some of the preparatory schools are not buying this; they fear the camel of state regulation will get more than his nose into the tent. They are not quite ready to rise above principle and accept "the Queen's shilling." There is a question whether the General Assembly can make state funds directly available to the nonpublic schools for this purpose. But driver training is even now given to youth enrolled in nonpublic schools by public school personnel using public school equipment. What is significant is that some nonpublic schools, in seeking funds, are reconciled to state prescription. As categorical aid continues, Congress will undoubtedly continue the demand for state prescription and evaluation. Some federal education officials foresee general aid replacing categorical aid, but even so, I believe the states will be called upon for assurance that the money is spent effectively. To the extent that nonpublic schools partipate in federal aid, they will be subject to prescription and evaluation of program, in short, to regulation.

Federal legislation is generated in response to needs that arise in the body politic, needs voiced by the electorate. Professional educators, educational foundations, educational organizations, and civic and political leaders have been calling for improvement, and nonpublic schools have been calling for assistance. One of the more arresting voices has been that of James Conant, whose writings over the past dozen years have criticized, constructively, in my opinion, the support and administration of the schools. He has been heard, and his 1964 effort, "Who Shapes Educational Policy," has brought into being the Commission of the States, an organization designed to encourage in each state a commission comprising the governor, members of the legislature, and educators. It is an attempt to combine political and educational leadership to secure greater political interest in and support for education at the state level, comparable to that emerging at the federal level. If the Commission is successful, it should strengthen the state's effort in education and have an impact on improving nonpublic as well as public schools.

The National Assessment Program to which more and more educators are becoming reconciled is unlikely to ignore the nonpublic schools. It is expected that such schools will be very much interested in participating.

The joint use by public and nonpublic schools of data processing for pupil accounting, of television, of computer-assisted instruction, in short, jointure in educational technology, is here already. As the nonpublic schools are swept up in this movement, they become more similar to public schools in programs and procedures.

Technology has a way of ironing out differences; it exerts a centripetal force. But so does our manner of living and working together. There is better communication between the public and private sectors. The barriers seem to be melting. In Connecticut, headmasters are encouraging their teachers to qualify academically for state certification. Institutions preparing nuns, priests, and brothers to teach in parochial schools have sought evaluation and approval of their programs, showing eagerness to have their students as well prepared for teaching as are candidates for public schools. Some of them are applying for provisional certificates, although these certificates are not required (a permanent certificate is available, however, only to those who have completed three years of successful experience in a public school).

The regulatory functions of the state should not be overemphasized. The state agency's greatest effectiveness is in improvement of education through its consultative service. However, it should set the standards for all elementary, secondary, and vocational education in consultation with all responsible educational interests in the state. It should help new nonpublic schools get started when they are needed, licensing those that give promise. Regional and professional accrediting associations are valuable, but they came about to fill a vacuum left by state inaction. There is even a question about the desirability of too great dependence upon the associations. In some instances, particularly, the professional associations may be inclined toward restraint of educational opportunity. There is a temptation for them to be protective of established schools, and of the interests of members of the profession, as unions are said to be, rather than of the public interest. While criticizing government agencies for being subject to political pressures, they are allegedly guilty of creating shortages of qualified professionals in the areas they represent.

However, there is change here, too. The professional associations, having gained strength while fighting for the benefit of their membership, may now be turning their concern to the public interest. If they are gaining maturity, so are the state agencies. Many state agencies, such as that in Connecticut, have become free of political pressures. If the Commission of the States succeeds in bringing together political and educational leaders, the politicians both in education and state government may become statesmen. They may learn, as many have already learned, to seek out the public interest and to be guided by it in the discharge of their responsibilities.

Regulation by government in which those who are regulated and their representative organizations have a part should not be onerous. The government regulates the sale of securities, interstate commerce, public utilities, the railroads, television, the airlines, etc. Education is big business and deserves similar treatment. Education involves everybody, and there is more and more involvement of private and public education with the federal and state governments. The federal government is not satisfied with the job being done by local school boards or the educational associations. President Johnson, in his budget message on February 28, recommended "legislation authorizing $15 million to help state and local governments evaluate their education programs and plan for the future." The government wants improvement, and is taking steps to bring it about directly, and through the states, by involving public and private school leadership in cooperative efforts to this end. There is no wall of separation between the government and the people; there just seems to be. In this age of massive involvement and electronic communication so dramatically described by Professor McLuhan in his "global village," the artificial or mythical walls are melting rapidly, as I have tried to show.

We can expect an acceleration of the pace of regulation of nonpublic as well as public schools, and, as the quality of all is raised, differences among them will diminish. "Excellence" and "quality," instead of being mere words to justify more expensive education, either public or private, may even be defined and measured in terms of achievement. I am much encouraged to think that perhaps in my own time I may see us move out of the night of educational nominalism into the clear dawn of pragmatic realism.

9 William B. Ball

A Roman Catholic Viewpoint

I think my comments can best be made under the following three headings: (1) the "control" question and the present position of the Catholic schools; (2) control and constitutional issues relating to it; (3) the nature and technique of education control.

The "Control" Question and the Present Position of the Catholic Schools

Catholic elementary and secondary schools now educate about one-seventh of the national school population. In some states the percentage is markedly higher. In Wisconsin it is nearly a quarter, in Pennsylvania and Massachusetts 22 per cent, in New York 21 per cent. This gigantic educational effort was never launched with the intention of creating a savings to the public, but one of the great realities which comes booming out of the so-called "parochial school question" is the pocketbook fact of the present absorption by supporters of the Catholic schools of about $2.25 billion in education cost per year. In Pennsylvania it is $310 million per year. In a financially worrisome national or state educational picture these amounts of money become important factors

The author, a specialist in constitutional law in Harrisburg, Pennsylvania, has represented Catholic educational interests and is an attorney for the National Committee for Amish Religious Freedom.

in all our educational planning — decisive factors in cities such as New York or Philadelphia, where the attempt to move any substantial number of parochial school children into public schools would trigger fiscal and educational chaos. I conclude that any phase-out of the Catholic schools, even if desired, would be a practical impossibility.

It is not my point today to argue extensively the issue of public aid to parochial schools. But since the issues of public aid and public control are interrelated, five conclusions respecting public aid to parochial schools are germane to the topic of this conference:

1. It is constitutionally permissible for government to support the achievement of *secular* objectives in church institutions — not only in hospitals, colleges, child care institutions, and homes for the aged, but indeed in elementary and secondary schools.

2. In view of the universally acknowledged national crisis in education, public policy will reflect the belief that it is financially cheaper and socially wiser to keep the bulk of the parochial schools in the game through partial public support.

3. Such partial support should never go beyond demonstrably secular objectives.

4. The proprietors of the church-related schools should judge the question of whether they should seek public support, not upon the basis of how much public support may be constitutionally permissible (because for secular objectives), but upon the basis of how little public support they will need in order to survive.

5. Diversion of tax dollars to other than the support of elementary, secondary, and higher education should be stopped at once. Let me briefly expand on this point. In state legislative and litigational squabbles over parochial school busing, textbook aid, etc., there has been a great outcry by the opponents of such aids over threatened "diversion" of the sacrosanct "public school fund." From this flows the familiar barrage of accusations about "weakening of our public schools." What the public does not understand is that, in all states, gross diversions of the "public school fund" to purposes neither closely nor properly related to *any* school purposes are constantly made. In Pennsylvania, for

example, what is blithely denominated the "public school fund" may (according to statute) be used for numerous *municipal* functions — the maintaining and operating of public museums, parental and other schools for adults, public lectures, and indeed public baths wherein all the adults of a school district may immerse themselves.[1] The buildup of diversions for recreational centers and for free trips of public school administrators to attend conferences held by state and national public school lobbies is also to be noted in this connection.

When we speak of public aid to church-related schools, we are brought directly to the problem of controls. I lay it down as a basic premise, that *what the public pays for it has the right to assure it gets.* There is no power in the public to expend its funds without such assurance. But "control" is, after all, a word susceptible of different meanings. These meanings should always be talked out, because the word "control" has lately been used as a bogeyman term in discussions of public aid to parochial schools. I have lately seen crocodile tears being shed by some absolutist separationists who have told the parochial schools: "If you receive public aid, you'll get controlled!" Then I have heard a few Catholics assert that the principle of religious liberty at once "commands" public aid to the church schools and precludes any vestige of "control." These people would have public aid but rule out even reasonable public inspection or reasonable accountability.

Perhaps the bogeyman can be dispelled by reference to a debate which recently took place in Pennsylvania over the question of the use of public funds for parochial school busing. Opponents of such use challenged proponents with this broad question: "If this public aid is granted, are you willing to accept control just as the public schools do?" The proponents answered — quite correctly, I feel: "We not only accept public control, we demand it — fully and completely — of the specific public aid furnished: namely, *the transportation.* We want buses with four wheels, all safety features required by law, and a state-qualified driver." The

1 Act of March 10, 1949, P.L. 30, art. IV, § 706, 24 P.S. § 7-706.

proponents rightly denied any power in the state to control *curriculum* upon the pretext that it was providing *busing*.

"*Any* aid justifies *all* control" is a slogan as dangerous as it is absurd. It should not be unthinkingly accepted. It finally leads to the idea that if the public but provides the whitewalls, the private must provide the Cadillac that goes with them. Controls ought always to be coterminous with the subject matter aided. If government supports a standard course of chemistry in a church-related institution, I should argue that this gives it no right to dictate a course in sex education in the same institution.

But what is the proper scope of public control over a school where the public provides no aid? This is, of course, the key constitutional question pertaining to Amish education. Here the only proper rule is one whereby the public is deemed restricted to narrow police power objectives — minimal controls respecting fire, safety, public morality, fraud, and absolutely rudimentary educational essentials. In the field of education the public should not be deemed to enjoy a broad reach of control over that which it refuses to support. Moreover, there ought to exist a live option upon the part of schools to avoid all but minimal police power control if they decide they do not want public aid. And the public then will not be empowered to wipe out schools which cannot afford the "standards" which state departments of public instruction, not encumbered by the economies imposed upon voluntary enterprise, are wont to dream up. This rule appeals to me as that which best safeguards both the public and the principle of voluntarism.

The statement of that rule leads me directly into the second division of my comment.

Control and Constitutional Issues Relating to It

Here I take as my text the statement of Justice Jackson in the Second Flag Salute Case:

> Probably no deeper division of our people could proceed from any provocation than from finding it necessary to

choose what doctrine and whose program public educational officials shall compel youth to unite in embracing.[2]

The question posed by Jackson is to me the most important question before this conference. It crackles in the presentations of Professor Henry, Professor Hostetler, Rabbi Kaminetzky, and others. It relates closely to the comments of Professor Dorsen. It accounts for my view that public control in education ought (1) to be limited strictly to the object aided and (2) that it should be largely absent where public aid is absent.

In the field of American education today, public control is so increasingly being urged in value-related areas of curriculum, instructional methods, and general program, that a third limiting principle should be stated: that the state, in exerting controls in value-related areas, should not be permitted to impose its own value judgments, its own consensus morality, or its own ordaining of religious values even in an honest effort to "teach about" religion. A definition of "religion," as that term is used in the First Amendment, long evolving in Supreme Court decisions, today equates that term with almost any sort of world outlook, moral code, or what anybody subjectively calls his own "religion," or what anybody calls his own values — even though he may claim these to be "nonreligious."[3] The new definition is extremely signicant both in widening the scope of protection to be accorded to the free exercise of religion and in broadening the ban of the No Establishment clause.

It is the latter effect of the new definition which must be considered when the state attempts to realize the best of all possible worlds in education by at once proclaiming that its schools shall be sterilized of any vestige of (traditional) "religion" and or-

2 West Virginia State Board of Education v. Barnette, 319 U.S. 624, 641 (1943).
3 The definition and its implications are examined at length in a paper presented by the author at the 1966 Harvard Conference on the Role of Religion in Public Education, now appearing as the chapter, "Religion and Public Education: Post-*Schempp*," in the volume devoted to the Harvard Conference, *Religion and Public Education* (New York: Houghton Mifflin, 1967).

daining its own substituted indifferentist, "neutral," secularist, or majoritarian values.[4]

One area of special concern, in connection with the constitutional position of the church-related schools, is the area of concerns posed by recent civil rights decisions. The *Pierce* case laid it down (hopefully, forever) that children are not required to accept instruction from public school teachers only. It also provides us with that memorable line, everlastingly quoted by advocates of aid to parochial schools, that "the child is not the mere creature of the state." This reference can be overdrawn. It is sometimes meaningless. Whose children *are* those millions of children who today have no family, are rootless and blown about through our slum streets like bits of loose trash? We may deplore the fact that these children are not raised in the secure Christian interdependence of an Amish community or that they were not raised in a God-fearing Irish or Polish family who "made it on their own" (but who were never chattels). But here these children are, and Professor Dorsen has rightly asked us to consider them as we ponder questions of freedom and control in education. He raises two basic questions: Should public controls be applied to require church-related schools to take children (a)

4 Most interesting, in this connection, is the case now on appeal to the Supreme Court of the United States from the court of Washington. There the University of Washington offered a course, English 390, on "The Bible as Literature." A taxpayers' suit has been brought to enjoin this state institution from continuing to offer the course, on the ground that it brings about in the mind of the student "destruction of the Bible as an infallible revelation from God to man." (Quoted from Brief of Respondent in the Supreme Court of the State of Washington in Calvary Bible Presbyterian Church of Seattle, *et al.* v. Board of Regents of the University of Washington, 436 P2d 189 [1967]). The plaintiffs in this suit did not contend that the state taught the Bible is *not* God's word; since the state did not teach that it *is* God's word, it effectively destroyed the concept of its being God's word. Perhaps the plaintiffs have a point when we consider the new definition of "religion," when we consider "power and prestige of the state" of which Justice Black wrote so stirringly in the Regents' Prayer case, when we consider all the fastidiousness of the Court in *Everson* and *McCollum* over not letting a cent of taxpayers' funds go, directly or indirectly, into the support of a smidgeon of religion.

without distinction as to race? (b) without distinction as to religion?

I should answer the first question as follows: they should not only take children without distinction as to race — that is elementary; they ought to be a prominent force in bringing about the enactment of state statutes barring all nonpublic schools from discriminating on account of race. I stress statutes both because statutes, as expressions of the will of the people, often have greater moral impact and educational value than court decisions, and because statutes are generally easier to effect as public policy than court decisions. Again, statutes can be precisely drafted, and thus judicial ruminating, which can convert things private into things public without proper basis therefor, can be avoided. The view of the *Poindexter* decision, as given by Professor Dorsen, that "any aid" creates such a conversion, leaves the church-related school in a most precarious position indeed. Is it "public" only so far as pupil selection is concerned? Why is it not then thought "public" for any and all purposes? In such case it will have lost its freedom to dictate its own religious curriculum — in fact, if it is "public," one must ask how it can have a religious curriculum. Again, the "any aid" doctrine (if "any" means "any") would have the effect of converting all church-related schools into public schools, whether or not they receive subsidy or bus service or other things popularly denominated as "aid." I say this because tax exemption, fire protection, and sewage service are, in actual fact, "aids," and these are almost universally provided to parochial schools *at the present*.

As to the second question posed by consideration of Professor Dorsen's paper, I can only state my own legal conclusion that no church-related school is under any constitutional requirement to abandon the practice of selecting its pupils solely on the basis of religion. Instead, it is clear that there is a constitutional right to selection on account of religion. To require that such a school not select upon the basis of religion is plainly to say both that religious schools may not exist and that parents and children thus do not have the right to choose a religious school. Such a doctrine at once destroys both corporate and individual rights. This is not the forum to argue this case, but to omit comment upon this broad avenue to total state control in education would be unpardonable upon the part of anyone devoted to liberty or religion and to freedom in education.

My comment, however, expresses no objection to voluntary experimentation with religious open enrollment by church-related schools (such as I understand is being undertaken by the Chicago Archdiocesan schools).

The Nature and Technique of Education Control

William J. Sanders (chapter 8) makes liberal use of such words and phrases as "goals," "according to standards," "supervision to assure achievement," "upgrading," "unfit teachers," and so on. All of this leaves me perplexed — as I suspect it does Professor Littell — and I am sure it does the Amish. I do not understand — nor do most citizens — what sort of "goals" public education has in mind, or how many different goals different public education departments may have decided are to be "*the*" goals, or by what popular processes, or according to what and whose philosophic presumptions the goals were ordained. I note unkind references to supervision of education by "the politicians" (and I can understand that), but I am eased over the lip of the frying pan when presented with the desired alternative, an elite who may freely prescribe for all education — that is to say, for the mind and soul of the nation.

Mr. Sanders' gentle plea on behalf of "standards" moves us rapidly away from that narrow area of the police power wherein alone I feel that the state may prescribe by law under very limited definitions of health, safety, etc. He moves us into an area in which it is very doubtful that the actual competence of the state is to do more than to perform research and to give us its recommendations. Law cannot do everything, and it had better not try. If the public authority seeks to lead education, let it do so as exemplar and with even-handed love of all education. As matters stand, public education in the United States resembles most of all a sect — large and militant, to be sure — but nevertheless a sect. Its public conferences recognize the efforts of no others; the public schools alone are the true font of education. And the much abused "politicians" repeat by rote the slogans of the monolith. In almost any state of the Union, a Governor's Message on Education will typically embrace unreality by ignoring even a line of reference to the nonpublic schools within the borders of his very state. This is utter fantasy in states where a sixth or more of all the children are in nonpublic schools — like a discussion of fruit which would compulsively have to omit mention of oranges. If "standards" are going to be saddled upon the nonpublic schools, then the "we-they" dichotomy is going to have to be be eased by the sense of reality (including both educational and fiscal reality) and by good manners.

Perhaps, however, it is providential that the church-related schools are relegated by the public authority to an outsider's role. Some Catholic educational leaders have gone quite overboard of late, proclaiming a "partnership" between public and private education. This gratuitous speech, too, is a flight to unreality. Though undoubtedly intended as an expression of cordial comradeship in the job of helping the nation's children, it triggers fears in some that Catholic education desires a management role in public education. But worse is the fact that the impulse which it really expresses, to attempt to be a "Catholic" part of public education, ought to have been well weighed before becoming a slogan to start feet marching.

I have debated throughout the country in favor of public aid to church-related education. I believe limited aid to such education both constitutionally permissible and wise. But Catholics must not approach the aid question with anything less than the most discriminating evaluation of what their schools will need in order to survive and the nature of the controls which will follow public dollars. We Catholics will lose a great deal if we too uncritically embrace public aid. One thing we may lose is the spirit of sacrifice and the salvific tension in which the need to sacrifice places us. In our later generations on these shores, the affluent society is ready for us Catholics. But do we ever really want to be ready for it? Shall Catholic parents give over their educational system, by and large, to the state so that they can even more fully experience luxury, attune their reflexes to advertising's every whim? I am not at all sure that we Catholics have plumbed the depths of our ability to give; my guess is that we have not. My certainty is that the Catholic of suburbia is able to give money to aid Catholic education among God's poor of the inner city. We will be sturdier and better for such sacrifice, for our willingness to give up Techne's baubles by taking care of our own.

Techne proffers more than toys, as Mr. Littell has pointed out. Catholic educators today are not a little anxious to "renew" Christian education. Some see the renewal as consisting of greater "relevance" in the teaching of religion and, beyond that, the mounting of drives for "excellence" — the content of that term being supplied, not by Christianity, but by those who, in education, are making our technologized society what it is. Some of these drives are becoming rather frantic, with nuns, priests, brothers, and lay teachers hot in pursuit of what some anonymous, impersonal mind prescribes as "standards" for teacher certification. The ultimate education resulting may, however, turn out to be a sort of shared time — Techne and Techne's values (whether imparted on the Catholic school premises or not) occupying most of the time, and the isolated religious element unable to do much sharing of itself with any other part of curriculum and having little impact on the pupil.

The very expression of such fears may seem both retrograde and ill-timed. Better, however, to have brought them out. We have all read shelf-fulls of books pointing up the need of Christianity to be relevant to the actual world of the twentieth century, to be in the marketplace — for Christians to be Christians in their milieu, lathe operators leading lathe operators back to Christ, and so on. Well and good. But before Catholic education is ir-

revocably committed to sanctifying the world as it finds it, perhaps it should take one last careful look at the Amish and reflect
upon the values of self help, of schools which are schools of god-
liness, perhaps even looking to civil disobedience in the defense
of Christian education, and a perfect willingness to embrace the
life of the pilgrim on this earth.

Participants in the discussion who are among the authors of preceding chapters of this volume are: Norman Dorsen, Donald A. Erickson, Jules Henry, and Franklin H. Littell. In addition, the following members of the conference contributed to the discussion: John Paul Carter, executive secretary, National Association of Episcopal Schools; Jere Farley, director, Adult Education, Tennessee State Department of Education; David F. Hanson, consultant, Accreditation and Approval, Michigan Department of Education; John A. Hostetler, professor of anthropology, Temple University; Joseph Kaminetsky, national director, National Society for Hebrew Day Schools; Neil G. McCluskey, professor of education, University of Notre Dame; William E. McManus, superintendent of schools, Catholic Archdiocese of Chicago; David C. Osborn, supervisor of accreditation, Maryland State Department of Education; Leo Pfeffer, professor and head, Department of Political Science, Long Island University; August W. Steinhilber, specialist for legislation, U.S. Office of Education; Anne H. Strickland, coordinator, Affiliate Program, American Civil Liberties Union; and T. Raber Taylor, attorney, Denver, Colorado.

10

Highlights of the Conference Discussion

Question from the floor:

I am not sure that I see the relevance of Jules Henry's remarks [chapter 4] to state regulation of nonpublic schools.

Jules Henry:

I have attempted to draw attention to the fact that there are fundamental reasons why our educational system is defective in many ways. We could therefore say, in regard to the Amish or any other group which desires to develop its own form of education, "Who are we to throw the first stone?" That is the point. That is the whole thrust of my argument. In view of the recognized weaknesses of our educational system, let us be circumspect about saying to anybody, "Your educational system must conform to ours." The title of this conference is "Freedom and Control in Education." Control always involves assumptions concerning the validity of the control to be exercised. The intent of my paper is to ask, "On what do you base your theory of superiority? On what do you base your right to exercise control over the education of any people wishing to pursue its own ends?"

Question from the floor:

How far can we push this principle of educational dissent without undoing the whole fabric of public education? Or perhaps you believe it would be a good thing if we did unravel the whole fabric of public education.

Mr. Henry:

I don't think that a desire to see public education unraveled can be inferred from my statements. It seems to me that our philosophical position must be similar to the one advocated by Governor Hughes [chapter 1]. In view of our own defects, we must move slowly. We must examine carefully the claims of any group wanting to develop its own system of education, and we must not assert blindly, as the press and various pressure groups in our society often do, that such a group must be made to conform.

Question from the floor:

Would you accept the position of John Stuart Mill in his "Essay on Liberty" that we favor giving the state power to demand that all children learn the English language and acquire some familiarity with the structure of government, but that other matters of education be left to parents and the groups to which they belong?

Mr. Henry:

We want the best thing for the Amish and other divergent groups. We want what will permit them to survive in a competitive economy — what will permit them to follow the way of life they desire. The orientation our educational system does not have is this: What is best for the kids? What is best for the particular group? Our educational system does not ask the question, "What is best for the child?" Our education system asks, "What is best for the political economy and the gross national product?" The Amish objection, I think, is an objection raised by all people interested in civil rights. The questions are the same. The Negroes want to know whether their kids are getting the education that is best for them, best in terms of desegregation and standards of education equivalent to those of whites. Each group wants what it considers best for its children. The Negro is treated in terms of what is best for whites; Amish schooling is evaluated in terms of the question, "What education is best for the contemporary, technical, consumer-oriented, war-oriented American culture?"

Leo Pfeffer:

Who is to make the judgment of what is best for the child? Is it to be an unreviewable judgment by the particular group of which the child is a member? Or is it to be decided by the total society, acting through its government? There are certain instances where perforce we have to say that the judgment is to be made by the larger group, as the courts have ruled in those cases where the health of the child was directly involved. The Jehovah Witnesses won't allow blood transfusions for their children because they believe this refusal is best for the child, but their judgment is superseded by the state, and the child is given a blood transfusion to save his life. Fifteen or twenty years ago, a small group of extremely orthodox Jews living in a very Hasidic center of Brooklyn insisted that their religion forbade them to partake in any secular education at any level, to speak any language other than Yiddish, or to study books other than the Bible and the sacred readings. That group felt it was best for their children to do nothing but study the Torah from morning to night, seven days a week. The state had proceedings brought to compel the parents to enrol the children in either a nonpublic or a public school offering a basic minimum secular education. The case went up to the United States Supreme Court, which upheld the decision of the state court that the judgment of what is best for the children has to be a collective judgment of the entire community, at least in respect to basic secular elementary subjects the whole community judges to be necessary.

The Amish make the decision more difficult. They accept a basic secular education at the lower level, but they resist formal education beyond age fifteen. But the expectations of the overall community are expanding. A hundred years ago, an education up to age fifteen would be considered a great luxury. It is now a bare necessity. Our standards have — I can't say risen — changed. When

I recently brought the question of the Amish to a group of very liberal lawyers, asserting that in my opinion a serious question of religious liberty was involved, I was alone. "What kind of religious liberty is this," my colleagues asked, "if parents deprive their kids of a high school education?" Applying the same standards applied to Jehovah Witnesses with reference to blood transfusions and applied to the Hasidic group with reference to elementary education, I don't know the answer. Ultimately there has to be a determination as to how our collective judgment as to what is good for the child can be exercised while maintaining individual values and parental responsibility.

Anne H. Strickland:

I think we are missing an important point if we ask merely what is best for the child and assume that the Amish parent and the Negro parent are in the same position in this regard. The Amish parent claims the right to educate his child under the Free Exercise Clause of the First Amendment. This claim has priority over the question of what is educationally best for the child. The Negro parent who feels his child is not getting an adequate education bases his claim to this on his right as a citizen of this country, not on the First Amendment. The argument can be made, of course, that the education the Amish child is getting in the Amish school is best for him, but this is not the primary reason he should be entitled to attend a sectarian school. He has this right under the First Amendment.

T. Raber Taylor:

I would suggest that the collective judgment of which Mr. Pfeffer speaks must be limited to specifying certain clear minimums. One of the indices on which we may all have agreement is expressed in the United States code requirement that aliens who want to become citizens of the United States, must learn to read, write, and speak the English language and must acquire some understanding of the principles of the formation of our government and our basic documents (8 USCA Sec. 1423).

These are the minimums. I am indebted to E. Dexter Galloway for a little knowledge of the facts in the *Kansas* v. *Garber* case. In this case you have a high-school-age girl who, if she were an alien, could qualify to become a citizen of the United States by learning English and developing some knowledge of the principles of our form of government. Probably the young lady from Kansas has already met this minimum requirement. She went to grade school. She has been taking courses from a correspondence school approved by the U.S. Office of Education. She probably is as fully educated as would be any alien seeking citizenship. Why should she not be permitted to take courses in American government at home, as do most people who apply for citizenship? Perhaps the states are not on as firm ground in demanding high school attendance as they are in demanding an elementary education.

Franklin H. Littell:

In this regard it may be possible to make a very fundamental distinction. The position taken by the Amish is comparable to that of alien residents in the land rather than citizens who take full part in government, hold public office, and so on. I would suggest, therefore, that this may be a very useful distinction in the entire discussion: those who propose to vote, hold office, etc., are subject to a certain basic requirement of political education, whether as immigrants from abroad or as "immigrants" from dissenting groups in this country, whereas, when you are dealing with groups like the Amish, the real question is how you shall treat the stranger in the land. These people in their theology and their entire history are deliberately aliens, for what they view as good reasons, from a society with the characteristics that Jules Henry indicated. How do you treat aliens who are strangers in the land? Are they to be subject to the statist thrust which is the sickness of modern society, or are we still a society of liberty in which we acknowledge that there are some differences of opinion as to where the ultimate commitments lie? If it is the state and the general consensus which is to control all of these things, then

America, once the land of liberty, is only in a matter of degree different from the generally totalitarian state. If however we admit, as has been maintained for generations in America, that we are still engaged in a lively dialogue as to ultimate commitment and that we defer to our neighbors as individuals and as groups as to where the ultimate may lie in their own self-government, then we are on a different spot.

John A. Hostetler:

Jules Henry has characterized the culture of our societal mainstream. It may be useful, in contrast, to highlight some pertinent aspects of the Amish culture.

For the first eleven years of my life, as an Amish boy, I saw the daylight in Pennsylvania, and for the next eleven years, in Iowa. As a child, I learned a little proverb that has always stayed with me, an epitome of the Amish outlook. The nearest translation goes something like this: Self-praise stinks. Or, put somewhat more eloquently: Self-promotion is dysfunctional.

The life view encapsulated in this aphorism encompasses virtually everything that is important to the Plain People. They think they possess something infinitely greater than the competitive individualistic fulfillment Jules Henry has discussed. There is a greater cause, the Amishman feels, than what *I* want to do. The individual is not pitted against the community in this little *gemeinschaft* society. A child learns that the fear of God is the beginning of wisdom, something greater than self-fulfillment. The child does not need to create his community nor strive to belong to it. He is born into a ready-made community. In the dominant society, in contrast, the youth must create this community to an important extent and must strive incessantly to belong to it. He does not belong until he has proved himself. For example, in the *gemeinschaft* society a girl does not have to prove, as she would have to do elsewhere, that she is a female and can function socially in her role in order to be accepted. Yet an Amish girl at thirteen can prepare, cook, and serve a meal to twenty threshers or quilters. Self-denial and impulse control have meaning in the *gemeinschaft* society. Life has meaning, work has meaning, heaven has meaning. The rejection of the pleasure principle is possible, as well as the rejection of consumptive spending Jules Henry talked about in his *Culture Against Man*.

I am often asked, "Does an Amish child have a chance to become an American child in the sense of being exposed to alternate values?" This is a very interesting question and I think a valid one. But we also need to ask whether the average American child is given meaningful alternatives. Does the suburban child today have a chance to become a decent human being in spite of his loss of community? In spite of his unstable family life? In spite of his deep inferiority about belonging to the human family? In spite of deviant behavior and crime? In spite of not having a father in many families — no one to identify with in the family context when one grows up?

Amish children, according to the limited studies available at the present time, genuinely aspire to do the things their parents are doing. They are not impoverished by their social institutions. They are not denied emotional participation in society at many levels.

In terms of this social participation, the Amish have reasons for resisting compulsory high school attendance that are commonly overlooked. The status of the Amish individual changes significantly when he reaches the age of fifteen. No longer regarded as a child, he is an adult or at least a semi-adult, accepted into the responsibilities of adulthood, given meaningful work identification and responsibility. To enforce attendance at the onset of high school may be helpful for some American children, but in the case of this *gemeinschaft* society the effect is to deprive the individual of his rightful social status as an adult. It is to deprive him of some of the most meaningful rewards in the process of maturing. To remain in school is for him to be punished and deprived. The Amish are not alone, of course, in holding that compulsory school attendance beyond the elementary grades is an inappropriate or even antithetical approach to preparing the young for the way of life their parents want them to acquire.

And incidentally, the parent's right to choose the kind of education his offspring shall be given has been emphasized in the Declaration of Human Rights of the United Nations.

Let me emphasize another often-misunderstood fact. *Gemeinschaft* communities do change. They are not as static as popular myth would suggest. They are organisms — living, moving cultures. They change slowly and selectively, but they do change. As Donald Erickson put it in his *Saturday Review* article, the Amish may be in the last car of the train, but they are moving, like everyone else. The fact that there are different stages of change and movement is responsible for diversity in American life. We cannot protect this diversity unless we permit people to vary in their modes of adaptation.

Finally, the misconception should be challenged that if people are permitted to prepare for life in the *gemeinschaft* community they will be unable to cope with life elsewhere. Experience indicates that the Amish, at least, do not struggle unsuccessfully to adjust to the larger culture when they defect from the Old Order. Their manual skills, their emotional training, their attitudes concerning hard work and self-reliance are scarce assets in the modern age. They have retained many qualities of the American past with which we can identify and sympathize, and if their simple style of life is soon to be extinct, as some of my colleagues claim, perhaps all humans are soon to lose much that is uniquely human. In my view, we shall always need to have conscience groups with us. It is salutary to be aware of the existence of groups that put interpersonal relationships first, groups that question the culture of consumption, money making, and self-praise.

David F. Hanson:

I want to relate for a minute to the question of the Amish child who can serve a meal for twenty threshers. What happens to this girl if she cannot serve this meal? The public itself is responsible for what happens to the child who can't live up to the demands of her group.

Mr. Hostetler:

I think that what happens is a most beautiful thing. Her mother helps her and her sisters help her until she acquires the confidence and skill she needs. Furthermore, her livelihood is not at stake. The strong take care of the weak. Interpersonal relationships are the most important element in the culture.

* * *

Mr. Pfeffer:

I don't expect to win any friends with what I am about to say. I assume that most of the people in this room are professionally concerned either with law or with religion or with private education, and what I have to say will not be happily received by any of those three classes.

I have spent most of my adult life earning a livelihood in the field of law — practicing law and, lately, teaching it. I feel a little bit like the astrologer who suddenly found out that the stars don't really do anything at all, but he had no other way of making a living and he continued practicing astrology. With respect to civil rights, I am regretfully, but I am afraid unavoidably, being forced to the conclusion that the laws may be pretty nearly futile. No state in the Union has more and better anti-discrimination and anti-segregation laws than my own native state, New York. For well-nigh three-quarters of a century racial segregation has been forbidden at public schools in New York. Twenty years ago, I was drafting the same model anti-discrimination laws that Norman Dorsen is now getting the uniform state people to adopt. But New York has more racial segregation in its public schools today than it had twenty years ago. There is more racial segregation in the United States in the schools generally than there was before *Brown* v. *Board of Education*, the Magna Carta of racial integration.

I am afraid equally futile and somewhat naïve is Dorsen's appeal [in chapter 6] for nonpublic schools to get into the battle for racial integration. I am not tactful and diplomatic. I don't know how to be. I am blunt. The best way for nonpublic schools, primarily the parochial schools, to help racial integration is to close their doors and go out of business. Nonpublic schools are not an aid to integration. They are a barrier and a handicap.

Now I am not saying that the nonpublic school *should* go out of business, because racial integration is not the only value in our society. Other values have to be considered. Religious freedom is one which I hold very dear. Values have to be balanced, and it may very well be that we have to pay the price of racial segregation in order to maintain religious freedom. But what I do ask is that the nonpublic schools stop kidding themselves, and stop kidding such good people as Norman Dorsen. If they were to take his advice and conduct a strenuous recruiting campaign for Negro students, much as they recruit seven-foot basketball players, their success would be the same in both cases. Each school would have a seven-foot basketball player and a Negro scholarship student.

I used to think that the trouble with Negroes was that they had black skins. I don't think that is the trouble with them now. The trouble with the Negroes is that they are poor. They don't have any money. If they only became rich like us Jews, they could take over American culture, American universities, become recipients of national adulation, as we Jews have done. When I was young, we Jews were still poor, so I went to the City College of New York. Now we Jews are rich, so my son goes to Harvard, and I ease my conscience by forbidding him to apply for scholarships.

We used to think of City College, we chauvinistic City College men, as the Jewish Harvard. Today the Jewish Harvard is Harvard. If the Negroes only could become rich, Harvard would become a Negro Harvard. Sammy Davis would not become a Jew, but Abraham Heschel would become a Negro.

The bare, unadulterated truth of the matter is that the nonpublic school is a major instrument of segregation. It is not, except in the South, purposefully racially segregated. Indeed, it is becoming less purposefully religiously segregated. Racial segregation in the nonpublic schools and, increasingly, religious segregation are a function of economic segregation. The nonpublic school is becoming the home of middle and upper classes. Negroes don't go to nonpublic schools, not because of the blackness of their skin, but because of the emptiness of their pockets. I can say for the Jewish group that there are unfortunately not a few who go to the Jewish day schools, not because they love God more, but because they love the public school less. The public school, in the big cities at least, is fast becoming the dumping ground for society's rejects. And for some reason or other, those rejects almost all have black skins.

Now my major concern is with the religious nonpublic schools. The secular nonpublic schools, of the type which belong to the National Association of Independent Schools, are a very small, insignificant proportion of the whole picture. They are growing, but it is easier to take on the aura of religion, to take the kid out of public school and put him into some religiously affiliated nonpublic school, than to put him into one of these "snobbish" secular schools. (You will accomplish the same purpose anyway.) I have been a religious person all my life, and I would hate to see religion play such an ignoble role. I would hate to see religion becoming the handmaid, the prostitute, of the Haves in order to protect their snobbery and their exclusiveness against the Have-Nots. I could comment about the church founded by the penniless Galilean carpenter but I think, in the interest of ecumenism, I won't mention it.

There are three areas in which this tragic development is going on: hospitals, housing and schools. In New York, we have hospitals which are city-owned and hospitals which are privately owned. We have Bellevue hospital, a New York City hospital. I don't know how many of you have ever been there. You should go in. It would be an experience. Bellevue hospital is the hospital for those who haven't got the money to get into a private hospital, even as ward or charity patients. Most Negroes go to Bellevue hospital, few to the Presbyterian hospital or Mt. Sinai. Hill-Burton funds (federal funds starting in 1946 for the support of public and private hospitals) are increasingly going to the private hospitals and decreasingly going to the public hospitals in proportion.

I remember when we were first fighting for racial integration in housing. I participated in the drafting of the first (and still today the standard) fair housing practices law. I remember we had a case in 1947–48 in which we tried to establish a sophisticated legal philosophy and theory concerning state action. We tried to establish that the Metropolitan Life Insurance Company, when it built the Stuyvesant town project for middle-income housing and got tax exemption and so on, was engaged in state action and therefore couldn't discriminate against Negroes. We lost four to three in the New York Court of Appeals and were heartbroken when the Supreme Court of the United States denied certiorari. Subsequently, we felt that the only way to achieve racial integration was to get a fair-housing practices act which would apply to everybody. Some six to seven years passed before we finally persuaded the state of New York to adopt such a law. In the meantime we put our energies into public housing. Public housing — there you would have integration, because state action would unquestionably be involved. We wouldn't need any law, for we had the Fourteenth Amendment. So we pumped for, and got, public housing. But over the years public housing has become Negro housing, so much so that we must close our eyes to the very laws we drafted (laws which forbid discrimination in housing) and encourage the public housing officials to discriminate against Negroes in admission to public housing, lest we reach the tipping point and all the whites move out. We have even urged that the income ceilings be raised so the whites need not move out as soon as they can afford the rent in a private development.

About three or four years ago, I attended a meeting in which I heard two representatives of church groups which are engaged in obtaining federal funds for housing for senior citizens. (Not a dime do they put into it. All financing comes from the federal government.) I asked the first speaker what tenants were getting in as these lovely new buildings were put up. He said, "Exclusively upper middle class and upper class." The second speaker came in late and didn't hear this. He made the most glib spiel I have heard. Like any salesman selling insurance, he told us: "You know what housing means? Housing is three things: One, shelter; two aesthetics; three, privacy. Obviously there isn't enough private money to do it. Therefore we have to have federal money. Now who is to do it? Which is the most efficient agency to do it? The churches have a long history of being involved. They're organized. They're qualified. They're the people to do it. None of this nonsense about church-state separation." Do what? Take federal money to build up segregated cities with walls to keep the poor out. (The poor are nearly always black-skinned.) This is done by whom? By churches, by those who allege they speak in the name of God.

Finally, in education. Everybody knows that the reason the Elementary and Secondary Education Act of 1965 was adopted after years and years of frustration was that the church had gotten what it wanted. It had been paid off. It withdrew its veto and we got education financed from the federal government. The law said that the purpose of this act was to help educationally deprived children, handicapped children, and defined them: they are those who come from a family where the annual family income in 1965 was (hold your breath) $2,000 or less. If you made more than $2,000, you're not economically disadvantaged and are not entitled to the benefits of the act. And what happens? In every single community taking part under the Act, the church has got to get its ransom before the money is available. I tell you that there are very few really poor children in parochial schools. If you look hard you might find a token poor child here and there. But the poor children, for whose benefit the Education Act was purportedly enacted, do not go to nonpublic schools. Children whose annual family income is $2,000 are not to be found in nonpublic schools except in numbers so small as to be not much more than tokenism, but the church schools have to get their ransom, all in the name of God. As I said, no one will love me for what I say, but as a religious person, I don't think that this is "Thy Will being done."

Norman Dorsen:

What Leo Pfeffer says is very moving, and it comes from a person who has a right, in my judgment, to speak as he does. But if I may say so with all respect, I think that the sincere shock and anger reflected in Mr. Pfeffer's remarks is a naïve reaction. Judging from my reading of history, I would be surprised if the majority of people behaved in any other way than to safeguard what they think is their children's and their immediate personal interests above all. I think it is naïve to expect most people to do differently when they are in the situation in which many of the parents find themselves.

But I do not stop at this point. I believe that there is a possibility of improvement. I believe it is possible that the situation will improve, as it has done in certain areas. And even if improvement is not possible, we must act as if it were possible. I hope I am not moving into a philosophical or theological plane for which I am not well equipped. But there seem to me many situations in life where frustrations and evil stand in the way of good results, and there is no alternative but to do one's best to improve things. I spent some time recently in the fight against capital punishment, and I had a little to do with the American Civil Liberties Union's change of position on that issue. It has been said that when you are fighting against capital punishment, for each person who is not executed you have won 100 per cent of the battle. Perhaps that is true of each Negro child in each of the 3,270 schools of the National Association of Independent Schools. There should be many more than $1\frac{1}{2}$ per cent; there should be 10, 15, or perhaps 20 or 30 per cent. I deplore the current situation, as Mr. Pfeffer does. Nevertheless, I draw a somewhat different conclusion than he does. I think our job is to do what we can do to improve the situation, and I think it can be improved.

Joseph Kaminetsky:

I must say I have mixed emotions in this regard. I have known Mr. Pfeffer for a long time, and I respect his concern for the poor of this country. However, I must differ with some of the things he said, because there may be some here who will otherwise go away with the wrong impression. I cannot argue with Mr. Pfeffer's concern for his fellow man. I have that same concern from a deeply religious strain in my makeup, but I cannot go along with his denigrating what has become a great hope for the culture of America and for my people.

There may be some people who patronize Jewish day schools because they do not want their children to attend the public schools, but one of the major purposes of Jewish day schools is to raise a generation of our children who will not have hatred for their fellow men. I know of no way to do this outside of the religious tradition. To me, the hope of raising people who will recognize the rights of their fellow man is through religious education, and the Jewish day school has proven the way to do this, along with the other religious schools.

Further, it is not true that there are no poor Jews in Jewish day schools. Our tradition teaches us to take in *all* children into our schools, especially the needy.

Our objective is study for its own sake and not for the purpose of learning a trade. We now have hundreds of young men who don't want to go to college, who do not even pursue a trade. Somehow they manage to get along, because they want to sit and study. We have many, many communities where Jews are struggling against tremendous odds to make ends meet and tax themselves to send their children to day schools. Why? Because that is the only way they know to offset all of the invidious forces in our culture that Mr. Henry so beautifully describes [chapter 4]. Whether or not we will ever solve the problem of desegregation in the schools I do not know. But to us there are certain values we want to get across to our young people who are searching for these values. I know their quality and the quality of the parents who are sending them to our schools because they are seeking desperately for a way to save their children from the emphasis on hedonism in our times. Our day schools represent a real opportunity to them to raise good Jews and loyal Americans.

Mr. Taylor:

Those of you who have ridden the New York subway may have seen a map there showing a New Yorker's view of the United States. It shows a very large Manhattan, some place called Albany, Chicago, and the Great Lakes, and a small amount of other land. I think we should in fairness keep the record straight. We have more states in the Union than New York. I come from Colorado. In our country, we have more acres than we do souls, but at the same time, we sometimes have a sense of freedom which is significant. The Colorado Constitution has specifically banned any type of racial or religious discrimination in the public educational system of our State since 1876. I say we have occasion for faith in the laws. We also have occasion for greater faith in the religiously oriented schools. We can recall that seven years before *Brown* v. *Board of Education* the parochial schools gave the leadership in establishing desegregation in education. Cardinal Ritter of St. Louis was the first to desegregate education in any large school system. With opposition from many, Archbishop Rummel of New Orleans, Louisiana, also gave leadership by desegregating the parochial schools in New Orleans.

As we get older, we sometimes feel there is lack of hope. Yet I feel that all of us, insofar as we recognize the fatherhood of God, should recognize that there must be hope for our children. Religiously oriented education has made great contributions and provided equal educational opportunities for all children regardless of color or minority status.

Neil G. McCluskey:

As an old friend of Mr. Pfeffer, I would like to make an observation on his very moving comments and then I would like to ask him a simple question. My observation is this: Mr. Pfeffer has made the statement that the principal barrier to integration has been the nonpublic — chiefly the religiously oriented — schools. I think he is failing to see the distinction between the independent and the parochial school. There is an enormous difference. The parochial school system, as established in the various Roman Catholic dioceses, is a kind of a counterpart to the public school system, making provision for all classes, etc. This is a terribly costly operation, though it is saving a rather important sum of tax funds, and Mr. Pfeffer is among those chiefly responsible for starving it. Had energies been turned toward finding constitutional ways of coping with the financial problems of church-related schools, maybe the serious situations Mr. Pfeffer alluded to would not have arisen. Independent schools are completely different. They are often operated for a profit or for some small class and special groups. Now a month ago I asked Mr. Pfeffer to do some homework for me. We were up in Mt. Holyoke at a conference, and he made the same observations he made this afternoon. I pointed out then that although the Catholic population of the United States is hardly 2 per cent Negro, in the two dioceses of New York City the Catholic school population is around 14 to 16 per cent Negro. Now this is rather significant, it seems to me. I would second what Mr. Taylor has said about the fact that New York is not the United States. I don't think the same serious hospital situation, the same serious school situation, exists across the country in the graphic terms Mr. Pfeffer has utilized. So my question then, Mr. Pfeffer, is simply this: You have made the very serious statement that private schools are the chief obstacle to racial integration. I would like to know on what study, what national survey, you base your charge. If there are any relevant studies available I would like to hear about them.

Mr. Pfeffer:

I don't know if I used the phrase, "chief obstacle." I said "a major obstacle." The nonpublic schools are an obstacle by their very existence. If they didn't exist, if there were only public schools, the problem of racial integration wouldn't be solved completely. Indeed, there would still be a tremendous amount to accomplish, because you would have your problem of de facto segregation, segregation which comes about within the public schools by reason of geographic factors. I tried to make the point that nonpublic schools and private housing and private hospitals are a community for middle-class and upper-middle-class people. Public housing, public schools, public hospitals are a community for the poor. It so happens in this country (in other countries it might be different) that the poor mostly have black skins, while middle-class people have white skins. Therefore, race segregation is a function of economic segregation. And in the cities, Negroes are getting poorer and the whites more affluent. I am not against parochial schools, as I said earlier, because religious liberty to me is perhaps the highest of all values. Where there is a conflict between religious liberty and racial integration, I choose religious liberty. So long as the religious convictions of a group require them to maintain their own schools, I would defend their right to do so even though the consequences were deplorable. But what I am urging you against is permitting religious groups to be used, not for the purpose of protecting religious liberty, but for the purpose of further widening the gap between the Haves and Have-Nots.

William E. McManus:

I am superintendent of the Roman Catholic school system in the Archdiocese of Chicago, with 355,000 pupils. I have been in the position for ten years. My question to Mr. Pfeffer is simple and direct: Mr. Pfeffer, What do you know about the pattern of segregation and integration in the Roman Catholic schools of the Archdiocese of Chicago?

Mr. Pfeffer:

I don't know anything specific about the Archdiocese and the schools of Chicago. What I know is the general pattern of the economic segregation in the parochial schools. Only two days ago, the Religious News Service reported that the parochial schools generally are middle-class and upper-middle-class schools. I didn't make this up. That is not the first time I have seen such a report. I have seen it many times. I know this as far as the Jewish schools are concerned, and certainly I don't know of any poor children going to the Episcopalian or Quaker schools, except, let us say, the token scholarship when you hunt high and low for it.

Furthermore, they pick for scholarships kids with exceptional ability. But the poor or average Negro ends up in the public school.

Mr. Dorsen:

I don't know anything about the Archdiocese of Chicago either. But I went to the expense of a few telephone calls to obtain some interesting statistics that were published by the Superintendent of Schools of the Archdiocese of New York within the last couple of months. The pattern of racial distribution is very similar to that of the public schools. I certainly don't look upon this as an attack upon the parochial schools. Most parochial schools are heavily imbalanced one way or the other, either predominately white or predominantly Negro and/or Puerto Rican. In the research that I did in preparation for this meeting, I also looked into the situation in Philadelphia and Pittsburgh. The pattern in these cities, again, is that the composition of the neighborhood determines the composition of the school. There are exceptions. There are deviations. But if you look at the figures as a whole, you don't see a very heartening situation. I am not throwing either the first or the last stone, I may say, but the balance in the schools in the area I studied is not uplifting. I'd be very interested, Father McManus, if you would tell us what the situation is in the Roman Catholic schools in the Archdiocese of Chicago.

Father McManus:

Fact number one is that the Archdiocese of Chicago has a policy of open enrollment at the high school level. On January 14 of this year, every one of ninety high schools in the two counties was open to any applicant and from any part of the city. Under that pattern, sixty-five of the schools have both white and Negro pupils. The total number applying is 23,500 youngsters. All will be accepted. The proportion of youngsters from the central city parishes going on to Catholic high schools is much higher than in the suburban areas. Virtually all of the Negro applicants have been accepted into the central city schools. The typical pattern is for 85 to 90 per cent of the graduates of the central city Roman

Catholic schools to go to the Roman Catholic high schools. There are much smaller percentages from outside of the city. The other side of the coin is, however, that open enrollment is not a complete answer to our problem of integrating the Catholic high schools. Under the policy of an open enrollment, which certainly has to do with freedom of education, the tendency has been for the Negro youngsters to go to the integrated schools closest to home and in the process to segregate them. Now we are confronted next year with the very difficult problem (one on which I hope to get some light in the course of this conference) of whether to resort to some computerized method of assigning youngsters to schools. Should we put 23,500 names into an,advanced type of programming, sort them out as if they were jelly beans, and disperse them all around the city? Or should we try to preserve the right of free choice on the part of all people, white and Negro, to go to the school of their choice? Unless we can persuade an increasingly large number of Negro youngsters to take a long journey from their regrettably segregated neighborhoods out to the suburban areas, open enrollment (which I think is freedom at its best in a school system) simply is not going to alleviate the substantial amount of racial segregation that we are destined to have in the Roman Catholic school system.

August W. Steinhilber:

It is apparent from the general conversation and discussions at this conference that there are a number of misconceptions about (1) the history of the passage of the Elementary and Secondary Education Act, and (2) which children are eligible for assistance under Title I of that Act.

First, contrary to what has been said here, there were no deals or arrangements to buy the support of parochial school leaders to obtain passage of the ESEA. Our principal concern was how to provide educational assistance to all those who were in need, whether they were in public school, nonpublic school, or attending no school at all (dropouts), while at the same time honoring our constitutional concepts of separation of church and state. The concept which was developed was one of extending the public school program to all in need regardless of the school they attended. Please note this is not the so-called "child benefit theory." I repeat, the theory was one of extending public school programs. In the church-state context, such programs could be dual enrollment or special public school classes conducted on parochial school property — provided, however, the latter programs were to be basically remedial, health, and therapeutic in nature.

If one were to ask what was the reason for the passage of the ESEA, I would say the biggest single answer was not related to the church-state issue but the overwhelming Democratic majority in Congress resulting from the great landslide victory of President Johnson. Parochial school support alone could not have gained passage of this law. While it is true parochial school leaders were consulted, so were church groups opposing aid to parochial schools, such as the National Council of Churches. But this is only reasonable, for it is not wise policy to run roughshod over any group, even when you have the votes. The goodwill developed through negotiations and consultations can become invaluable at a later time.

The second misconception I have heard is as follows: "Only children from families having an income of less than $2,000 should be included in Title I programs." I realize, of course, I am oversimplifying the comments, but the foregoing statement is basically what we have heard.

This misunderstanding undoubtedly originates from the fact that funds are distributed to school districts on the basis of the relative number of children coming from low-income families residing in the district. This device of distributing funds is used solely for the purpose of placing funds where the educational needs are greatest. Family income data by counties throughout the nation are available. Uniform statistics on educational disadvantages or underachievement are not available. Because of the close correlation between educational achievement and low income, family income data are considered an effective means of distributing money for the purpose of meeting the educational needs of disadvantaged or educationally deprived children.

The normal procedure calls for the selection of target schools in areas having concentrations of low-income families. Once appropriate schools have been selected, any child in attendance at such school who is in need of the educational services is eligible for participation. As a practical matter, we have found our original theory to be true: There is a high relationship between economic and educational deprivation.

The House Committee on Education and Labor in a report made in 1966 underscored this difference between educational and economic deprivation when it said, "*No means test is required by the law and none should be imposed* on public or nonpublic school children" [emphasis is the committee's].

Jere Farley:

I would like to put a little different wrinkle in this sheet. We state department people find our problem is not with the parochial schools. The problem in my state, Tennessee, happens to be with people who want to start an independent school for various reasons, as Norman Dorsen pointed out [chapter 6]. Now do we as a society have an obligation to protect ourselves against this kind of knavery? What is our duty when we go out and look at a budding independent school that is taking advantage of the people, taking advantage of the students, and circumventing the laws that we are attempting to establish on civil rights and similar matters? In Tennessee it happens to be strongly segregationist schools that are developing. Somewhere we need come to grips with this thing. How can we control, for society, things that we need to control and yet preserve the things that are dear to us that Mr. Pfeffer alludes to?

* * *

John Paul Carter:

If a state department wishes to regulate nonpublic schools in more enlightened fashion, how can it obtain the necessary expertise? Is the necessary information available, and is there any mechanism through which the state department personnel may obtain it?

Mr. Littell:

I'm not sure that I quite agree with the stating of the question. I feel that the issue has to do with whether we have final answers or whether we are in an exploratory period. My colleague Mr. Erickson put that point very well. My conclusion is this: Before any further power and authority be granted to state departments of public instruction, two things must be achieved: one, a return to a sound doctrine of teacher stewardship and second, a recovery of balance in the training of teachers and in the program of the schools, so that both the pursuit of wisdom and the achievement of technical proficiency are encompassed. The Amish and other sectarian Protestants are not about to blow up the world, even though they may slow up its vaunted onrush of progress a bit. On the other hand, the most dangerous man in the modern world, whether he fancies himself a nuclear physicist or a human engineer, is, as Mr. Justice Jackson said at the Nurenberg trials, the technically competent barbarian. Now I think that this is where the issue lies, in essence, in any discussion of our present educational systems, and I am not prepared to say that the problem is to accommodate the private school systems to public instructional standards. I think the issue is to get the educational discussion back into the forum of responsible stewardship and of emphasis upon the heritage of wisdom and the oral tradition as well as technical proficiency. When we get that balance restored, we will discover that there are some things to be learned from such tiny groups as the Amish as well as from the Manhattan Project.

Donald A. Erickson:

I think that one way of accomplishing what Mr. Littell is after here is dialogue. Really, if someone were to ask me what was the most distressing part of the current situation, it is that some people in the state departments are assuming that they know the answers and are not talking with those who could communicate with them concerning the goals and the philosophies of schools of different types. I think there are people who can speak for the kind of viewpoint Mr. Littell is urging. There are the Cary Potters, for example, who can speak for the independent schools. There are people like Bishop McManus, who can explain what the Catholic schools are trying to do. And there are spokesmen for the Amish, not only the Amish themselves, but scholars like Mr. Hostetler, like Mr. Littell, and others, who have taken the time to understand the Amish culture. So I think this is a most apt question. Can we get at the kind of expertise we need? Well, I don't think we're going to come up with conclusive answers, but I am sure that by talking with people of these types, state department officials can gain enough understanding about independent schools so that they will approach them at least much better than they are approaching them now.

Mr. Littell:

But I think we don't agree as to the nature of the stewardship. It is a fundamental point of Protestant, Catholic, and Jewish conviction that the school and the teachers are an extension of *parental* responsibility. Bishop Dibelius put this very well in a book he wrote after the war, discussing his controversy with the Nazis and then with the Communists, on the cornerstone and the style of education. He said the issue, the question, does not lie between the parents and the Ministry of Education, but between the parents and God. Now over against this question we have the statist philosophy, represented not only by the Nazis and the Communists but also by ideological secularists, not persons supporting secular schools and secular governments and the rest of it (I am one), but persons who have embraced the secularist *ideology*, which finally lodges authority in the instruments of the state. This is something we are not really agreed upon, and this is where, in the fundamental sense, the controversy lies. This is what is at stake when somebody says the society has a right to do so and so, by which it is meant that the department of public instruction, the instrument of the society, has the right to define ultimate commitments. This I don't accept and I don't see how any believing Protestant, Catholic, or Jew can accept it. The alternative, however, is not chaos. The alternative is precisely the kind of lively public discussion involving the various elements to which Mr. Erickson pointed in his paper, and this is what we don't get. Speaking specifically of Iowa, I think it is very revealing that there is no representative on the registration list from the Department of Public Instruction. We have had as a participant here Iowa's governor, one of the most enlightened governors in the country, who is a statesman, who is a pragmatic man, who is not an idealist at all, yet the Department of Public Instruction — not only in relation to the Amish but in half a dozen other policies affecting all of us — is not in the dialogue and apparently doesn't care to participate in the dialogue. Now how do you get them where they *must* dialogue? That is the real question.

David C. Osborn:

What fundamental criteria may safely be used to determine the rights of the nonpublic school?

Mr. Littell:

I would like to suggest the distinction which I introduced earlier. It was a new thought to me, coming out of the discussion, but I think it was a fairly reasonable one. Perhaps we should make a distinction between groups which have no intention to participate in the exercise of a sovereignty and the self-government of the open society and groups which *do* propose to participate in politics and have their members hold office. There really is a fundamental distinction between the Amish, shall we say, who are by their own intention and basic religious commitment strangers in the land, and groups which claim to be training citizens and which participate fully in the political process. I would suggest that the Amish and like groups, such as the Hasidic group to which Mr. Pfeffer called our attention, come under a distinct line of argument entirely. The real question is whether they are free to pursue their own apolitical objectives, being no peril to the rest of us as long as they obey the law. One thing you have to say is these people are law-abiding residents. The society may make standardizing regulations much more clearly in relation to schools that claim to be developing citizens. Then you can say English language, American history, basic government courses, even practical experience in running committee meetings, might reasonably be part of the educational process if people are being equipped to participate in the making of the public opinion and in the exercise of popular sovereignty. But even there I would prefer to err in the direction of liberty for the simple reason that I have yet to encounter any agency or department or board of education — even of the Methodist church, let alone the state! — to which I am prepared to give final authority in the definition of elementary and secondary education. Maybe I've been protected but I haven't encountered such infallible groups yet. I've encountered a number that apparently claimed a certain infallibility, but that makes them even more suspect as far as my philosophy is concerned. And in the cases in which we should set certain basic standards, the best way to set them seems to me to be in a colloquium of citizens of the state in a committee or a public commission which uses such tools of liberty as the handbook which my imaginative colleague Erickson proposed as standardizing influences. Let us not give final and arbitrary authority concerning ultimate commitments to any group. Our fathers were wise enough to suspect that if you gave such power to any group the power would eventually be abused.

There is one footnote to this discussion that we have to keep in mind, on the other side. Many of the people who are speaking so strongly for the public school system in our country have in the back of their minds the importance of the public school as a unifying force in the life of the country as a whole. And they have of course in mind the very questionable historical experience of the Netherlands, where the principal of pillarization (Versaeulung) has developed completely separate school systems from the kindergarten through graduate school in the university. As you know, in the Netherlands, in 1911, around 80 per cent of the youngsters were still in the common schools; today, as the result of the pluralistic policy of the society and the granting of tax monies, the balance has shifted very powerfully in the other direction, so that you have parochial school systems from the cradle to the grave — a Catholic political party, a Calvinist radio and T.V. stations, etc. They even have factories where laborers and directors all belong to one confessional bloc. The Christian Reformed, as we call them, even have a goat-breeding society on confessional lines. I haven't yet been able to figure out what that means! And then the Humanists and Socialists have their pillar. Now I am not prepared to say that it is a matter of indifference that we should adopt a completely pillarized approach. If the only alternative is to cut each others' throats in wars of religion, then obviously the pillarization process is a better way of doing things. But I hope that God has something else better in store for the American republic than pillarization. Therefore I would be prepared to say that our weight should be thrown toward the public school system. But the question we confront in many cases is not whether we should maintain a weight in the direction of the common school system, which the present tax structures do, but whether the public school should be given an exclusive and monolithic weight. How do we find the middle ground? How do we emphasize the function of the public school system without sliding into some kind of monolithic and statist direction?

* * *

Miss Strickland:

There are two areas of consideration, it seems to me, that have received inadequate attention in the previous chapters of this volume. Both derive from the First Amendment. One concerns state regulations which may affect religious freedom. The other concerns practices which may amount to unconstitutional aid to religion.

All of us would agree, I think, that the state has the right to regulate in the interest of public welfare, and its regulations are ordinarily constitutionally valid so long as they bear any rational relationship to the promotion of the legitimate interests of the state. What has not been emphasized here is that the right of the state to regulate may be subject to severe limitations when the interest asserted against the state is one of the prized values of the First Amendment, such as freedom of speech, press, assembly, and in this case, religion.

Given this general thesis, what is the proper interest of the state, in regulating nonpublic schools? The state can legitimately regulate nonpublic schools in four areas:

First, it can regulate for the health and safety of the occupants of the physical school premises.

Second, the state may enforce regulations to protect parents against fraud by ensuring that the school fulfill its stated purpose.

Third, the state may legitimately provide criteria by which to chose quality nonpublic schooling, as Mr. Elson pointed out [chapter 5]. That is, the state may provide an accreditation or approval system by which to inform the public of the quality of education offered by different schools, all of which it permits to exist under its regulations.

Fourth, the state may constitutionally regulate minimum standards of competence for two reasons. It is in the interest of the public order and the continuation of democratic government to have a minimally educated citizenry, for democratic self-government will not long survive without it. Minimum standards of competence are also essential to protect the interests of the child. That is, a child will not be able to exercise freedom of choice in adult life if he has not learned the skills and grasped the tools essential to functioning on a productive level in this complex society.

In the ordinary case, state regulation of nonpublic schools is valid if it bears any rational relation to advancing any one of these four interests. For example, it may require teacher certification in nonpublic schools in an attempt to ensure minimum standards of competence even though the effect may be to exclude some very good teachers. The state may likewise require education through age sixteen or any one of a number of other requirements.

But when an interest protected by the First Amendment is asserted, a different standard must apply. Mr. Justice Jackson aptly stated it in *West Virginia* v. *Barnette*, the famous flag salute case: When First Amendment freedoms are asserted the state can regulate "only to prevent a grave and immediate danger to interests which the state may lawfully protect." This means that, even against the claim of religious liberty, a state may close down a private school that is housed in a fire trap or contains sanitation hazards to the health of the children. The state may also close down even a sectarian school which induces attendance by fraudulent claims. Moreover, the state's accreditation or approval function for the purposes of information does not seem to interfere with religious liberty, unless discriminatorily carried out.

But where there are claims of religious liberty under the First Amendment, the state's interest in attainment of a minimum competence must be satisfied by using different criteria in judging that competence. That is, where a state normally, for its own legitimate convenience, uses objective, definable standards, such as teacher certification and minimum hours for certain courses to insure this competence, it may now be confined to purely result-oriented tests. Let us take two examples to illustrate this point:

The Amish assert that their religious liberty is infringed when they are forced to adhere to state standards of education. They seek an alternative — to send their children to private schools serving purely the interests of their religious community. No one claims that these schools do not provide an adequate preparation for life in the Amish community. Likewise no one claims they do provide an adequate preparation for life in the mainstream of American society. But no school — Amish or state-supported secular school — is neutral in teaching values. It is not tenable to insist in a society that respects religious liberty that the Amish should be compelled to educate their children in one set of values rather than another. Moreover, the state's interest in the public order is not threatened by the Amish, who prepare their young for productive agricultural lives with minimum risks of their becoming delinquents or public charges.

I suspect that the genuine heat generated by the controversy over the Amish schools arises from the fact that Amish values are not merely different from those which most of us accept, but are antithetical to them, and therefore felt as a direct threat.

But let us consider what is in some respects a much harder example. Suppose a Catholic or Lutheran school (I use both for my example because of their seemingly opposite theological positions concerning state aid to parochial schools), operating because of the strong religious preference of the parents, is too poor to provide the resources, teachers, and textbooks necessary to meet the admittedly legitimate criteria of the state. Such a school is different from the Amish school in two important respects. First, the members of these denominations seem to concede the necessity to use the public schools when their resources are inadequate to provide a religious education for all their children. Theirs is a religious preference, not a conscientious objection to nonparochial education. Second, their objective is not merely to educate for life in a religiously isolated community. They purport to prepare their students for life in the mainstream of American society.

It might be argued, on the basis of these differences, that such schools may be regulated by the state without regard to religious objections. But the interests claimed on their behalf are still religious interests, and the state may properly be held to adopting the alternative least offensive to these interests.

One such alternative might be to allow an academically inferior religious school to operate, but without state accreditation or approval. This would serve to inform parents that if they chose to send their children to this school as a matter of religious preference they would do so without the assurances that the state's accreditation or approval would provide. If the state is worried that to adopt this procedure is tantamount to abdicating its responsbility regarding its citizens, I suggest that when the state has ensured an *adequate* education for all of the children attending public schools, including schools located in slums and lower-class neighborhoods (and these children have no religious objections to an adequate education, I assure you), then it is soon enough for the state to worry about the possible substandard education being given to children with a religious objection to more education, or to children with a religious preference for parochial education.

But if a private school education were so inferior as to amount to a fraud on parents who relied on the private school for an adequate secular education, this would be another matter entirely, and the state should certainly exercise its power to close that school.

Another alternative, of course, would be the one suggested by Governor Hughes: to use public funds to upgrade private schools, thereby enabling them to meet state standards. Governor Hughes, you recall, undertook to meet the Amish religious objections by supplying accredited teachers at state expense to what are essentially their private sectarian schools [chapter 1]. And Professor Erickson suggested that the state might undertake to operate rural Amish schools [chapter 7]. These alternatives, however, raise very serious questions under the prohibition against religious establishment of the First Amendment.

I do not propose to dwell on this at length, for I do not think the purpose of this conference is to settle that thorny problem. But it is so important that I would not be doing justice to my agreement to comment honestly if I did not at least mention it.

In the case of Governor Hughes's proposal, the religious objections of the Amish are truly met by their being permitted to conduct their own private schools — they didn't ask for certified teachers. The state has not established that certified teachers are essential to an education of the kind which the Amish require, and it just does not seem necessary for the state to move into the business of providing teachers for religious education when the interests of religious liberty could be protected more simply. If I understand Mr. Elson's paper correctly [chapter 5], Iowa is one of only six states which regard teacher certification as an essential requirement for private schools.

The danger, of course, is not only to the First Amendment but also to the nonpublic school, for the so-called "solution" to upgrading inferior religious education may get the whole camel of which Commissioner Sanders speaks [chapter 8] into the tent of the nonpublic school, bringing the whole tent down to the ground. He is indeed correct that state aid gives the state power to regulate, and he has pointed out the movement of nonpublic schools to become more similar to public schools in program and procedure, as the differences among them diminish. But nonpublic schools, at least the sectarian schools, are established precisely because they offer an education which is substantially different from that offered in the public schools. May not this price become too great for sectarian schools to pay? Certainly the Amish think so.

In summary, the state may legitimately regulate nonpublic schools to insure the health and safety of the occupants of the school premises, to protect parents against fraud, to provide criteria of quality education, and to seek minimum standards of competence in the interests of the state and the interests of the child. But the state's legitimate interests in regulating nonpublic schools are subjected to substantially more rigid tests when a claim of religious liberty is made against the state's regulations. Indeed, it would seem that until the state can insure that all children attending public schools will not receive an academically inferior education, children attending a sectarian school through either conscientious conviction or religious preference should be allowed to do so, even at the risk that they will receive what government officials may regard as a comparably inferior education.

Index